Managing [...] [...]00 Network Environment Exam Cram

This Cram Sheet contains the distilled, key facts about the Managing a Microsoft Windows 2000 Network Environment exam. Review this information last thing before entering the test room, paying special attention to those areas where you feel you need the most review. You can transfer any of the facts onto the provided blank piece of paper before beginning the exam.

NETWORKING PROTOCOLS

1. Addressing protocols: AppleTalk, Internet Protocol (IP), Internet Packet Exchange (IPX), NetBIOS Enhanced User Interface (NetBEUI).

2. TCP/IP Suite: FTP, HTTP, IP, POP3, PPP, PPTP, SLIP, SMTP, SNMP, TCP, Telnet, UDP.

3. IP addressing: network address, host address, subnet mask, CIDR notation (<IP Address>/<mask bits>).

4. Host identification: FQDN (myserver.mycorp.com), IP (128.46.197.101), MAC (AF-04-2B-11-69-43), NetBIOS (myserver).

5. Address classes: A (001–126.0.0.0/255.0.0.0), B (128–191.x.0.0/255.255.0.0), C (192–223.x.x.0/255.255.255.0), Reserved: D (224–239), E (240–255), localhost (127.0.0.1). Private network ranges: 10.0.0.0/8, 172.16.0.0/16,192.168.0.0/24 (a zero in the host address refers to a complete subnet).

6. Subnetting means to take an available block of addresses and designate additional network address bits in order to create smaller, contiguous numerical groupings. The remaining bits provide available host addresses within a subnet, from which one gateway and one broadcast address are unavailable for host identification. If the network addresses match, then the two IP addresses are in the same subnet.

ACTIVE DIRECTORY STRUCTURE

7. Active Directory is a multimaster hierarchical structure composed of one or more contiguous namespaces, also called trees.

8. Global Catalog is a distributed multimaster database containing information and settings for references to objects such as users, computers, groups, and shared resources.

9. Flexible Single Master Operation (FSMO) roles: Domain Naming Master, Infrastructure Master (not on Global Catalog Server), PDC Emulator, RID Master, Schema Master.

10. Trusts are logical connections between domains. They can be one-way or two-way, and transitive or nontransitive (Windows 2000 default: two-way transitive).

11. Forests contain one or more trees; trees contain one or more domains sharing a hierarchical name space; domains contain users, computers, groups, and organizational units (OUs); OUs contain users, computers, groups, and other OUs.

12. Groups allow inheritance of permissions by members. OUs allow granting of subdomain administrative capability.

13. Sites are made up of one or more IP subnets closely connected using dependable connections. Intersite replication is accomplished through a bridgehead server, and may be scheduled manually for off-peak times.

NAME RESOLUTION

14. FQDN name resolution: Hierarchical naming resolved using DNS or HOSTS file (located in %SystemRoot%\WINNT\System32\drivers\etc). HOSTS entries look like this: 128.167.244.10 myserver.mycorp.com.

15. NetBIOS: Flat namespace resolved using WINS or LMHOSTS file. LMHOSTS entries look like this: 128.167.244.10 myserver #PRE (#PRE designates a preload into cache at boot).

16. Lightweight Directory Access Protocol (LDAP) is used to browse the directory. Objects are listed using a distinguished name (CN=myserver,OU=sales,DC=mycorp,DC=com) whose relative distinguished name is the most unique portion (CN=myserver).

69. System monitoring can be performed using the Task Manager, System Monitor, and Network Monitor.

70. Network diagnostic utilities include the ping, tracert, pathping, ipconfig, netdiag, nbtstat, and nslookup utilities, as well as the **net** commands.

71. Microsoft publishes regular security updates called hotfixes, which are combined with other non-security-related updates into Service Packs. The hfnetchk tool can be used to scan a system or domain for needed hotfixes, and the qchain utility can be used to apply multiple hotfixes at one time.

REMOTE ACCESS

72. A small number of public IP addresses can be shared by a larger number of private addresses using either network address translation (NAT) or Internet connection sharing (ICS). ICS can be configured for on-demand dialing.

73. WAN protocols include: ARAP, RAS, and the Point-to-Point Protocol (PPP). VPNs include LT2P and PPTP.

74. Authentication protocols include: Challenge Handshake Authentication Protocol (CHAP), MS-CHAP, MS-CHAP v2, PAP (low security), and SPAP (medium security). The Extensible Authentication Protocol (EAP) allows the use of smart cards and biometric security devices.

75. Encryption protocols include IPSec, which is used over L2TP connections, and MPPE, which is used over PPTP connections.

76. Remote access settings can be configured on the user account or using Group Policy.

77. Terminal Services provides remote terminal sessions on a central server.

78. The **route add <*IP address*> mask <*mask*> <*gateway*>** command adds a static route to the routing table. The **route delete <*IP address*> mask <*mask*>** command removes it.

SECURITY

79. Auditing allows security-related information to be written to the Security log.

80. Event logs include: Application, Security, System, Directory Service (domain controllers only), and File Replication Service (domain controllers only).

17. WINS static mapping types: domain name, group, Internet group, multihomed, and unique.

18. WINS replication can be push, pull, or push/pull.

19. DNS servers can be primary, secondary (read-only copy), or cache-only.

20. DNS querying can be iterative or recursive.

21. Zones can be forward lookup (name to IP) or reverse lookup (IP to name), and can be Active Directory integrated (Win2K domain controllers only), standard (file-based), primary, or secondary.

22. DNS resource record types: A (HOST), CNAME (alias), MX (mail exchanger), NS (name server), PTR (pointer for reverse lookup), SOA (start of authority), or SRV (service).

DHCP CONFIGURATION

23. DHCP lease process: discovery, offer, client request, and acknowledgement.

24. Default lease duration is eight days—longer for mobile users, shorter for rapid reuse.

25. DHCP servers must be authorized to provide addresses for domain members.

26. A scope must be set up for each subnet supported, with an address pool, reservations, and any scope parameters (start and end IP address, exclusion range, lease duration, subnet mask, gateway, domain name, DNS, and WINS). Scopes must be activated to become available.

ACTIVE DIRECTORY ADMINISTRATION

27. Access permissions can be explicitly allowed, explicitly denied, or implicitly denied (default). Explicit denial overrides any allowal grants.

28. Access permissions are inherited from containers, so group membership can simplify mass-assignment and rapid change.

29. The Delegation Of Authority Wizard allows delegation of basic administrative tasks.

30. MMC consoles can be created and distributed with snap-ins, along with the adminpak.msi file from the Windows 2000 Server CD, to allow local administrators access to customized interfaces.

31. Taskpads are user-friendly versions of the MMC that hide administrative complexity behind simple task shortcuts.

GROUP POLICY

32. Group policies specify settings, configuration information, and software deployment packages for users and computers to centralize management and configuration of large networks based on container-level assignment at the site, domain, and OU level.

33. Group policy objects are made up of the group policy container, which is an Active Directory object, and the group policy template, which is a hierarchical folder structure located in %SystemRoot%\WINNT\SYSVOL\sysvol\<domain>\Policies\.

34. Group Policy setting types: Administrative Templates, Folder Redirection, Internet Explorer Maintenance, Remote Installation Services, Scripts, Security Settings, and Software Installation.

35. Multiple group policies can be linked to each container, and each group policy can be linked to multiple containers. Resolution is handled from the highest-level container to lowest, with same-container resolution handled in list order from bottom to top.

36. Block inheritance prevents all inheritance from above, except settings configured with the No Override option. You can filter by group by removing the Read and Apply Group Policy permissions on the group policy link.

37. Group policy can identify a slow network as one communicating under 500Kbps, limiting evaluation to Administrative Templates, Security, and Encrypted File System settings only.

38. Administrative template types: Control Panel, Desktop, Network, Printers, Start Menu & Taskbar, System, and Windows Components. Settings can be configured as Disabled, Enabled, or Not Configured.

39. Default security templates are provided for basic, secure, and high security configurations.

40. Account policies can be configured for specific password and account lockout settings. All three of the account lockout policies must be configured to work.

41. Password policy settings include: Enforce History, Maximum Age, Minimum Age, Minimum Length, Must Meet Complexity Requirements, and Whether To Store Using A Reversible Encryption.

42. Account lockout policies include: Duration, Threshold, and Reset Counter After.

43. Scripting allows multiple commands to be enacted at logon/logoff (users) or startup/shutdown (computers). Scripts are placed within the Group Policy template under the appropriate GPO_GUID and object type (user or computer).

44. Folder redirection applies to Application Data, Desktop, My Documents, My Pictures, and Start Menu, and may be applied the same way to all, differently by group, or specifically to a user using the *%username%* variable.

45. Software life cycle:

    a. Preparation of the MSI Windows Installer Package using third-party software.

    b. Deployment of the package using Group Policy to publish or assign packages.

    c. Maintenance of the package using Group Policy to publish or assign updates.

    d. Removal of the package using forced or optional removal via Group Policy.

RESOURCE MANAGEMENT

46. Publishing a resource creates a reference to the object within the Global Catalog. A resource can have several published links, each with its own DACL.

47. Location specification for published resources has a maximum of 260 characters, with a 32-character limit for each name: general/less general/more precise/.

48. Shared folders have the Change, Read, and Full Control access permissions. Those without the Read permission will not be able to see the published resource when browsing the catalog.

49. When resolving access permissions, share permissions are evaluated for the most favorable combination, NTFS permissions are evaluated for the most favorable combination, and then the results of both are evaluated for the least favorable combination. A denial will override all access allowal grants.

50. Shared printer options: Connect (allows installation), Move, Open (allows job management), and Properties (driver and print queue management).

SYSTEM CONFIGURATION

51. Disks can be basic or dynamic. Basic disks have from one to four primary partitions and up to one extended partition on which logical drives can be created. Dynamic disks have one or more volumes, which can be extended, spanned, striped, or mirrored.

52. RAID types supported by Windows 2000:

    • RAID-0 (striping)—Not fault tolerant, but fast access due to simultaneous read/write capability.

    • RAID-1 (mirroring)—Fault tolerant. Inefficient use of storage but faster than RAID-5.

    • RAID-5 (striping with parity)—Fault tolerant. Slower access speed and moderate storage efficiency.

53. The **dcpromo** command allows a member server to be converted to a domain controller, or an existing DC to be reduced to a member server.

54. Domains can be in mixed mode, which allows NT 4 BDCs, or native mode, which requires that all domain controllers be Windows 2000.

55. Computer accounts can be precreated to allow new computers to join into OU containers other than the default Computers container.

INTERNET INFORMATION SERVICES

56. Virtual sites can be identified using one or more unique IP addresses, host headers, or custom ports.

57. Each IIS server can support multiple FTP, Web, NNTP, and SMTP virtual sites. Each site is uniquely identified and addressable using a browser client.

58. Virtual directories create links to folders located outside of the root site folder, but act as if they were located within the site folder hierarchy.

59. The IUSR_*<computername>* account is used for anonymous authentication and the IWAM_*<computername>* account is used to run some Web applications.

60. IIS authentication types: Anonymous (no password or logon), Basic, Digest (W2K Active Directory server and IE5+ only), and Integrated Windows (IE required, and will not function through HTTP proxy connections). FTP sites can only use Anonymous and Basic authentication.

61. Web permissions include General permissions (Directory Browsing, Read, Write, and Script Source Access) and Execute permissions (None, Scripts Only, Scripts And Executables).

62. The Permissions Wizard is used to set both Web and NTFS permissions at once. Two default templates are available: Public Web site and Secure Web site.

63. Access to Web resources is evaluated by first authenticating the user, then Web permissions, and finally NTFS access permissions.

64. Web sites are accessed using port 80 by default; FTP sites use port 21.

65. WebDAV connections allow the use of Web folders, creating remote file shares through port 80.

66. It is sometimes necessary to configure IE to bypass HTTP proxy servers for local intranet addressing.

TROUBLESHOOTING

67. The Advanced Startup Options include: Command Prompt Only, Debugging Mode, Enable VGA Monitor, Last Known Good Configuration (only useful to the last successful logon), Logged, Safe Mode, Safe Mode With Command Prompt, Safe Mode With Networking, and Step-By-Step.

68. The Recovery console can be used after all advanced startup options are unsuccessful, and can recover damaged boot sectors with the **fixboot** command or corrupted master boot records using the **fixmbr** command.

Managing a Windows 2000 Network Environment

Kalani Kirk Hausman

CERTIFICATION

MCSA Managing a Windows 2000 Network Environment Exam Cram2 (Exam 70-218)

Copyright © 2003 by Que Certification

International Standard Book Number: 0-7897-2866-4

Library of Congress Catalog Card Number: 20-02113787

Printed in the United States of America

First Printing: November 2002

05   04   03   02   4   3   2   1

Trademarks

Warning and Disclaimer

Publisher
Paul Boger

Executive Editor
Jeff Riley

Development Editor
Marta Justak

Managing Editor
Thomas F. Hayes

Project Editor
Carol Bowers

Production Editor
Megan Wade

Indexer
Brad Herriman

Proofreader
Justak Literary Services

Team Coordinator
Rosemary Lewis

Multimedia Developer
Michael Hunter

Page Layout
Ayanna Lacey

Graphics
Tammy Graham
Oliver L. Jackson, Jr.

CERTIFICATION

Que Certification • 201 West 103rd Street • Indianapolis, Indiana 46290

A Note from Series Editor Ed Tittel

You know better than to trust your certification preparation to just anybody. That's why you, and more than two million others, have purchased an Exam Cram book. As Series Editor for the new and improved Exam Cram2 series, I have worked with the staff at Que Certification to ensure you won't be disappointed. That's why we've taken the world's best-selling certification product—a finalist for "Best Study Guide" in a CertCities reader poll in 2002—and made it even better.

As a "Favorite Study Guide Author" finalist in a 2002 poll of CertCities readers, I know the value of good books. You'll be impressed with Que Certification's stringent review process, which ensures the books are high-quality, relevant, and technically accurate. Rest assured that at least a dozen industry experts—including the panel of certification experts at CramSession—have reviewed this material, helping us deliver an excellent solution to your exam preparation needs.

We've also added a preview edition of PrepLogic's powerful, full-featured test engine, which is trusted by certification students throughout the world.

As a 20-year-plus veteran of the computing industry and the original creator and editor of the Exam Cram series, I've brought my IT experience to bear on these books. During my tenure at Novell from 1989 to 1994, I worked with and around its excellent education and certification department. This experience helped push my writing and teaching activities heavily in the certification direction. Since then, I've worked on more than 70 certification-related books, and I write about certification topics for numerous Web sites and for *Certification* magazine.

In 1996, while studying for various MCP exams, I became frustrated with the huge, unwieldy study guides that were the only preparation tools available. As an experienced IT professional and former instructor, I wanted "nothing but the facts" necessary to prepare for the exams. From this impetus, Exam Cram emerged in 1997. It quickly became the best-selling computer book series since "...*For Dummies*," and the best-selling certification book series ever. By maintaining an intense focus on subject matter, tracking errata and updates quickly, and following the certification market closely, Exam Cram was able to establish the dominant position in cert prep books.

You will not be disappointed in your decision to purchase this book. If you are, please contact me at etittel@jump.net. All suggestions, ideas, input, or constructive criticism are welcome!

Ed Tittel

Taking You to the 70-218 Finish Line!

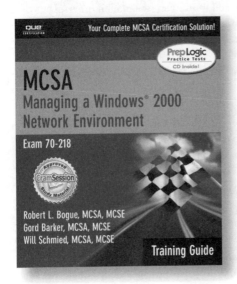

MCSA 70-218 Training Guide

Robert L. Bogue, Gord Barker, and Will Schmied
ISBN 0-7897-2766-8
$49.99 US/$77.99 CAN/£36.50 Net UK

Before you walk into your local testing center, make absolutely sure you're prepared to pass your exam. In addition to the Exam Cram2 series, consider our Training Guide series. Que Certification's Training Guides have exactly what you need to pass your exam:

- Exam Objectives highlighted in every chapter
- Notes, Tips, Warnings, and Exam Tips advise what to watch out for
- Step-by-Step Exercises for "hands-on" practice
- End-of-chapter Exercises and Exam Questions
- Final Review with Fast Facts, Study and Exam Tips, and another Practice Exam
- A CD that includes PrepLogic Practice Tests for complete evaluation of your knowledge
- Our authors are recognized experts in the field. In most cases, they are current or former instructors, trainers, or consultants – they know exactly what you need to know!

About the Author

Kalani Kirk Hausman (MCSE+I, MCSD, MCDBA, MCSA, MCT, CCNA, CIW-A, A+, Network+, I-Net+) has been an IT professional for more than 20 years in the roles of consultant, trainer, programmer, security administrator, database administrator, IT manager, and network administrator. He is currently working as a Computer Systems Manager for Texas A&M University, where he provides network planning and security support. He is also employed as the North American Online Manager for Fujitsu's online training division, KnowledgePool, Inc.

Mr. Hausman's studies include security, computer science, electronics technology, electrical engineering, mechanical engineering, and philosophy, as well as consulting in the IT field. His hobbies include designs in high-speed transportation, submersible propulsion, cosmology, interactive telepresence, technology in education, and virtual reality for use by those with disabling conditions.

One of his current projects includes the development of a shared interactive telepresence system that is designed to allow remote experience of widely varying environments by students, regardless of geographic location or disabling conditions. He is also working on implementing a zoological wireless telepresence system that is capable of allowing remote observation of animals in both natural and human-created environments, along with many other ongoing projects. Kirk can be reached at **kkhausman@hotmail.com**.

Dedication

To Ralph and Barbara Hausman for that first computer.

Contents at a Glance

Introduction   xv

Self Assessment   xxviii

Chapter 1   Microsoft Certification Exams   1

Chapter 2   Networking Basics   23

Chapter 3   Active Directory Structure   39

Chapter 4   Name Resolution   57

Chapter 5   DHCP Configuration   89

Chapter 6   Active Directory Administration   109

Chapter 7   Group Policy   129

Chapter 8   Resource Management   159

Chapter 9   System Configuration   177

Chapter 10   Internet Information Services (IIS)   199

Chapter 11   Troubleshooting   227

Chapter 12   Remote Access   253

Chapter 13   Network Security   277

Chapter 14   Sample Test   301

Chapter 15   Answer Key   325

Appendix A   What's on the CD-ROM   347

Appendix B   Using the *PrepLogic Practice Tests, Preview Edition* Software   351

Glossary   359

Index   365

Table of Contents

. . . .

Introduction xv

Self-Assessment xxviii

Chapter 1
Microsoft Certification Exams 1
Assessing Exam-Readiness 2
What to Expect at the Testing Center 3
Exam Layout and Design: New Case Study Format 4
  Multiple-Choice Question Format 5
  Build-List-and-Reorder Question Format 6
  Create-a-Tree Question Format 8
  Drag-and-Connect Question Format 10
  Select-and-Place Question Format 11
Microsoft's Testing Formats 13
Strategies for Different Testing Formats 15
  Case Study Exam Strategy 15
  Fixed-Length and Short-Form Exam Strategy 16
  Adaptive Exam Strategy 18
Question-Handling Strategies 18
Mastering the Inner Game 19
Additional Resources 20

Chapte 2
Networking Basics 23
Overview 24
Networking Protocols 25
Host Identification 27
IP Network Addressing 29
  Address Class 29
  Subnetting 30
Name Resolution 31
  NetBIOS Name Resolution 31
  FQDN Name Resolution 32

Practice Questions   33
Need to Know More?   38

Chapter 3
Active Directory Structure **39**

Active Directory Structure Overview   40
  Domain Controllers   40
Active Directory   41
Global Catalog   41
Flexible Single-Master Operation (FSMO) Roles   42
Trusts   43
Logical Structure   46
Domains   46
  Organizational Units   48
  Trees   49
  Forests   50
Physical Structure   50
Practice Questions   51
Need to Know More?   55

Chapter 4
Name Resolution **57**

Overview   58
  NetBIOS Naming   58
  FQDN Naming   59
NetBIOS Naming   60
  NetBIOS Name Cache   61
  LMHOSTS File   61
  WINS Resolution   62
  WINS Service Configuration   64
FQDN Host Naming   67
  DNS Cache   68
  HOSTS File   68
  DNS Server Types   70
  DNS Service Configuration   72
Command-Line Utilities   76
  ipconfig   77
  nbtstat   78
  net   78
  nslookup   79
  ping   79
  tracert   80

Practice Questions   81
Need to Know More?   87

Chapter 5
DHCP Configuration 89

Overview   90
  Static Addressing   90
  Dynamic Addressing   91
DHCP Leasing   91
  DHCP Lease Generation   92
  DHCP Lease Duration   94
DHCP Server Setup   95
  Server Authorization   96
  Scope Configuration   97
Practice Questions   103
Need to Know More?   108

Chapter 6
Active Directory Administration 109

Overview   110
Delegated Permissions   110
  Permissions   111
  Access Rights   112
  Assignment   114
  Delegation of Authority   115
Management Tools   118
  Custom Consoles   118
Practice Questions   124
Need to Know More?   128

Chapter 7
Group Policy 129

Overview of Group Policies   130
  Group Policy Structure   130
  Group Policy Scope   132
  Group Policy Application   134
  Site-Level Settings   134
  Modifying Default Inheritance   136
  Creating and Linking Group Policy Objects   138
  Specifying the Domain Controller   141
  Slow Network Connections   142
Administration Using Group Policy   142

Administrative Templates   143
Group Policy Settings   144
Group Policy Scripting   144
Folder Redirection   145
Software Deployment Using Group Policy   147
Software Lifecycle   147
Group Policy Software Management   149
Practice Questions   151
Need to Know More?   157

Chapter 8
Resource Management **159**

Overview   160
Sharing Resources   160
Location References   161
File Sharing   163
Shared Folders   163
Permissions Resolution   168
Printer Sharing   169
Practice Questions   171
Need to Know More?   176

Chapter 9
System Configuration **177**

Overview   178
Adding Windows Components   178
Terminal Services Configuration   179
Storage   180
Drive Configuration   180
Dynamic Volumes   182
Domain Configuration   185
Server Configuration   185
Account Management   188
Practice Questions   191
Need to Know More?   197

Chapter 10
Internet Information Services (IIS) **199**

IIS Overview   200
Intranets, Extranets, and the Internet   200
IIS Installation   203
Server Configuration   204

User Authentication   205
Access Permissions   207
Site Creation   210
Master Properties   210
Creating a Site   211
Creating a Virtual Folder   214
Folder Web Sharing   215
Accessing Web Sites   216
Establishing a Connection   216
Configuring Internet Explorer to Use a Proxy Server   218
IIS Maintenance   219
Practice Questions   220
Need to Know More?   225

Chapter 11
Troubleshooting **227**
System Startup   228
Initialization   228
Windows 95/98 Startup   228
Windows NT/2000/XP Startup   229
Advanced Startup Options   231
Recovery Console   233
System Monitoring   234
System Configuration   234
Performance and Resource Utilization   235
Event Viewer   238
Network Diagnostics   238
Network Connectivity   238
Replication   242
Security Updates   242
Qchain.exe   243
Hfnetchk.exe   243
Personal Security Advisor   244
IISLockDown   244
Practice Questions   245
Need to Know More?   251

Chapter 12
Remote Access **253**
Overview of Remote Acess   254
Private Networks   254
Remote Access   256

Authentication Protocols   258
Encryption Protocols   259
Configuring Remote Access   260
Enabling Inbound Connections   260
Configuring Ports for VPN Connections   263
Remote Access Policies   264
User Account Dial-In Settings   265
Remote Access Policy Properties   265
Configuring Client Connections   269
Dialing Up to a Private Network   269
Connecting to a Private Network Through the Internet   270
Practice Questions   271
Need to Know More?   276

Chapter 13
Network Security 277

Introduction to Network Security   278
Terminology   278
Securing the Network   279
Security Using Group Policy   281
Security Templates   282
Account Policies   285
Auditing for Security   287
Configuring Auditing   288
Event Logs   289
Practice Questions   292
Need to Know More?   299

Chapter 14
Sample Test 301

Test Questions   302

Chapter 15
Answer Key 325

Appendix A
What's on the CD-ROM...347

Appendix B
Using the *PrepLogic Practice Tests, Preview Edition* Software 351

Glossary 359

Index 365

We Want to Hear from You!

As the reader of this book, *you* are our most important critic and commentator. We value your opinion and want to know what we're doing right, what we could do better, what areas you'd like to see us publish in, and any other words of wisdom you're willing to pass our way.

As an executive editor for Que Certification, I welcome your comments. You can email or write me directly to let me know what you did or didn't like about this book—as well as what we can do to make our books better.

Please note that I cannot help you with technical problems related to the *topic* of this book. We do have a User Services group, however, where I will forward specific technical questions related to the book.

When you write, please be sure to include this book's title and author as well as your name, email address, and phone number. I will carefully review your comments and share them with the author and editors who worked on the book.

Email:	**feedback@quepublishing.com**
Mail:	Jeff Riley
	Executive Editor
	Que Certification
	201 West 103rd Street
	Indianapolis, IN 46290 USA

For more information about this book or another Que Certification title, visit our Web site at **www.quepublishing.com**. Type the ISBN (excluding hyphens) or the title of a book in the Search field to find the page you're looking for.

Introduction

. . . .

Welcome to *MCSA Managing a Microsoft Windows 2000 Network Environment*. Whether this is your first or your fifteenth *Exam Cram* book, you'll find information here and in Chapter 1 that will help ensure your success as you pursue knowledge, experience, and certification. The purpose of this book is to help you get ready to take—and pass—Microsoft Certification Exam 70-218: Managing a Microsoft Windows 2000 Network Environment. This Introduction explains Microsoft's certification programs in general and how the *Exam Cram* series can help you prepare for Microsoft's MCSA Certification Exams.

Exam Cram books help you understand and appreciate the subjects and materials you need to pass Microsoft certification exams. *Exam Cram* books are aimed strictly at test preparation and review. They do not teach you everything you need to know about a topic. Instead, I present and dissect the questions and problems I've found that you're likely to encounter on the Microsoft Certification Exams.

Nevertheless, to completely prepare yourself for any Microsoft test, you should begin by taking the Self-Assessment that immediately follows this Introduction. This tool will help you evaluate your knowledge base against the requirements for an MCSE or MCSA certification under both ideal and real circumstances.

Based on what you learn from this exercise, you may decide to begin your studies with some classroom training or some background reading. On the other hand, you may decide to read one of the many study guides available from Microsoft or third-party vendors on certain topics, including Que Certification's own *Training Guide* series.

I also strongly recommend that you install, configure, and play with the software that you'll be tested on, because nothing beats hands-on experience and familiarity when it comes to understanding the questions you're likely to encounter on a certification test. Book learning is essential, but hands-on experience is the best teacher.

Microsoft Certified Professional (MCP) Program

The Microsoft Certified Professional (MCP) program is undergoing a major restructuring that will allow the maintenance of existing and former certification tracks. For details on the changes as they occur, please visit **www.microsoft.com/traincert/mcp/**. In its current form, it currently includes the following separate tracks, each of which boasts its own special acronym (as a certification candidate, you need to have a high tolerance for alphabet soup of all kinds):

➤ *MCP (Microsoft Certified Professional)*—This is the least prestigious of all the certification tracks from Microsoft. Passing one of the major Microsoft exams qualifies an individual for the MCP credential. Individuals can demonstrate proficiency with additional Microsoft products by passing additional certification exams.

➤ *MCP+I (Microsoft Certified Professional + Internet)*—All exams for this certification have been retired, although individuals who have already earned the MCP+I certification remain certified.

➤ *MCP+SB (Microsoft Certified Professional + Site Building)*—This certification has been noted as pending retirement and one or more of its required exams have already been retired, although individuals who have already earned the MCP+SB certification remain certified.

➤ *MCSA (Microsoft Certified Systems Administrator)*—This newly created certification program is designed for individuals who have experience in implementing and administering Microsoft Windows 2000 networks. This credential is designed to prepare individuals to plan, implement, troubleshoot, and maintain networks and inter-networks built around Microsoft Windows 2000 and Windows .NET Server 2003 technologies within network environments of up to 26,000 users and 100 physical locations.

To obtain an MCSA, an individual must pass one core Operating System exam, two core networking exams, and one elective exam. The Operating System exams require that individuals prove their competence with the installation and maintenance of user operating systems such as Windows XP or Windows 2000 Professional.

In order to fulfill the networking core exam requirements, a candidate may have completed the Accelerated exam, 70-240: Microsoft Windows 2000 Accelerated Exam for MCPs Certified on Microsoft Windows NT

4.0, as an option. This free exam covers all of the material tested in the Core Four exams. The hitch in this plan is that you can take the test only once, and the exam is scheduled for retirement on December 31, 2001. Alternately, a candidate may take 70-215: Installing, Configuring, and Administering Microsoft Windows 2000 Server or the soon to be released 70-275: Installing, Configuring, and Administering Microsoft Windows .NET Server 2003. In addition to 70-240 or 70-215, an MCSA candidate must also pass Exam 70-218: Managing a Microsoft Windows 2000 Network Environment or the soon to be released 70-278: Managing a Microsoft Windows .Net Server Network Environment.

You are also required to take one elective exam. An elective exam can be from a variety of Microsoft exam options or by providing proof of having attained both A+ and Network+, or A+ and Server+ CompTIA certifications.

Note that the exam covered by this book is a core requirement for the MCSA certification. Table 1 shows the requirements for the MCSA certification.

➤ *MCSE (Microsoft Certified Systems Engineer)*—Anyone who has a current MCSE is warranted to possess a high level of networking expertise with Microsoft operating systems and products. This credential is designed to prepare individuals to plan, implement, maintain, and support information systems, networks, and inter-networks built around Microsoft Windows 2000 and its BackOffice Server 2000 family of products.

To obtain an MCSE, an individual must pass four core Operating System exams, one optional core exam, and two elective exams. The Operating System exams require that individuals prove their competence with desktop and server operating systems and networking/internetworking components.

For a Windows NT 4 MCSE, the Accelerated exam, 70-240: Microsoft Windows 2000 Accelerated Exam for MCPs Certified on Microsoft Windows NT 4.0. Alternately, the Core Four exams are 70-210: Installing, Configuring, and Administering Microsoft Windows 2000 Professional, 70-215: Installing, Configuring, and Administering Microsoft Windows 2000 Server, 70-216: Implementing and Administering a Microsoft Windows 2000 Network Infrastructure, and 70-217: Implementing and Administering a Microsoft Windows 2000 Directory Services Infrastructure.

To fulfill the fifth core exam requirement, you can choose from three Design exams: 70-219: Designing a Microsoft Windows 2000 Directory Services Infrastructure, 70-220: Designing Security for a Microsoft

Windows 2000 Network, or 70-221: Designing a Microsoft Windows 2000 Network Infrastructure. You are also required to take two elective exams. An elective exam can be from any number of subject or product areas, primarily BackOffice Server 2000 components. The two Design exams that you don't select as your fifth core exam also qualify as electives. If you are on your way to becoming an MCSE and have already taken some exams, visit **www.microsoft.com/traincert/** for information on how to complete your MCSE certification.

If you are an MCP or MCSE and want to review how the certification tracks are changing, please visit **www.microsoft.com/traincert/**.

New MCSE candidates must pass seven tests to meet the MCSE requirements. It's not uncommon for the entire process to take over a year, and many individuals find that they must take a test more than once to pass. The primary goal of the *Training Guide* and *Exam Cram* test preparation books is to make it possible, given proper study and preparation, to pass all Microsoft certification tests on the first try. Table 2 shows the required and elective exams for the Windows 2000 MCSE certification.

➤ *MCSE+I (Microsoft Certified Systems Engineer + Internet)*—This certification has been noted as pending retirement, although individuals who have already earned the MCSE+I certification remain certified.

➤ *MCSD (Microsoft Certified Solution Developer)*—These individuals are qualified to design and develop custom business solutions by using Microsoft development tools, technologies, and platforms. The new track includes certification exams that test users' abilities to build Web-based, distributed, and commerce applications by using Microsoft products such as Microsoft SQL Server, Microsoft Visual Studio, and Microsoft Component Services.

To become an MCSD, you must pass a total of four exams: three core exams and one elective exam. Each candidate must choose one of these three desktop Application exams: 70-016: Designing and Implementing Desktop Applications with Microsoft Visual C++ 6.0, 70-156: Designing and Implementing Desktop Applications with Microsoft Visual FoxPro 6.0, or 70-176: Designing and Implementing Desktop Applications with Microsoft Visual Basic 6.0.In addition, one of these three distributed Application exams are required: 70-015: Designing and Implementing Distributed Applications with Microsoft Visual C++ 6.0, 70-155: Designing and Implementing Distributed Applications with Microsoft Visual FoxPro 6.0, or 70-175: Designing and Implementing Distributed Applications with Microsoft Visual Basic 6.0. The third core exam is 70-100: Analyzing Requirements and Defining Solution Architectures.

Elective exams cover specific Microsoft applications and languages, including Visual Basic, C++, the Microsoft Foundation Classes, Access, SQL Server, Excel, and more.

For the new MCSD for .NET Technologies, another set of requirements and exams should be followed. For this MCSD the candidate must pass four core exams and one elective exam. The elective exam is added to show a mastery of a Microsoft Server topic along with the development requirements of the .NET version of the MCSD. The core exams provide a measure of technical proficiency in developing and administering enterprise applications created with Microsoft development tools, technologies, and platforms like Visual Studio .NET.

➤ *MCAD (Microsoft Certified Application Developer)*—The Microsoft Certified Application Developer (MCAD) for Microsoft .NET credential is for professionals who use Microsoft technologies to develop and maintain department-level applications, components, Web or desktop clients, or back-end data services. MCAD candidates must pass two core exams and one elective exam in a specialization area. To find out more about the MCAD and the requirements for achieving this certification, see **http://www.microsoft.com/traincert/mcp/mcad/requirements.asp**.

➤ *MCDBA (Microsoft Certified Database Administrator)*—The MCDBA credential reflects the skills required to implement and administer Microsoft SQL Server databases. To obtain an MCDBA, an individual must demonstrate the ability to derive physical database designs, develop logical data models, create physical databases, create data services by using Transact-SQL, manage and maintain databases, configure and manage security, monitor and optimize databases, and install and configure Microsoft SQL Server.

To become an MCDBA, you must pass a total of three core exams and one elective exam. The required core exams are 70-028: Administering Microsoft SQL Server 7.0 or 70-228: Installing, Configuring, and Administering Microsoft SQL Server 2000 Enterprise Edition; 70-029: Designing and Implementing Databases with Microsoft SQL Server 7.0 or 70-229: Designing and Implementing Databases with Microsoft SQL Server 2000 Enterprise Edition; and 70-215: Installing, Configuring, and Administering Microsoft Windows 2000 Server.

The elective exams that you can choose from cover specific uses of SQL Server and include 70-015: Designing and Implementing Distributed Applications with Microsoft Visual C++ 6.0, 70-019: Designing and Implementing Data Warehouses with Microsoft SQL Server 7.0, 70-155: Designing and Implementing Distributed Applications with Microsoft

Visual FoxPro 6.0, 70-175: Designing and Implementing Distributed Applications with Microsoft Visual Basic 6.0, and one exam relating to Windows 2000: 70-216: Implementing and Administering a Microsoft Windows 2000 Network Infrastructure.

If you have taken the three core Windows NT 4 exams on your path to becoming an MCSE, you qualify for the Accelerated exam (it replaces the Network Infrastructure exam requirement). The Accelerated exam covers the objectives of all four of the Windows 2000 core exams. In addition to taking the Accelerated exam, you must take only the two SQL exams (70-228 and 70-229): Administering and Database Design.

➤ *MCT (Microsoft Certified Trainer)*—Microsoft Certified Trainers are deemed able to deliver elements of the official Microsoft curriculum, based on technical knowledge and instructional ability. Thus, it is necessary for an individual seeking MCT credentials (which are granted on a course-by-course basis) to pass the related certification exam for a course, complete the official Microsoft training in the subject area, and demonstrate an ability to teach.

This teaching skill criterion may be satisfied by proof of training certification (from Novell, Banyan, Lotus, the Santa Cruz Operation, or Cisco) or by taking a Microsoft-sanctioned workshop on instruction. Microsoft makes it clear that MCTs are important cogs in the Microsoft training channels. Instructors must be MCTs before Microsoft allows them to teach in any of its official training channels, including Microsoft's affiliated Certified Technical Education Centers (CTECs) and its online training partner network. As of October 31, 2001, MCT candidates must also possess a current MCSE, MCSD, or MCDBA certification, as well as fulfilling classroom instruction and continuing educational credit requirements before renewal in October, 2002.

Microsoft has announced that the MCP+I and MCSE+I credentials will not be continued with the MCSE exams for the Windows 2000 program because the skill set for the Internet portion of the program has been included in the new MCSE program. For details on these tracks, go to **www.microsoft. com/traincert/**.

Technology continues to change, and new products replace older ones. When a Microsoft product becomes obsolete, MCPs typically have to recertify on current versions. If they want to remain competitive in the modern job market.

For the most current information on Microsoft's certification programs, go to **www.microsoft.com/traincert/**. Because Microsoft's Web site changes often, this URL may not work, so try the Search tool on Microsoft's site using either MCP or the quoted phrase Microsoft Certified Professional as a search string.

Taking a Certification Exam

After you've prepared for your exam, you need to register for the exam with a testing center. Contact one of the following testing groups for current pricing and registration information, as pricing and testing centers can change over time. In the United States and Canada, tests are administered by Sylvan Prometric and by Virtual University Enterprises (VUE). Here's how you can contact them:

➤ Sylvan *Prometric*—You can sign up for a test through the company's Web site at **www.2test.com**. Within the United States and Canada, you can register by phone at (800) 755-EXAM. If you live outside this region, check the company's Web site for the appropriate phone number.

➤ *Virtual University Enterprises*—You can sign up for a test or get the phone numbers for local testing centers through the Web page at **www.vue.com/ms/**.

To sign up for a test, you may pay with a valid credit card or by check (only in the United States). Contact the company for mailing instructions if paying by check. Your payment must be verified before you can actually register for a test.

To schedule an exam, call the company or visit its Web page at least one day in advance (it is even better to do so at least several days before the day you wish to test). To cancel or reschedule an exam, you must call before 7 P.M. Pacific Standard Time the day before the scheduled test time (if you don't contact the company, you may be charged even if you don't take the test). When you want to schedule a test, have the following information ready:

➤ Your name, organization, and mailing address.

➤ Your Microsoft Test ID. (In the United States, your Test ID is your Social Security number; citizens of other nations should call ahead to find out what type of identification number is required to register for a test.)

➤ The name and number of the exam you want to take.

➤ A method of payment. (As I've already mentioned, a credit card is the most convenient method, but alternate means can be arranged in advance, if necessary.)

After you have signed up for a test, you'll be informed when and where the test is scheduled. Try to arrive at least 15 minutes early. You must supply two forms of identification—one of which must be a photo ID—to be admitted into the testing room.

All exams are completely closed-book. You may not take anything with you into the testing area, but you will be furnished with a blank sheet of paper and a pen or, in some cases, an erasable plastic sheet and an erasable pen. I suggest that you immediately write down on that sheet of paper all of the information you've memorized for the test. In *Exam Cram* books, this information appears on a tear-out sheet inside the front cover of each book. You will have some time to compose yourself, record this information, and take a sample orientation exam before you begin the real thing. I suggest you take the orientation test before taking your first exam. However, you probably won't need to do this more than once because the exams are fairly identical in layout, behavior, and controls.

When you complete a Microsoft Certification Exam, the software lets you know whether you've passed or failed. If you need to retake an exam, you'll have to schedule a new test with Sylvan Prometric or VUE and pay another fee.

 The first time you fail a test, you can retake the test the next day. However, if you fail a second time, you must wait 14 days before retaking that test. The 14-day waiting period remains in effect for all retakes after the second failure.

Tracking MCP Status

As soon as you pass any Microsoft exam (except Networking Essentials), you'll attain Microsoft Certified Professional (MCP) status. Microsoft also generates transcripts that indicate which exams you have passed. You can view a copy of your transcript at any time by going to the MCP secured site and selecting Transcript Tool. This tool allows you to print a copy of your current transcript and confirm your certification status.

After you pass the necessary set of exams, you are certified. Official certification normally takes anywhere from six to eight weeks, so don't expect to get your credentials overnight. When the package for a qualified certification arrives, it includes a Welcome Kit that contains a number of elements (see Microsoft's Web site for other benefits of specific certifications):

➤ A certificate suitable for framing, along with a wallet card and lapel pin.

➤ A license to use the MCP logo, thereby allowing you to use the logo in advertisements, promotions, and documents, and on letterhead, business cards, and so on. Along with the license, you'll receive an MCP logo sheet, which includes camera-ready artwork. (Note: Before using any of the artwork, individuals must sign and return a licensing agreement that indicates they'll abide by its terms and conditions.)

➤ A subscription to *Microsoft Certified Professional Magazine*, which provides ongoing data about testing and certification activities, requirements, and changes to the program.

Many people believe that the benefits of MCP certification go well beyond the perks that Microsoft provides to newly anointed members of this elite group. An increasing number of job listings request or require applicants to have an MCP, MCSE, and so on, and many individuals who complete the program qualify for increases in pay and/or responsibility. As an official recognition of hard work and broad knowledge, an MCP credential is a badge of honor in many IT organizations.

Preparing for a Certification Exam

To prepare for any Microsoft Windows-related test (including 70-218: Managing a Microsoft Windows 2000 Network Environment), you must obtain and study materials designed to provide comprehensive information about the product and its capabilities. The following list of materials will help you prepare:

➤ The exam preparation content, practice tests, and review materials found in Que Certification's *Exam Cram* and *Training Guide* products.

➤ The Windows 2000 Server and Workstation product CDs include comprehensive online documentation and related materials. This should be a primary resource when you are preparing for the test. Another valuable resource is the Windows 2000 Resource Kit, which contains exhaustive documentation necessary to the understanding of network administrators.

➤ The exam preparation materials, practice tests, and self-assessment exams on the Microsoft Training and Services page at **www.microsoft.com/traincert/**. The Testing Innovations article at **www.microsoft.com/TRAINCERT/mcpexams/faq/innovations.asp**

includes a downloadable series of demonstrations and samples of the new question types found on the Windows 2000 MCSE exams. Find the materials, download them, and use them.

In addition, you'll probably find the following materials useful in your quest for Windows 2000 expertise:

➤ *Microsoft TechNet CD*—This monthly CD-based publication delivers numerous electronic titles that include coverage of Windows 2000 and related topics on the Technical Information (TechNet) CD. Its offerings include product facts, technical notes, tools and utilities, and information on how to access the Seminars Online training materials for Windows 2000 networks. A subscription to TechNet costs $299 per year, but it is well worth the price. Visit **www.microsoft.com/technet/** and check out the information under the TechNet Subscription menu entry for more details.

➤ *Study guides*—Several publishers offer Windows 2000 titles. Que Certification series includes the following:

➤*The Exam Cram series*—These books give you information about the material you need to know to pass the tests.

➤*The Training Guide series*—These books provide a greater level of detail than the *Exam Cram* books and are designed to teach you everything you need to know from an exam perspective. Each book comes with a CD that contains interactive practice exams from PrepLogic in a variety of testing formats.

➤ *Classroom training*—CTECs, online partners, and third-party training companies (such as Wave Technologies, Learning Tree, Data-Tech, and others) all offer classroom training on Windows 2000 networking. The aim of these companies is to help you prepare to pass and score well on Exam 70-218. Although the cost of such training is approximately $350 per day, most individuals find it to be quite worthwhile.

➤ *Other publications*—There's no shortage of materials available about Microsoft Windows 2000. Refer to the resource sections at the end of each chapter in this book for additional sources of information.

About This Book

Each topical *Exam Cram* chapter follows a regular structure, along with graphical cues about important or useful information. Here's the structure of a typical chapter:

➤ *Opening hotlists*—Each chapter begins with a list of the terms, tools, and techniques that you must learn and understand before you can be fully conversant with that chapter's subject matter. Following the hotlists are one or two introductory paragraphs that explain what will be discussed in the chapter.

➤ *Topical coverage*—After the opening hotlists, each chapter covers a series of topics related to the chapter's subject title. Throughout this section, topics or concepts likely to appear on a test are highlighted using a special Exam Alert layout, like this:

This is what an Exam Alert looks like. Normally, an Exam Alert stresses concepts, terms, software, or activities that relate to one or more certification test questions.

Pay close attention to material flagged as an Exam Alert because this indicates that the information is really important. Most of the information that appears on The Cram Sheet appears as Exam Alerts within the text. You'll also find that the meat of each chapter is worth knowing, too, when preparing for the test. Because material in this book is very condensed, I recommend that you use this book along with other resources to achieve the maximum benefit.

In addition to the Exam Alerts, tips are provided that will help you build a better foundation for Microsoft Windows 2000 Network Administration knowledge. Although the information may not be on the exam, it is related and will help you become a better test-taker.

This is how tips are formatted. Keep your eyes open for these, and quickly you'll become a Windows 2000 guru.

➤ *Practice questions*—Although I talk about test questions and topics throughout the book, a section at the end of each chapter presents a series of mock test questions and explanations of both correct and incorrect answers.

➤ *Details and resources*—Every chapter ends with a section titled Need to Know More? This section provides direct pointers to Microsoft and third-party resources offering more details on the chapter's subject. In addition, this section rates the quality and thoroughness of the topic's coverage by each resource. Select the resources you find most useful in this collection, but don't feel compelled to use all of them. I recommend only resources that I use on a regular basis, so none are a waste of your time or money (however, purchasing them all at once probably represents an expense that many network administrators and would-be MCPs and MCSAs may find hard to justify).

The bulk of the book follows this chapter structure slavishly, but there are a few other elements that I'd like to point out. Chapter 15 includes a sample test that provides a good review of the material presented throughout the book to ensure you're ready for the exam. Chapter 16 is an answer key to the sample test that appears in Chapter 15. In addition, you'll find a handy glossary and an index.

Finally, the tear-out Cram Sheet attached to the inside front cover of this *Exam Cram* book represents a condensed and compiled collection of facts and tips that are useful to memorize before taking the test. Because you can write this information onto a piece of paper before taking the exam, you can master this information by brute force—you need to remember it only long enough to write it down when you walk into the test room. I suggest that you review it just before you walk in to take the test.

How to Use This Book

I've structured the topics in this book to build on each other. Therefore, some topics in later chapters make more sense after you've read earlier chapters. That's why I suggest you read this book from front to back for your initial test preparation. If you need to brush up on a topic or you have to bone up for a second try, use the index or table of contents to go straight to the topics and questions that you need to study. Beyond helping you prepare for the test, this book serves as a tightly focused reference to some of the most important aspects of Microsoft Windows 2000 networks.

Given all the book's elements and its specialized focus, I've tried to create a tool that will help you prepare for—and pass—Microsoft Exam 70-218. Please share your feedback on the book with us, especially if you have ideas about how I can improve it for future test-takers. I'll consider everything you say carefully, and I'll respond to all suggestions.

Send your questions or comments to me at **wargod@tca.net**. Please remember to include the title of the book in your message so I won't have to guess which book you're writing about. Also, be sure to check out the Web pages at **www.quepublishing.com**, where you'll find information updates, commentary, and certification information.

Thanks, and enjoy the book!

Self-Assessment

The purpose of this Self-Assessment is to help you evaluate your readiness to tackle Microsoft Certified Systems Engineer (MCSE) or Microsoft Certified Systems Administrator (MCSA) certification. It should also help you understand what you need to know to master the topic of this book—namely, Exam 70-218: Managing a Microsoft Windows 2000 Network Environment. Before you take this Self-Assessment, you should think about the concerns you have about pursuing an MCSE or MCSA for Windows 2000 and what an "ideal" candidate is.

MCSEs in the Real World

The next section describes the "ideal" candidate, although very few real candidates meet all of the requirements. In fact, some of those requirements may seem impossible to fulfill, especially with the ongoing changes made to the program to support Windows 2000. Although the requirements for obtaining an MCSE may seem formidable, they are by no means unattainable. However, it does take time, involves some expense, and requires real effort to get through the process.

Increasing numbers of people are attaining Microsoft certifications, and you can also reach that goal. If you're willing to tackle the process seriously and work toward obtaining the necessary experience and knowledge, you can take—and pass—all of the certification tests involved in obtaining an MCSE. In fact, Que Certification designed our *Training Guide* series, the companion *Exam Crams*, and partnered with *PrepLogic* to bring you state-of-the-art practice exams to assist you in studying for these exams.

In addition to MCSE, other Microsoft certifications include the following:

➤ *Microsoft Certified Systems Administrator (MCSA)*, which is designed for network administrators and requires one operating system exam, two networking exams, plus one elective exam drawn from a list of options.

➤ *Microsoft Certified Solution Developer (MCSD)*, which is aimed at software developers and requires one specific exam, two more exams on client and distributed topics, plus a fourth elective exam drawn from a different, but limited, pool of options.

➤ Microsoft certifications that require one test, such as Microsoft Certified Professional (MCP), or several tests, such as Microsoft Certified Database Administrator (MCDBA), Microsoft Certified Application Developer (MCAD), and Microsoft Certified Solution Devloper (MCSD).

Who Is an Ideal Windows 2000 MCSE Candidate?

Just to give you some idea of the qualifications an ideal MCSE candidate should have, here are some relevant statistics about background and experience. Don't worry if you don't meet these qualifications, or don't come that close—this is a far from ideal world, and if you fall short, it just means that you simply have more work to do in those areas.

➤ Academic or professional training in network theory, concepts, and operations. This includes everything from networking media and transmission techniques through network operating systems, services, and applications.

➤ Three-plus years of professional networking experience, including experience with Ethernet, token ring, modems, and other networking media. This must include installation, configuration, upgrade, and troubleshooting experience.

➤ Two-plus years in a networked environment that includes hands-on experience with Windows 2000 Server, Windows 2000 Professional, Windows NT Server, Windows NT Workstation, and Windows 95 or Windows 98. A solid understanding of each system's architecture, installation, configuration, maintenance, and troubleshooting is also essential.

The Windows 2000 MCSE program is much more rigorous than the previous NT MCSE program; therefore, you'll really need some hands-on experience. Some of the exams require you to solve real-world case studies and network design issues, so the more hands-on experience you have, the better.

➤ Knowledge of the various methods for installing Windows 2000, including manual and unattended installations.

➤ A thorough understanding of key networking protocols, addressing, and name resolution, including TCP/IP, IPX/SPX, and NetBEUI.

➤ A thorough understanding of NetBIOS naming, browsing, and file and print services.

➤ Familiarity with key Windows 2000 TCP/IP-based services, including HyperText Transfer Protocol (HTTP), Dynamic Host Configuration Protocol (DHCP), Windows Internet Naming Service (WINS), Domain Name Service (DNS), plus familiarity with one or more of the following: Internet Information Server (IIS), Index Server, and Proxy Server.

➤ An understanding of how to implement security and auditing for key network data in a Windows 2000 environment.

➤ Working knowledge of NetWare 3.x and 4.x, including IPX/SPX frame formats; NetWare file, print, and directory services; and both Novell and Microsoft client software. Working knowledge of Microsoft's Client Services for NetWare (CSNW), Gateway Services for NetWare (GSNW), NetWare Migration Tool (NWCONV), and NetWare Client for Windows (NT, 95, and 98) is essential.

➤ A good working understanding of Active Directory. The more you work with Windows 2000, the more you'll realize that this new operating system is quite different from Windows NT. New technologies such as Active Directory have really changed the way that Windows is configured and used. I recommend that you find out as much as you can about Active Directory and acquire as much experience using this technology as possible. The time you take learning about Active Directory will be time very well spent!

Fundamentally, this boils down to a bachelor's degree in computer science, plus three years' experience working in a position involving network design, installation, configuration, and maintenance. Que Certification believes that well under half of all certification candidates meet these requirements, and that most meet less than half of these requirements—at least, when they begin the certification process. However, many candidates have survived this ordeal and become certified. You can also survive it—especially if you heed what our Self-Assessment can tell you about what you already know and what you need to learn.

Put Yourself to the Test

The following series of questions and observations is designed to help you determine what you must do to pursue Microsoft certification and what kinds of resources you may consult on your quest. Be absolutely honest in your answers, or you'll end up wasting money on exams that you're not yet ready to take. There are no right or wrong answers—only steps along the path to certification. Only you can decide where you really belong in the broad spectrum of aspiring candidates.

At the very minimum, you should have the following:

➤ Some background in computer science, even a limited one

➤ Hands-on experience with Microsoft products and technologies

Educational Background

Following are some questions to help you determine if you need further education and training before attempting to take an exam:

1. Have you ever taken any computer-related classes? [Yes or No]

 ➤ If Yes, proceed to Question 2; if No, proceed to Question 4.

2. Have you taken any classes on computer operating systems? [Yes or No]

 ➤ If Yes, you will probably be able to handle Microsoft's architecture and system component discussions. If you're rusty, brush up on basic operating system concepts, especially virtual memory, multitasking regimes, user mode versus kernel mode operation, and general computer security topics.

 ➤ If No, consider some basic reading in this area. I strongly recommend a good general operating systems book, such as *Operating System Concepts, 5th Edition*, by Abraham Silberschatz and Peter Baer Galvin (John Wiley & Sons, 1998, ISBN 0-471-36414-2). If this title doesn't appeal to you, check out reviews for other, similar titles at your favorite online bookstore.

3. Have you taken any networking concepts or technologies classes? [Yes or No]

 ➤ If Yes, you will probably be able to handle Microsoft's networking terminology, concepts, and technologies (brace yourself for frequent departures from normal usage). If you're rusty, brush up on basic networking concepts and terminology, especially networking media, transmission types, the OSI Reference Model, and networking technologies such as Ethernet, Token Ring, FDDI, and WAN links.

➤ If No, you may want to read one or two books in this topic area. The two best books that I know of are *Computer Networks, 3rd Edition*, by Andrew S. Tanenbaum (Prentice Hall, 1996, ISBN 0-13-083617-6) and *Computer Networks and Internets, 2nd Edition*, by Douglas E. Comer and Ralph E. Droms (Prentice Hall, 1998, ISBN 0-130-83617-6).

➤ Skip to the next section, "Hands-on Experience."

4. Have you done any reading on operating systems or networks? [Yes or No]

➤ If Yes, review the requirements stated in the first paragraphs after Questions 2 and 3. If you meet those requirements, move on to the next section. If No, consult the recommended reading for both topics. A strong background will help you prepare for the Microsoft exams better than anything else.

Hands-On Experience

The most important key to success on all of the Microsoft tests is hands-on experience, especially with Windows 2000 Server and Professional, plus the many add-on services and BackOffice components around which so many of the Microsoft certification exams revolve. After taking this Self-Assessment, you should learn at least this—there's no substitute for time spent installing, configuring, and using the various Microsoft products on which you'll be tested repeatedly and in depth.

5. Have you installed, configured, and worked with the following:

➤ Windows 2000 Server? [Yes or No]

➤ If Yes, make sure that you understand the basic concepts as covered in Exam 70-215. You should also study the TCP/IP interfaces, utilities, and services for Exam 70-216, plus implementing security features for Exam 70-220.

 You can download objectives, practice exams, and other data about Microsoft exams from the Training and Certification page at **www.microsoft.com/traincert/**. Use the "Exam Resources" link to obtain specific exam information.

➤ If you haven't worked with Windows 2000 Server, you must obtain one or two machines and a copy of Windows 2000 Server. Then, learn the operating system and whatever other software components on which you'll also be tested.

➤ In fact, I recommend that you obtain two computers—each with a network interface—and set up a two-node network on which to practice. With decent Windows 2000-capable computers selling for about $500 to $600 apiece these days, this shouldn't be too much of a financial hardship. You may have to scrounge to come up with the necessary software, but if you scour the Microsoft Web site you can usually find low-cost options to obtain evaluation copies of most of the software that you'll need.

6. Windows 2000 Professional? [Yes or No]

➤ If Yes, make sure you understand the concepts covered in Exam 70-210.

➤ If No, you should obtain a copy of Windows 2000 Professional and learn how to install, configure, and maintain it. You can use Que Certification's *MCSE Windows 2000 Professional Exam Cram* and our *MCSE Training Guide (70-210): Installing, Configuring, and Administering Windows 2000 Professional* to guide your activities and studies or work straight from Microsoft's test objectives if you prefer.

For any and all of these Microsoft exams, the Resource Kits for the topics involved are a good study resource. You can purchase softcover Resource Kits from Microsoft Press (search for them at **http://mspress.microsoft.com/**), but they also appear on the TechNet CDs (**www.microsoft.com/technet/**). Along with *Exam Crams*, I believe that Resource Kits are among the best tools you can use to prepare for Microsoft exams.

7. For any specific Microsoft product that is not itself an operating system (for example, Exchange 2000), have you installed, configured, used, and upgraded this software? [Yes or No]

➤ If Yes, skip to the next section. If No, you must get some experience. Read on for suggestions on how to do this.

➤ Experience is a must with any Microsoft product exam, be it something as simple as FrontPage 2000 or as challenging as Exchange 2000. For trial copies of other software, search Microsoft's Web site using the name of the product as your search term. Also, search for bundles like "BackOffice" or "Small Business Server."

If you have the funds, or your employer will pay your way, consider taking a class at a Certified Training and Education Center (CTEC) or at an Authorized Academic Training Partner (AATP). In addition to classroom exposure to the topic of your choice, you get a copy of the software that is the focus of your course, along with a trial version of whatever operating system it needs and the training materials for that class.

➤ Before you even think about taking any Microsoft exam, make sure that you've spent enough time with the related software to understand how it may be installed and configured, how to maintain such an installation, and how to troubleshoot that software when things go wrong. This will help you in the exam, and in real life!

Testing Your Exam-Readiness

Whether you attend a formal class on a specific topic to get ready for an exam or use written materials to study on your own, some preparation for the Microsoft certification exams is essential. At $100, or better—because exam prices can go up over time, you want to do everything you can to pass on your first try. That's where studying comes in.

I have included a practice exam in this book, so if you don't score well on the test, you can study more and then take the test again. Que Certification also offers *PrepLogic, Preview Edition* as a solid practice exam engine.If you still don't hit a score of at least 75 to 80 percent after these tests, you'll want to investigate other practice test resources, such as *www.preplogic.com* and *www.cramsessions.com* where you can affordably purchase a good number of practice questions. Use these questions and extensive review study to brush up on your weak areas as you draw closer to passing your exam.

For any given subject, consider taking a class if you've tackled self-study materials, taken the test, and failed. The opportunity to interact with an instructor and fellow students can make all the difference in the world, if you can afford that privilege. For information about Microsoft classes, visit the Training and Certification page at **www.microsoft.com/traincert/**. Or take a look at **www.microsoft.com/education/?ID=ctec** for information on Microsoft Certified Education Centers or **www.microsoft.com/education/?ID=aatp** for Microsoft Authorized Training Providers.

If you can't afford to take a class, visit the Training and Certification page anyway, because it also includes pointers to free practice exams and to Microsoft Certified Professional Approved Study Guides and other self-study tools. If you can't afford to spend much at all, you should still invest in some low-cost practice exams from commercial vendors.

8. Have you taken a practice exam on your chosen test subject? [Yes or No]

➤ If Yes, and you scored 75 to 80 percent or better, you're probably ready to tackle the real thing. If your score isn't above that threshold, keep at it until you break that barrier.

➤ If No, obtain all of the free and low-budget practice tests you can find and start working. Keep at it until you can break the passing threshold comfortably.

When it comes to assessing your test readiness, there is no better way than to take a good-quality practice exam and pass with a score of 75 percent or better. When I'm preparing myself, I shoot for 85-plus percent, just to leave room for the "weirdness factor" that sometimes shows up on Microsoft exams.

Assessing Readiness for Exam 70-218

In addition to the general exam-readiness information in the previous section, there are several things you can do to prepare for the Managing a Microsoft Windows 2000 Network Environment exam.

You can also cruise the Web looking for "braindumps" (recollections of test topics and experiences recorded by others) to help you anticipate topics that you're likely to encounter on the test. The MCSE mailing list is a good place to ask where the useful braindumps are.

You can't be sure that a braindump's author can provide correct answers. Thus, use the questions to guide your studies, but don't rely on the answers in a braindump to lead you to the truth. Double-check everything you find in any braindump.

Microsoft also recommends checking the Microsoft Knowledge Base (available on its own CD-ROM as part of the TechNet collection or on the Microsoft Web site at **http://support.microsoft.com/support/**) for "meaningful technical support issues" that relate to your exam's topics. Although I'm not sure exactly what the quoted phrase means, I have also noticed some overlap between technical support questions on particular products and troubleshooting questions on the exams for those products.

Onward, Through the Fog!

Once you've assessed your readiness, undertaken the right background studies, obtained the hands-on experience that will help you understand the products and technologies at work, and reviewed the many sources of information to help you prepare for a test, you'll be ready to take a round of practice tests. When your scores come back positive enough to get you through the exam, you're ready to go after the real thing. If you follow this assessment regime, you'll know what you need to study and when you're ready to make a test date at Sylvan Prometric or VUE. Good luck

Microsoft Certification Exams

- -

Terms you'll need to understand:

✓ Case study
✓ Multiple-choice question formats
✓ Build-list-and-reorder question format
✓ Create-a-tree question format
✓ Drag-and-connect question format
✓ Select-and-place question format
✓ Fixed-length tests
✓ Simulations
✓ Adaptive tests
✓ Short-form tests

Techniques you'll need to master:

✓ Assessing your exam-readiness
✓ Answering Microsoft's varying question types
✓ Altering your test strategy depending on the exam format
✓ Practicing (to make perfect)
✓ Making the best use of the testing software
✓ Budgeting your time
✓ Guessing (as a last resort)

Exam-taking is not something that most people anticipate eagerly, no matter how well prepared they may be. In most cases, familiarity helps offset test anxiety. In plain English, this means you probably won't be as nervous when you take your fourth or fifth Microsoft certification exam as you'll be when you take your first one.

Whether it's your first exam or your tenth, understanding the details of taking the new exam (how much time to spend on questions, the environment you'll be in, and so on) and the new exam software will help you concentrate on the material rather than on the setting. Likewise, mastering a few basic exam-taking skills should help you recognize (and perhaps even outfox) some of the tricks and snares you're bound to find in some exam questions.

This chapter explains the exam environment and software and describes some proven exam-taking strategies that you can use to your advantage.

Assessing Exam-Readiness

I strongly recommend that you read through and take the Self-Assessment included with this book (it appears just before this chapter). This will help you compare your knowledge base to the requirements for obtaining an MCSE or MCSA, and it will also help you identify parts of your background or experience that may need improvement, enhancement, or further learning. If you get the right set of basics under your belt, obtaining Microsoft certification will be that much easier.

After you've gone through the Self-Assessment, you can remedy those topical areas in which your background or experience may be lacking. You can also tackle subject matter for individual tests at the same time, so you can continue making progress while you're catching up in some areas.

After you've worked through an *Exam Cram*, have read the supplementary materials, and have taken the practice test, you'll have a pretty clear idea of when you should be ready to take the real exam. Although I strongly recommend that you keep practicing until your scores top the 75 percent mark, 80 percent is a better goal because it gives some margin for error when you are in an actual, stressful exam situation. Keep taking practice tests and studying the materials until you attain that score. You'll find more pointers on how to study and prepare in the Self-Assessment. But now, on to the exam itself.

What to Expect at the Testing Center

When you arrive at the testing center where you scheduled your exam, you must sign in with an exam coordinator and show two forms of identification, one of which must be a photo ID. After you've signed in and your time slot arrives, you'll be asked to deposit any books, bags, cell phones, or other items you brought with you. Then, you'll be escorted into a closed room.

All exams are completely closed-book. Although you are not permitted to take anything with you into the testing area, you are furnished with a blank sheet of paper and a pen (in some cases, an erasable plastic sheet and an erasable pen). Immediately before entering the testing center, try to memorize as much of the important material as you can, so you can write that information on the blank sheet as soon as you are seated in front of the computer. You can refer to this piece of paper during the test, but you'll have to surrender the sheet when you leave the room. Because your timer does not start until you begin the testing process, it is best to do this first while the information is still fresh in your mind.

You will have some time to compose yourself, write down information on the paper you're given, and take a sample orientation exam before you begin the real thing. I suggest you take the orientation test before taking your first exam (because the exams are generally identical in layout, behavior, and controls, you probably won't need to do this more than once).

Typically, the room has one to six computers, and each workstation is separated from the others by dividers. Most test rooms feature a wall with a large picture window. This permits the exam coordinator to monitor the room, prevent exam-takers from talking to one another, and observe anything out of the ordinary. The exam coordinator will have preloaded the appropriate Microsoft certification exam (for this book, Exam 70-218), and you'll be permitted to start as soon as you're seated in front of the computer.

All Microsoft certification exams allow a certain maximum amount of time in which to complete your work (this time is indicated on the exam by an on-screen counter/clock, so you can check the time remaining whenever you like). All Microsoft certification exams are computer-generated. In addition to multiple choice, you'll encounter select and place (drag and drop), create a tree (categorization and prioritization), drag and connect, and build list and reorder (list prioritization) on most exams. The questions are constructed to check your mastery of basic facts and figures about Microsoft Windows 2000 Network Administration and to require you to evaluate one or more sets of circumstances or requirements. Often, you'll be asked to give more than one answer to a question. You may also be asked to select the best or most effective solution to a problem from a range of choices, all of which are technically correct. Taking the exam is quite an adventure, and it involves real thinking. This book shows you what to expect and how to deal with the potential problems, puzzles, and predicaments.

In the next section, you'll learn more about the format of Microsoft test questions and how to answer them.

Exam Layout and Design: New Case Study Format

The format of Microsoft exams can vary. For example, many exams consist of a series of case studies, with six types of questions regarding each presented case. Other exams may have the same six types of questions but no complex multi-question case studies.

For the Design exams, each case study presents a detailed problem that you must read and analyze. Figure 1.1 shows an example of what a case study looks like. You must select the different tabs in the case study to view the entire case.

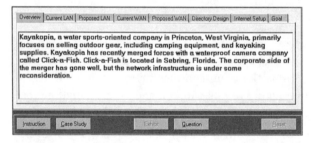

Figure 1.1 This is a typical case study.

Following each case study is a set of questions related to the case study. These questions can be one of six types (which are discussed next). Careful attention to details provided in the case study is the key to success. Be prepared to toggle frequently between the case study and the questions as you work. Some of the case studies also include diagrams (called *exhibits*) that you'll need to examine closely to understand how to answer the questions.

After you complete a case study, you can review all of the questions and your answers. However, when you move on to the next case study, you cannot return to the previous case study and make any changes.

Following are the six types of question formats:

➤ Multiple-choice, single answer

➤ Multiple-choice, multiple answers

➤ Build list and reorder (list prioritization)

➤ Create a tree

➤ Drag and connect

➤ Select and place (drag and drop)

 Exam formats may vary by test center location. You may want to call the test center to see if you can find out which type of test you'll encounter. Some exams will be offered in both forms on a random basis which cannot be pre-determined.

Multiple-Choice Question Format

Some exam questions require you to select a single answer, whereas others ask you to select multiple correct answers. The following multiple-choice question requires you to select a single correct answer. Following the question is a brief summary of each potential answer and why it is either right or wrong.

Question 1

You have three domains connected to an empty root domain under one contiguous domain name: **tutu.com**. This organization is formed into a forest arrangement with a secondary domain called **frog.com**. How many Schema Masters exist for this arrangement?

○ a. 1

○ b. 2

○ c. 3

○ d. 4

The correct answer is a, because only one Schema Master is necessary for a forest arrangement. The other answers (b, c, and d) are misleading because you are led to believe that Schema Masters may be in each domain, or that you should have one for each contiguous domain namespace.

This sample question format corresponds closely to the Microsoft Certification Exam format (of course, questions are not followed by answer keys on the exam). To select an answer, you position the cursor over the radio button next to the answer and click the mouse button to select the answer.

Let's examine a question where one or more answers are possible. This type of question provides checkboxes rather than radio buttons for marking all appropriate selections.

Question 2

How can you seize FSMO roles? [Check all correct answers]
- ❑ a. The ntdsutil.exe utility
- ❑ b. The Replication Monitor
- ❑ c. The secedit.exe utility
- ❑ d. Active Directory Domains and FSMOs

Answers a and b are correct. You can seize FSMO roles from a server that is still running through the Replication Monitor, or in the case of a server failure, you can seize roles with the ntdsutil.exe utility. The secedit.exe utility is used to force group policies into play; therefore, answer c is incorrect. Active Directory Domains and Trusts are a combination of truth and fiction; therefore, answer d is incorrect.

For this particular question, two answers are required. Microsoft sometimes gives partial credit for partially correct answers. For Question 2, you have to check the boxes next to answers a and b to obtain credit for a correct answer. Notice that picking the right answers also means knowing why the other answers are wrong.

Build-List-and-Reorder Question Format

Questions in the build-list-and-reorder format present two lists of items: one on the left and one on the right. To answer the question, you must move items from the list on the right to the list on the left. The final list must then be reordered into a specific order.

These questions can are usually in the form, "From the following list of choices, pick the choices that answer the question. Arrange the list in a certain order." To give you practice with this type of question, some questions of this type are included in this study guide. Here's an example of how they appear in this book; for a sample of how they appear on the test, see Figure 1.2.

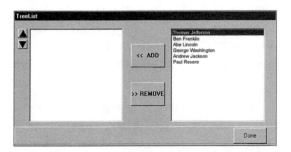

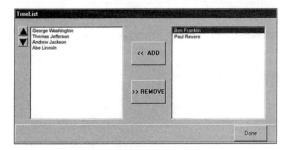

Figure 1.2   This is how build-list-and-reorder questions appear.

Question 3

From the following list of famous people, pick those that have been elected President of the United States. Arrange the list in the order in which they served.

Thomas Jefferson

Ben Franklin

Abe Lincoln

George Washington

Andrew Jackson

Paul Revere

The correct answer is:

> George Washington
>
> Thomas Jefferson
>
> Andrew Jackson
>
> Abe Lincoln

On an actual exam, the entire list of famous people would initially appear in the list on the right. You would move the four correct answers to the list on the left and then reorder the list on the left. Notice that the answer to the question did not include all items from the initial list. However, this may not always be the case.

To move an item from the right list to the left list, first select the item by clicking on it and then clicking the Add button (left arrow). Once you move an item from one list to the other, you can move the item back by first selecting the item and then clicking the appropriate button (either the Add button or the Remove button). After items have been moved to the left list, you can reorder the list by selecting an item and clicking the up or down button.

Create-a-Tree Question Format

Questions in the create-a-tree format also present two lists: one on the left and one on the right. The list on the right consists of individual items, and the list on the left consists of nodes in a tree. To answer the question, you must move items from the list on the right to the appropriate node in the tree.

These questions are basically a matching exercise. Items from the list on the right are placed under the appropriate category in the list on the left. Here's an example of how they appear in this book; for a sample of how they appear on the test, see Figure 1.3.

Question 4

The calendar year is divided into four seasons:

Winter

Spring

Summer

Fall

Identify the season when each of the following holidays occurs:

Christmas

Fourth of July

Labor Day

Flag Day

Memorial Day

Washington's Birthday

Thanksgiving

Easter

The correct answer is:

> Winter
>
>> Christmas
>>
>> Washington's Birthday
>
> Spring
>
>> Flag Day
>>
>> Memorial Day
>>
>> Easter
>
> Summer
>
>> Fourth of July
>>
>> Labor Day
>
> Fall
>
>> Thanksgiving

In this case, all of the items in the list were used. However, this may not always be the case.

To move an item from the right list to its appropriate location in the tree, you must first select the appropriate tree node by clicking on it. Then, you select the item to be moved and click the Add button. If one or more items have been added to a tree node, the node is displayed with a "+" icon to the left of the node name. You can click this icon to expand the node and view whatever was added. If any item has been added to the wrong tree node, you can remove it by selecting it and clicking the Remove button (see Figure 1.3).

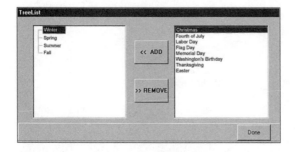

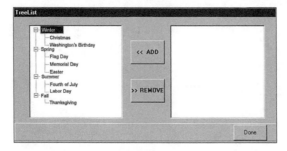

Figure 1.3 This is how create-a-tree questions appear.

Drag-and-Connect Question Format

Questions in the drag-and-connect format present a group of objects and a list of "connections." To answer the question, you must move the appropriate connections between the objects.

This type of question is best described using graphics. Here's an example.

Question 5

The following objects represent the different states of water:

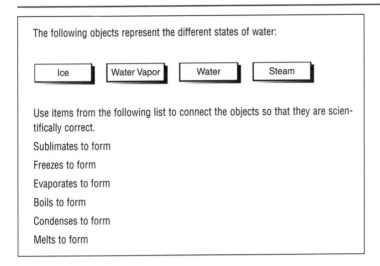

Use items from the following list to connect the objects so that they are scientifically correct.

Sublimates to form

Freezes to form

Evaporates to form

Boils to form

Condenses to form

Melts to form

The correct answer is:

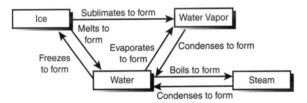

For this type of question, it's not necessary to use every object, but each connection can be used multiple times by dragging the answer to multiple locations. Dragging an answer away from its position removes it.

Select-and-Place Question Format

Questions in the select-and-place (drag-and-drop) format present a diagram with blank boxes and a list of labels that must be dragged to fill in the blank boxes. To answer the question, you must move the labels to their appropriate positions on the diagram.

This type of question is best described using graphics. Here's an example.

Question 6

Place the items in their proper order, by number, on the following flowchart. Some items may be used more than once, and some items may not be used at all.

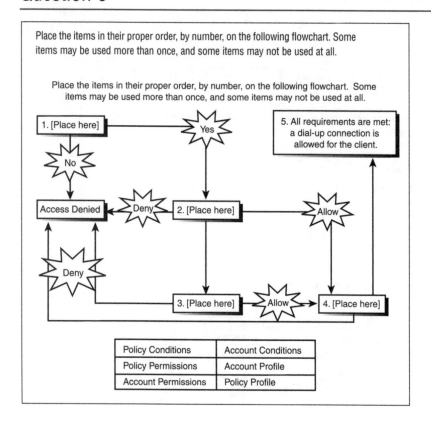

The correct answer is:

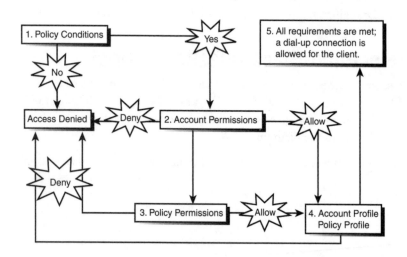

Microsoft's Testing Formats

Currently, Microsoft uses four different testing formats:

➤ Case study

➤ Fixed length

➤ Adaptive

➤ Short form

As mentioned earlier, the case study approach is used with many of the newer Microsoft exams. These exams consist of a set of case studies that you must first analyze to answer questions related to the case studies. Such exams include one or more case studies (tabbed topic areas), each of which is followed by 4 to 10 questions. The question types for exams will be: multiple choice, build list and reorder, create a tree, drag and connect, and select and place. Depending on the test topic, some exams are totally case-based, whereas others are not at all.

Other Microsoft exams employ advanced testing capabilities that may not be immediately apparent. Although the questions that appear are primarily multiple-choice, the logic in *fixed-length tests*, which use a fixed sequence of questions, is more complex than that in older Microsoft tests. Some questions employ a sophisticated user interface (which Microsoft calls a *simulation*) to test your knowledge of particular software and systems in a simulated "live" environment that behaves just like the original. The Testing Innovations article at **www.microsoft.com/TRAINCERT/mcpexams/faq/innovations.asp** includes a downloadable series of demonstrations and samples.

For some exams, Microsoft has turned to a well-known technique, called *adaptive testing*, to establish a test-taker's level of knowledge and product competence. Adaptive exams look the same as fixed-length exams, but they determine the level of difficulty at which an individual test-taker can correctly answer questions. Test-takers with differing levels of knowledge or ability see different sets of questions; individuals with high levels of knowledge or ability are presented with a smaller set of more difficult questions, whereas individuals with lower levels of knowledge are presented with a larger set of easier questions. Two individuals may answer the same percentage of questions correctly, but the test-taker with a higher knowledge or ability level scores higher because his or her questions are weighted more heavily.

Also, lower-level test-takers may answer more questions than more-knowledgeable colleagues. This explains why adaptive tests use ranges of values to define the number of questions and the amount of time needed to complete the tests.

Adaptive tests work by evaluating the test-taker's most recent answer. A correct answer leads to a more difficult question (also raising the test software's estimate of the test-taker's knowledge and ability level). An incorrect answer leads to a less difficult question (also lowering the test software's estimate of the test-taker's knowledge and ability level). This process continues until the test targets the test-taker's true ability level. The exam ends when the test-taker's level of accuracy meets a statistically acceptable value (in other words, when his or her performance demonstrates an acceptable level of knowledge and ability) or when the maximum number of items has been presented (in which case, the test-taker is almost certain to fail).

Microsoft also introduced a short-form test for its most popular tests. This test consists of 25 to 30 questions, with a time limit of exactly 60 minutes. This type of exam is similar to a fixed-length test because it allows readers to jump ahead or return to earlier questions and to cycle through the questions until the test is done. Microsoft does not use adaptive logic in this test; it claims that statistical analysis of the question pool is such that the 25 to 30 questions delivered during a short-form exam conclusively measure a test-taker's knowledge of the subject matter in much the same way as an adaptive test. The short-form test is like a "greatest hits exam" (that is, the most important questions are covered) version of an adaptive exam on the same topic.

Some of the Microsoft exams may contain a combination of adaptive and fixed-length questions.

Because you won't know in which form the Microsoft exam may be, you should be prepared for an adaptive exam instead of a fixed-length or a short-form exam: The penalties for answering incorrectly are built into the test itself on an adaptive exam, whereas the layout remains the same for a fixed-length or short-form test, no matter how many questions you answer incorrectly.

The biggest difference between adaptive tests and fixed-length or short-form tests is that you can mark and revisit questions on fixed-length or short-form tests after you've read them. On an adaptive test, you must answer the question when it is presented and cannot go back to that question later.

Strategies for Different Testing Formats

Before you choose a test-taking strategy, you must determine what type of test it is: case studies, fixed length, short form, or adaptive.

➤ Case study tests consist of a tabbed window that allows you to navigate easily through the sections of the case.

➤ Fixed-length tests consist of 50 to 70 questions with a checkbox. You can return to these questions if you want.

➤ Short-form tests have 25 to 30 questions with a checkbox. You can return to these questions if you want.

➤ Adaptive tests are identified in the introductory material of the test. They have no checkbox and can be visited (and answered) only once.

Some tests contain a variety of testing formats. For example, a test may start with a set of adaptive questions, followed by fixed-length questions.

You'll be able to tell for sure if you are taking an adaptive, fixed-length, or short-form test by the first question. Fixed-length or short-form tests include a checkbox that allows you to mark the question for later review. Adaptive test questions include no such checkbox and can be visited (and answered) only once.

Case Study Exam Strategy

Most test-takers find that the case study type of exam is the most difficult to master. When it comes to studying for a case study test, your best bet is to approach each case study as a stand-alone test. The biggest challenge you'll encounter is that you'll feel that you won't have enough time to get through all of the cases that are presented.

Each case provides a lot of material that you'll need to read and study before you can effectively answer the questions that follow. The trick to taking a case study exam is to first scan the case study to get the highlights. Make sure you read the overview section of the case so that you understand the context of the problem at hand. Then, quickly move on and scan the questions.

As you are scanning the questions, make mental notes to yourself or notes on your paper so that you'll remember which sections of the case study you should focus on. Some case studies may provide a fair amount of extra information that you don't really need to answer the questions. The goal with this scanning approach is to avoid having to study and analyze material that is not completely relevant.

When studying a case, read the tabbed information carefully. It is important to answer each and every question. You will be able to toggle back and forth from case to questions, and from question to question within a case testlet. However, after you leave the case and move on, you may not be able to return to it. I suggest that you take notes while reading useful information to help you when you tackle the test questions. It's hard to go wrong with this strategy when taking any kind of Microsoft certification test.

Fixed-Length and Short-Form Exam Strategy

A well-known principle when taking fixed-length or short-form exams is first to read through the entire exam from start to finish. Answer only those questions that you feel absolutely sure you know. On subsequent passes, you can dive into more complex questions more deeply, knowing how many such questions you have left and the amount of time remaining.

 There's at least one potential benefit to reading the exam over completely before answering the trickier questions: Sometimes, information supplied in later questions sheds more light on earlier questions. At other times, information you read in later questions may jog your memory about facts, figures, or behavior that helps you answer earlier questions. Either way, you'll come out ahead if you answer only those questions on the first pass that you're absolutely confident about.

Fortunately, the Microsoft exam software for fixed-length and short-form tests makes the multiple-visit approach easy to implement. At the top-left corner of each question is a checkbox that permits you to mark that question for a later visit.

Marking questions makes later review easier, but you can return to any question by clicking the Forward or Back button repeatedly.

Here are some question-handling strategies that apply to fixed-length and short-form tests. Use them if you have the chance:

➤ When returning to a question after your initial read-through, read every word again; otherwise, your mind can miss important details. Sometimes, revisiting a question after turning your attention elsewhere lets you see something you missed, but the strong tendency is to see what you've seen before. Try to avoid that tendency at all costs.

➤ If you return to a question more than twice, try to articulate to yourself what you don't understand about the question, why answers don't appear to make sense, or what appears to be missing. If you chew on the subject awhile, your subconscious may provide the missing details, or you may notice a "trick" that points to the right answer.

As you work your way through the exam, another counter that Microsoft provides comes in handy—the number of questions completed and questions outstanding. For fixed-length and short-form tests, it's wise to budget your time by making sure that you've completed roughly one-quarter of the questions one-quarter of the way through the exam period, and three-quarters of the questions three-quarters of the way through.

If you're not finished when only five minutes remain, use that time to guess your way through any remaining questions. Remember, guessing is potentially more valuable than not answering. Blank answers are always wrong, but a guess may turn out to be right. If you don't have a clue about any of the remaining questions, pick answers at random or choose all a's, b's, and so on. Questions left unanswered are counted as answered incorrectly, so a guess is better than nothing at all.

At the very end of your exam period, you're better off guessing than leaving questions unanswered.

Adaptive Exam Strategy

If there's one principle that applies to taking an adaptive test, it's "Get it right the first time." You cannot elect to skip a question and move on to the next one when taking an adaptive test, because the testing software uses your answer to the current question to select whatever question it plans to present next. You also cannot return to a question because the software gives you only one chance to answer the question. You can, however, take notes as you work through the test. Sometimes, information supplied in earlier questions may help you answer later questions.

Also, when you answer a question correctly, you are presented with a more difficult question next, to help the software gauge your level of skill and ability. When you answer a question incorrectly, you are presented with a less difficult question, and the software lowers its current estimate of your skill and ability. This continues until the program settles into a reasonably accurate estimate of what you know and can do.

The good news is that if you know the material, you'll probably finish most adaptive tests in 30 minutes or so. The bad news is that you must really know the material well to do your best on an adaptive test. That's because some questions are so convoluted, complex, or hard to follow that you're bound to miss one or two, at a minimum. Therefore, the more you know, the better you'll do on an adaptive test, even accounting for the occasionally strange or unfathomable questions that appear on these exams.

 Because you can't always tell in advance if a test is fixed length, short form, adaptive, or a combination, you should prepare for the exam as if it were adaptive. That way, you will be prepared to pass, no matter what kind of test you take. If the test turns out to be fixed length or short form, remember the tips from the preceding section, which will help you improve on what you could do on an adaptive test.

If you encounter a question on an adaptive test that you can't answer, you must guess an answer quickly. (However, you may suffer for your guess on the next question if you guess correctly, because the software will give you a more difficult question next!)

Question-Handling Strategies

For those questions that have only one right answer, usually two or three of the answers will be obviously incorrect, and two of the answers will be plausible. Unless the answer leaps out at you (if it does, reread the question to look for a trick; sometimes those are the ones you're most likely to get wrong), begin the process of answering by eliminating those answers that are most obviously wrong.

At least one answer out of the possible choices for a question can usually be eliminated immediately because it matches one of these conditions:

➤ The answer does not apply to the situation.

➤ The answer describes a nonexistent issue, an invalid option, or an imaginary state.

After you eliminate all answers that are obviously wrong, you can apply your retained knowledge to eliminate further answers. Look for items that sound correct but refer to actions, commands, or features that are not present or not available in the situation that the question describes.

If you're still faced with a blind guess among two or more potentially correct answers, reread the question. Try to picture how each of the possible remaining answers would alter the situation. Be especially sensitive to terminology; sometimes the choice of words ("remove" instead of "disable") can make the difference between a right answer and a wrong one.

You should guess at an answer only after you've exhausted your ability to eliminate answers and are still unclear about which of the remaining possibilities is correct. An unanswered question offers you no points, but guessing gives you at least some chance of getting a question right; just don't be too hasty when making a blind guess.

If you're taking a fixed-length or a short-form test, you can wait until the last round of reviewing marked questions (just as you're about to run out of time or unanswered questions) before you start making guesses. You will usually have the same option within each case study testlet (but once you leave a testlet, you may not be allowed to return to it). If you're taking an adaptive test, you'll have to guess to move on to the next question if you can't figure out an answer some other way. Either way, guessing should be your technique of last resort!

Numerous questions assume that the default behavior of a particular utility is in effect. If you know the defaults and understand what they mean, this knowledge will help you cut through many Gordian knots. Simple 'final' actions may be critical as well. If a utility must be restarted before proposed changes take effect, a correct answer may require this step as well.

Mastering the Inner Game

In the final analysis, knowledge gives confidence, and confidence breeds success. If you study the materials in this book carefully and review all of the practice questions at the end of each chapter, you should become aware of those areas where additional learning and study are required.

After you've worked your way through the book, take the practice exam in the back of the book. Taking this test provides a reality check and helps you identify areas to study further. Make sure you follow up and review materials related to the questions you miss on the practice exam before scheduling a real exam. Don't schedule your exam appointment until after you've thoroughly studied the material and feel comfortable with the whole scope of the practice exam. You should score 80 percent or better on the practice exam before proceeding to the real thing (otherwise, obtain some additional practice tests so you can keep trying until you hit this magic number).

If you take a practice exam and don't get at least 80 to 85 percent of the questions correct, keep practicing. Microsoft provides links to practice exam providers and also self-assessment exams at **www.microsoft.com/traincert/mcpexams/ prepare/**.

Armed with the information in this book and with the determination to augment your knowledge, you should be able to pass the certification exam. However, you need to work at it, or you'll spend the exam fee more than once before you finally pass. If you prepare seriously, you should do well.

The next section covers other sources you can use to prepare for the Microsoft Certification Exams.

Additional Resources

A good source of information about Microsoft Certification Exams comes from Microsoft itself. Because its products and technologies—and the exams that go with them—change frequently, the best place to go for exam-related information is online.

If you haven't already visited the Microsoft Certified Professional site, do so right now. The MCP home page resides at **www.microsoft.com/ traincert/default.asp** (see Figure 1.4).

This page may be replaced by something new and different by the time you read this, because things change regularly on the Microsoft site. Should this happen, please read the sidebar titled "Coping with Change on the Web."

Figure 1.4   The Microsoft Certified Professional Training and Certification home page.

Coping with Change on the Web

Sooner or later, all of the information I've shared with you about the Microsoft Certified Professional pages and the other Web-based resources mentioned throughout the rest of this book will go stale or be replaced by newer information. In some cases, the URLs you find here may lead you to their replacements; in other cases, the URLs will go nowhere, leaving you with the dreaded "404 File not found" error message. When that happens, don't give up.

There's always a way to find what you want on the Web if you're willing to invest some time and energy. Most large or complex Web sites (such as the Microsoft site) offer a search engine. On all of Microsoft's Web pages, a Search button appears along the top edge of the page. As long as you can get to the Microsoft site (it should stay at **www.microsoft.com** for a long time), use this tool to help you find what you need.

The more focused you can make a search request, the more likely the results will include information you can use. For example, you can search for the string

```
"training and certification"
```

to produce a lot of data about the subject in general, but if you're looking for the preparation guide for Exam 70-218, "Managing a Microsoft Windows 2000 Network Environment," you'll be more likely to get there quickly if you use a search string similar to the following:

```
"Exam 70-218" AND "preparation guide"
```

Likewise, if you want to find the Training and Certification downloads, try a search string such as this:

```
"training and certification" AND "download page"
```

Finally, feel free to use general search tools—such as **www.search.com**, **www.altavista.com**, and **www.excite.com**—to look for related information. Although Microsoft offers great information about its certification exams online, there are plenty of third-party sources of information and assistance that need not follow Microsoft's party line. Therefore, if you can't find something immediately, intensify your search.

Networking Basics

Terms you'll need to understand:

✓ Transmission Control Protocol/Internet Protocol (TCP/IP)
✓ Local Area Network (LAN)
✓ Wide Area Network (WAN)
✓ NetBIOS
✓ Fully qualified domain name (FQDN)
✓ Windows Internet Naming Service (WINS)
✓ Domain Name System (DNS)
✓ LMHOSTS
✓ HOSTS
✓ Network ID
✓ Host ID
✓ Subnet mask

Techniques you'll need to master:

✓ Recognizing the standard TCP/IP protocols and, where applicable, their default port numbers
✓ Identifying the four host identification methods for hosts within an IP network
✓ Associating an IP address with its default class and recognizing the use of private address values
✓ Formatting an entry in an LMHOSTS or HOSTS file and understanding the use of each

Modern computing is no longer defined as the stand-alone operation of a single monolithic system. Almost all businesses and many individual homes are increasingly interconnected in a large heterogeneous network of systems commonly known as the Internet or the World Wide Web.

In order to tap into the fundamental capabilities present in networked computing solutions, all systems involved must be able to uniquely identify one another, and to communicate using an agreed-upon standard of communication (also called a *communications protocol*).

This chapter provides an overview of the requirements for interconnectivity, as well as more detailed coverage of the most common cross-platform communications protocols in use: *Transmission Control Protocol/Internet Protocol (TCP/IP)*. This chapter focuses on the underlying basis of networking and the concept of name resolution. Additional references are listed at the end of this chapter.

Overview

The original ARPANET, a product of the Defense Advanced Research Projects Agency (DARPA), has evolved from its humble beginnings as a switched network using dedicated lines to connect a few key centers of research and development, to become a globally spanning architecture of incredible complexity. Now a commercially supported system of high-speed networking components, the Internet provides a generally available solution for interconnectivity almost anywhere in the world.

Internetworking of systems in the Windows 2000 environment provides security of access, auditing, grant and revocation of user access rights, file and printer sharing, and a host of other functions that rely on the capability of many distributed systems to communicate and coordinate effectively with others. The processing power of powerful servers may provide support for lightweight client systems, worldwide commerce may be undertaken by leveraging Internet technologies in an e-commerce setting, and many other forms of coordinated processing may be enacted according to client requirements.

As a network administrator, your job will focus on the details required for interconnecting distributed systems. These systems may all be present in a small geographic area, also called a *Local Area Network (LAN)*, or may be located anywhere in the world and connected via *Wide-Area Network (WAN)* connectivity. Widely distributed systems may be interconnected using dedicated links or, more commonly, across the Internet where local networking is supported by in-house Information Technology assets and wide area connectivity is provided by access to the Internet through an Internet Service Provider (ISP).

Regardless of the platform in use, the communications protocols in use must be able to uniquely identify a given system, and to provide a mechanism by which one system may establish a communications channel to another. The protocol that has evolved to become the Internet standard for connectivity is TCP/IP networking. Although somewhat more complex than other networking protocols, TCP/IP has proved to be scalable from small single office solutions up to globally spanning network deployments involving satellite and even wireless cellular connections.

 This chapter will provide an understanding of the most basic aspects of networking. For experienced network administrators, some topics may be "old hat," but a good understanding of the details presented herein may assist in rapidly identifying blatantly false questions on the exam.

Networking Protocols

When two or more people converse, they must understand a common language or effective communication is impossible. Similarly, two or more computers must also speak the same language (protocol) in order to communicate effectively. A variety of protocols have been proposed and several adopted by different hardware and operating system vendors. Table 2.1 provides a listing of the most common network protocols.

Table 2.1 Network addressing protocols.	
Protocol	**Description**
AppleTalk	The native communications protocol for Apple computer networks.
Internet Protocol (IP)	The default communications protocol for Windows and Unix networks. This is also considered the fundamental "native language" for the Internet, which shares its name.
Internetwork Packet Exchange (IPX)	The native communications protocol for Novell NetWare networks.
NetBIOS Enhanced User Interface (NetBEUI)	A Microsoft communications protocol useful in small networks without significant traffic. NetBEUI is not often used anymore, as it is not a routable protocol.

As previously mentioned, TCP/IP is actually a suite of communications protocols named for the two most common of its protocols. *Internet Protocol (IP)* addressing provides unique identifiers for each network and host, and is used in combination with others for specific purposes, as noted in Table 2.2.

Table 2.2 TCP/IP suite.		
Protocol	**Alias**	**Description**
File Transfer Protocol	FTP	Client/server protocol used in order to transfer files between two computers in a TCP/IP network, typically operating on port 21.
HyperText Transfer Protocol	HTTP	Client/server protocol used in World Wide Web transactions for the exchange of HTML documents, typically operating on port 80.
Internet Protocol	IP	Network protocol that provides connectionless interconnectivity using packet routing, fragmentation, and re-assembly of packets at the destination.
Post Office Protocol v3	POP3	Communications protocol useful in retrieving electronic mail from a server, typically operating on port 110.
Point-to-Point Protocol	PPP	Network protocol that encapsulates different network protocols (AppleTalk, IP, IPX) and transmits them over serial point to point lines. This protocol is similar to SLIP (see below) but also includes error detection and other improvements.
Point to Point Tunneling Protocol	PPTP	Similar to PPP, PPTP establishes connections for Remote Access Server (RAS) communications and for Virtual Private Networking (VPN).
Serial Line Internet Protocol	SLIP	Network protocol that provides connectionless networking over serial lines. Error detection must be provided by high level protocols when using SLIP connectivity.

(continued)

Table 2.2 TCP/IP suite *(continued)*		
Protocol	**Alias**	**Description**
Simple Mail Transfer Protocol	SMTP	Communications protocol used to transfer electronic mail between two computers, typically operating on port 25.
Simple Network Management Protocol	SNMP	Standard protocol designed to allow remote management of heterogeneous equipment connected to TCP/IP networks, typically operating on port 161.
Transmission Control Protocol	TCP	Communications protocol used over IP connectivity in order to add connection-oriented communication, flow control, and other improvements in connectivity at the cost of higher network packet overhead.
Telnet	TELNET	Communications protocol that allows remote terminal connections to computers, routers, and other TCP/IP network equipment, typically operating on port 23.
User Datagram Protocol	UDP	Connectionless communications protocol similar to TCP used over IP connectivity in order to add checksum and addressing information.

The PPTP protocol does not directly provide encryption of transferred data. Additional encryption is required in order to provide a secure connection.

Host Identification

In order to establish communications between two systems, it is first necessary to be able to uniquely distinguish each host from all others. Identification involves IP addressing for each host, along with mechanisms to provide translation of network IP addresses to the proper *media access control (MAC)* identifier assigned to a particular *network interface card (NIC)* via the *address resolution protocol (ARP)*.

A MAC address is assigned to each network interface card by its manufacturer. In theory, these are unique and no two identical MAC addresses are possible. A MAC address is the same as the Ethernet address in Ethernet networks, and appears in the form of six pairs of hexadecimal digits (for example, 01-02-5A-0F-1B-F7). Lists of MAC addresses and the IP addresses associated with them provide proper routing between two or more systems. These lists are dynamically updated in routers and other forms of network hardware in order to allow the resolution of an IP address to the proper target NIC.

An IP address is made up of four bytes of binary data, which are generally entered in their decimal value form (for example, 11000000. 10101000.00000001.00001010 translates to 192.168.1.10, which is a private address range IP address). This will be discussed in greater detail later in this chapter under IP Network Addressing.

Given the sheer number of systems present on the Net, it is often necessary to give a computer an identifier more readily remembered by a human operator than a string of numbers, such as a name like *mailserver*. The process of resolution of each name to its appropriate IP address then becomes an issue.

NetBIOS naming is used in small networks, and provides the translation of names to IP addresses with a flat namespace. This means that there may never be more than one machine named *mailserver*, for example. Though this might work well in a small office, it is obviously unsuitable to today's modern networks which may be comprised of tens of thousands of systems, many of which may serve in similar roles for various portions of an organization.

In order to expand naming solutions to accommodate modern needs, hierarchical naming schemes are used. In this way, a given company's domain might be *mycompany.com*, with subdomains grouped according to geographical location (*dallas.mycompany.com*), by function (*purchasing.mycompany.com*), or by any other desired breakdown that will provide ease in management of a large network. In this way, there might be systems named *mailserver. dallas.mycompany.com* and *mailserver.austin.mycompany.com* that are uniquely identifiable one from the other. This naming scheme involving *fully qualified domain names (FQDNs)* for each system is far better suited to a modern deployment, and forms the basis for Windows 2000 domain design.

Table 2.3 details the various types of host identification.

Table 2.3 Host identification methods.		
Type	**Example**	**Description**
FQDN	*myserver.mycorp.com*	Hierarchical naming scheme that is scalable to include any number of domains and sub-domains. This is the basis for Windows 2000 domain organization. Resolved by DNS and HOSTS file association.
IP	128.46.197.101	Machine identification used for TCP/IP resolution, associated statically or dynamically to a particular MAC address in routing tables.
MAC	AF-04-2B-11-69-43	Unique hardware-level identifier assigned to each network interface card by its manufacturer.
NetBIOS	*myserver*	Flat naming scheme useful for access to local resources in smaller network deployments. Resolved by WINS and LMHOSTS file association.

Resolution mechanisms DNS, HOSTS, LMHOSTS, and WINS are discussed later in this chapter as well as in Chapter 4.

IP Network Addressing

Each computer or device (also called a *host* or *node*) in a TCP/IP network is uniquely identified by an IP address, consisting of a *network ID* and a *host ID*. Hosts with the same network ID belong to the same subnet and may communicate with one another without having to pass through a router. If the two network IDs are different, then the hosts must communicate through a router or network gateway.

Address Class

The class of an address determines which part of the IP address is the network ID and which part the host ID. The class may be determined by the decimal value of the first address byte.

Table 2.4 covers the three main classes of IP addresses.

Table 2.4	IP address classes.			
Class	First Byte	Network ID	Host ID	Default Subnet Mask
A	001-126	x.-.-.-	-.x.x.x	255.0.0.0
B	128-191	x.x.-.-	-.-.x.x	255.255.0.0
C	192-223	x.x.x.-	-.-.-.x	255.255.255.0

Address classes D (224-239) and E (240-255) are reserved and will not be used for host identification. The address 127.0.0.1 is reserved for local loop-back connections.

Three IP ranges have been allocated for private (local) addressing. These addresses are not externally routable:

10.0.0.0

172.16.0.0

192.168.0.0

A zero in the host position refers to an entire subnet and is not used for addressing.

Obviously, fewer hosts may be present in class B than in class A subnets, just as class C subnets will have fewer hosts than class B subnets. This allows for a more efficient allocation of addressing to clients requiring a smaller number of unique addresses.

The first IP address within a subnet is allocated for the subnet's gateway, whereas the last IP address within a subnet is reserved for broadcast traffic (information sent to all IP addresses within the subnet).

For example, a class C subnet with a default subnet mask might have the following configuration:

Subnet: 200.128.10.0
Range: 200.128.10.1-255
Gateway: 200.128.10.1
Hosts: 200.128.10.2-254
Broadcast: 200.128.10.255

Subnetting

Network subnetting beyond the default address class division is accomplished by the use of custom *subnet masks*. In order to further divide available subnets, a subnet mask may be applied to the network addressing in order to define how many bits are used for the network ID and how many remain for the host ID. The number of bits (counted from the left) in a subnet mask defines the number of bits used for the network ID.

As an example, if a subnet mask of 255.255.255.224 is applied to a class C address, the result is six subnets of 30 hosts each (for each subnet, one IP address is allocated as the gateway and one as the broadcast address). This functions in the following manner:

```
Mask:     11111111.11111111.11111111.11100000
```

This defines the network address as being 27 bits in length, and the host address being 5 bits in length. This gives a maximum possible number of addresses for each subnet as 2^5, or 32 addresses. Because the first and last are reserved, 30 hosts may share each subnet. If two addresses are compared, then if all network bits match, they are in the same subnet and may communicate without passing through a router.

 An understanding of the proper use of subnet masks may allow the rapid identification of many incorrect answers during the exam. Make sure you understand the "cost" of subnetting—each subnet consumes two addresses for gateway and broadcast, so the smaller the subnet, the greater the percentage of addresses "lost" to this overhead.

Name Resolution

Obviously, bits and bytes are easier for computers to remember than for most of us. In order to provide an easier method for meaningful identification by the living portion of the user/machine interface, textual naming may be associated with a host IP address. Translation of textual naming to an associated IP address is referred to as *name resolution*.

Name resolution may be dynamically accomplished by querying a Windows Internet Naming Service (WINS) or Domain Name System (DNS) server. Static name associations for a small number of systems that do not change often may also be accomplished using HOSTS and LMHOSTS files located in the **<root>\WINNT\System32\drivers\etc** folder of a system.

NetBIOS Name Resolution

Windows operating systems announce themselves when they boot and at routine intervals thereafter. The NetBIOS name of a system is registered in a local WINS server when available, along with its associated IP address. Queries against a WINS server would function to resolve host naming such as *myserver* to an IP address such as 128.167.244.10.

Static associations of NetBIOS naming may also be made using an LMHOSTS file. Entries in this file are checked before WINS queries are made when a NetBIOS name resolution is attempted.

An example of an LMHOSTS entry is:

```
128.167.244.10    myserver #PRE
128.167.244.29    mailserver
```

The #PRE designation causes Windows to preload this association into memory during boot, rather than having to refer to the LMHOSTS file each time.

FQDN Name Resolution

In order to provide naming beyond a small workgroup setting, FQDN naming is required. Windows 2000 utilizes this hierarchical naming scheme in its domain organization. The FQDN name of a system may be statically registered in a DNS system along with its associated IP address, or dynamically registered when the system boots. Queries against a DNS server would function to resolve FQDN host naming such as *myserver.mycompany.com* to an IP address such as 128.167.244.10.

Static associations of FQDN naming may also be made using a HOSTS file. Entries in this file are checked before DNS queries are made when an FQDN name resolution is attempted.

An example of a HOSTS entry is:

```
128.167.244.10    myserver.mycompany.com
```

Although HOSTS and LMHOSTS files may be used for static name resolution in stand-alone systems, Windows 2000 Active Directory mandates an available DNS server.

Detailed configuration of client and server systems for name resolution is covered in Chapter 4.

Practice Questions

Question 1

> Which of the following are valid TCP/IP suite protocols? [Check all correct answers]
>
> ❏ a. FTP
> ❏ b. IPX
> ❏ c. SNMP
> ❏ d. WINS
> ❏ e. UDP

Answers a, c, and e are correct. The TCP/IP suite includes the FTP, SNMP, and the UDProtocol. Answer b is incorrect because the IPX protocol is a Novell Netware native protocol and not part of the TCP/IP suite. Answer d is incorrect because WINS is a name resolution service and not a communications protocol.

Question 2

> Several of the TCP/IP suite protocols are associated with default port numbers, including:
>
> ➤ FTP
> ➤ HTTP
> ➤ POP3
> ➤ SMTP
> ➤ SNMP
> ➤ Telnet
>
> Match the following ports with the appropriate protocol:
>
> ➤ 21
> ➤ Port 23
> ➤ Port 25
> ➤ Port 80
> ➤ Port 110
> ➤ Port 161

The correct answers are:

➤ FTP

  ➤ Port 21

➤ HTTP

  ➤ Port 80

➤ POP3

  ➤ Port 110

➤ SMTP

  ➤ Port 25

➤ SNMP

  ➤ Port 161

➤ Telnet

  ➤ Port 23

Question 3

> Which of the following statements about the PPTP are true? [Check all correct answers]
>
> ❑ a. Creates a secure connection between two devices.
> ❑ b. Provides serial-line connections to Remote Access Server connections.
> ❑ c. Used to establish VPN connections.

Answers b and c are correct. Answer a is incorrect because PPTP connections do not provide encrypted secured connections inherently.

Question 4

> You are the administrator of a Windows Exchange server that provides electronic mail support for several salespersons in the field. In order to allow clients to read and send mail through the Exchange server, you have had the security group open port 110 through the firewall for your Exchange server.
>
> Will this solution provide the desired access for your remote clients?
>
> ○ a. Yes
> ○ b. No

Answer b is correct. Port 110 is used by the POP3 protocol, which is useful for receiving electronic mail. In order to send email through your Exchange server, you must also have port 25 opened in order to allow SMTP transactions to occur as well.

Question 5

> It is important to make sure to *never* assign the same MAC address to two NICs, in order to prevent resolution conflicts when using an LMHOSTS file as well as a WINS server for name resolution.
>
> ○ a. True
> ○ b. False

Answer b is correct. This is something of a trick question because the MAC address for a NIC is a unique address, assigned by the manufacturer. There should never be an occasion in which two identical MAC addresses exist.

Question 6

> The four types of host identification within an IP network are:
>
> ➤ FQDN
> ➤ IP
> ➤ MAC
> ➤ NetBIOS
>
> Match the following identifications with the appropriate type:
>
> ➤ 128.46.197.101
> ➤ AF-04-2B-11-69-43
> ➤ myserver
> ➤ myserver.mycompany.com

The correct answers are:

➤ FQDN

   ➤ myserver.mycompany.com

➤ IP

   ➤ 128.46.197.101

➤ MAC

   ➤ AF-04-2B-11-69-43

➤ NetBIOS

   ➤ myserver

Question 7

> Which of the following IP addresses are reserved as private addresses? [Check all correct answers]
>
> ❑ a. 1.10.1.10
> ❑ b. 10.10.10.10
> ❑ c. 128.194.166.5
> ❑ d. 192.168.15.4
> ❑ e. 200.200.200.200

Answers b and d are correct. The private address ranges are 10.0.0.0, 172.16.0.0, and 192.168.0.0. Answer a is incorrect because 1.0.0.0 would make this a class A address. Answer c is incorrect because 128.0.0.0 would make this a class B address. Answer e is incorrect because 200.0.0.0 would make this a class C address.

Question 8

> Given the IP address 191.145.221.16 with a default subnet mask, which part of this address is the host ID?
>
> ○ a. 16
> ○ b. 145.221.16
> ○ c. 191
> ○ d. 191.145
> ○ e. 191.145.221.16
> ○ f. 221.16

Answer f is correct. The address is a class B address with a default subnet mask of 255.255.0.0, so the first 16 bits are used as the network ID (191.145) and the last 16 bits for the host ID (221.16). Answer a is incorrect because only the last 8 bits are used for the host ID. Answer b is incorrect because the last 24 bits are used for the host ID. Answers c and d are incorrect because the first bits always specify a network ID and not a host ID. Answer e is incorrect because it is a complete IP address and does not specify only the host ID.

Question 9

Which of the following may be used for name resolution? [Check all correct answers]

❑ a. DNS

❑ b. HOSTS

❑ c. LMHOSTS

❑ d. MAC

❑ e. WINS

Answers a, b, c, and e are correct. Answer d is incorrect because the MAC address is a hexadecimal value assigned to identify a particular network interface card. Name resolution involves the translation of textual naming to an associated IP address value rather than to a MAC address value directly.

Question 10

Which of the following might be found as an entry in a HOSTS file?

○ a. 128.167.244.10   myserver.mycorp.com

○ b. 128.167.244.10   myserver

○ c. 128.167.244.10   myserver   #PRE

○ d. myserver.mycorp.com   128.194.244.10

Answer a is correct. Answers b and c are incorrect because they specify name resolution for a flat namespace naming scheme and should be used with an LMHOSTS entry instead. Answer d is incorrect because the order of the name and IP address are reversed.

Need to Know More?

 Stanek, William R.: *Microsoft Windows 2000 Administrator's Pocket Consultant.* Microsoft Press, Redmond, WA, 2000. ISBN 0-7356-0831-8. A helpful reference for network administrators to keep close at hand. The soft-cover trade-sized book is a condensed, easily carried version of many larger tomes of information.

 Microsoft Windows 2000 Server Resource Kit. Microsoft Press, Redmond, WA, 2000. ISBN 1-5723-1805-8. An exhaustive library covering detailed information on all aspects of Windows 2000 Server implementations. An invaluable reference for IT departments supporting Microsoft Windows 2000 networks.

 www.microsoft.com/windows2000/techinfo/proddoc/default. asp. *Windows 2000 Product Documentation Online* is a complete online copy of the documentation for all versions of the Windows 2000 operating system.

3

Active Directory Structure

Terms you'll need to understand:

✓ Active Directory
✓ Domain controller
✓ Trust
✓ Organizational unit
✓ Global catalog
✓ FSMO roles
✓ Domain
✓ Tree
✓ Forest
✓ Site
✓ Bridgehead server

Techniques you'll need to master:

✓ Describing the purpose of the Windows 2000 Active Directory global catalog
✓ Identifying the FSMO roles and their basic purposes
✓ Recognizing the different types of trusts including one- and two-way, as well as transitive and nontransitive trusts
✓ Identifying the levels of administrative grouping, including organizational units, domains, trees, and forests

Windows 2000 utilizes a decentralized database in which all *security principles* such as users, computers, and printers are registered in order to provide centralized access and management of resources within a distributed network environment. This database is referred to as the *Active Directory*.

This chapter covers the physical and logical structure of Active Directory deployment scenarios, as well as a basic understanding of the uses of each level of grouping in the centralized administration over widely distributed resources.

Active Directory Structure Overview

Users of Windows NT and earlier operating systems may be familiar with the idea of a peer-to-peer network of computers, often referred to as a *workgroup*. In a workgroup, each computer maintains its own list of users and the access to local resources granted to each. None of the systems in this configuration provide administration over the whole—all act as equals (peers). Although this may work for up to 5 or 10 computers, the problems of administration, configuration, and deployment of systems in larger configurations mandate some form of centralized administration and coordination.

Domain Controllers

In Windows NT, the concept of the *domain* was introduced. A domain is a grouping of resources including computers, printers, groups, and users that are maintained in a centralized database of resources located on a supervisory machine called a *domain controller (DC)*. In Windows NT, all updates to this database occurred within one domain controller designated as the *primary domain controller (PDC)*, with all other domain controller servers designated as *backup domain controllers (BDCs)*. The backup domain controllers receive updates to their local copy of the listing from the primary domain controller on a regular schedule.

In order to provide support for larger-scale deployments in which the security principles (such as users) in one domain may be granted access to resources located in another domain, multiple domains can be joined via a connection called a *trust*. Trusts will be covered in greater detail later in this chapter in the section titled "Trusts."

The limitation of the NT domain system was that all updates to the database had to occur on the primary domain controller, and only then would be propagated out to all backup domain controllers on the next scheduled update cycle. This can cause significant delays before changes are propagated to all remote backup domain controllers, and may prevent changes outright if a network connection to the primary domain controller is unavailable. Additionally, the process may be somewhat bandwidth-intensive if a full-domain synchronization of domain controllers is enacted, as the primary domain controller must update the local copy of the domain database on all backup domain controllers throughout the domain. This can prove to be a serious bottleneck when a deployment is distributed over a large number of servers or a broad geographic area.

Active Directory

In Windows 2000, a different system of registration is used for security principles distributed throughout the enterprise—the *Active Directory (AD)*. A decentralized database of objects is used in order to provide much more scalability to accommodate more modern deployment and management scenarios involving hundreds or thousands of security principles potentially distributed throughout a global-scale enterprise.

In order to provide granular administration of the security principals within such a structure, Windows 2000 improves on the NT domain model by adding smaller and larger aggregate groupings. Within each domain are many *organizational units (OUs)*, which may in turn contain other nested organizational units themselves. Domains may be grouped into parent/child relationships creating *trees*, and multiple trees may be joined via trusts in order to create the enterprise-level collection known as a *forest*.

The logical structure of the Windows 2000 Active Directory will be discussed in greater detail later in this chapter in the section called "Logical Structure."

Global Catalog

Unlike the centralized NT domain database maintained on the primary domain controller, the Active Directory database is stored as a *global catalog (GC)* on all domain controllers that have been designated as global catalog hosts throughout the enterprise. Updates to the listing of security principles may be enacted through any copy of the global catalog and then propagated to all others as each cycle of updates occurs until all copies of the global catalog contain the new changes. Obviously, in a global deployment scenario, this would provide greater redundancy in the event of inaccessibility or loss of function of a domain controller, as well as minimizing the potential for a replication bottleneck, as it is no longer necessary for a single primary domain controller to update all other backup domain controllers.

Using Windows 2000 Active Directory, all domain controllers perform the same tasks, such as user login authentication and resource management, equally. Unlike Windows NT 4.0 Domain controllers, all Windows 2000 Domain Controllers are peers, providing the same services. In order to provide backward compatibility to legacy servers, one server in each domain is assigned the role of *PDC Emulator*, but the global catalog functions identically on all domain controllers designated as global catalog servers. The PDC Emulator provides a centralized point for replication of data to NT 4.0 Backup Domain controllers, which remain in mixed-mode domains. (Native-mode and mixed-mode domains are discussed in greater detail in Chapter 9.)

 If conflicting changes occur (such as in the case where two administrators modify the attributes on a single entity), the change made later will be the one that is kept.

Flexible Single-Master Operation (FSMO) Roles

The Active Directory global catalog is a multimaster database in which all global catalog servers participate equally. However, for some specific roles, Windows 2000 maintains the single-master model seen in NT domains. These roles involve changes that could potentially result in conflict affecting identification of users or computers, and also provide legacy support for pre-Windows systems maintained within a Windows 2000 Active Directory deployment. Only a single domain controller within a domain or forest may assume these operations master roles.

Table 3.1 details the Flexible Single-Master Operation (FSMO) roles.

Table 3.1 Windows 2000 FSMO roles.	
Role	**Purpose**
Domain Naming Master	This forest-level operations master role is assigned to the domain controller responsible for making changes to domain naming within the catalog. It is the only domain controller that may add or remove child domains.

(continued)

Table 3.1 Windows 2000 FSMO roles *(continued)*	
Role	**Purpose**
Infrastructure Master	This forest-level operations master role is assigned to the domain controller responsible for updating the name and security ID (SID) for objects referenced between domains.
PDC Emulator	This domain-level operations master role is assigned to the domain controller responsible for time synchronization, which is required by the Kerberos authentication protocol. The PDC Emulator in the root domain of each forest should be directed to an external time service, and all subdomain PDC Emulators will synchronize with their parent-domain. Additionally, the PDC Emulator role is used in support of legacy operating systems maintained within a Windows 2000 domain. The PDC Emulator for a given domain is preferentially given the duty of handling password changes, account lockout, and password failure notification.
RID Master	When a new security principle is created, it is assigned a unique SID that is a combination of the domain SID and a unique Relative ID (RID). The domain-level RID Master role is assigned to the domain controller responsible for ensuring that each domain controller is provided with a unique pool of Relative IDs.
Schema Master	This directory-level master role is assigned to the one domain controller responsible for changes to the schema of the directory, such as the addition of new attributes available for security principles. Once schema changes are made to the global catalog on this domain controller, they are propagated to all other global catalog servers throughout the enterprise.

 The Infrastructure Master role should not be assigned to a server also designated as a global catalog server, or it will fail when attempting to update name and SID information and generate errors in the event log.

Trusts

Two domains must be linked via a connection called a *trust* in order to allow resources in one domain to be made available to users in the other. Trusts may be *one-way* or *two-way* (see Figure 3.1), and *nontransitive* (see Figure 3.2) or *transitive* (see Figure 3.3).

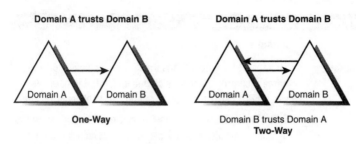

Figure 3.1 One-way and two-way trusts.

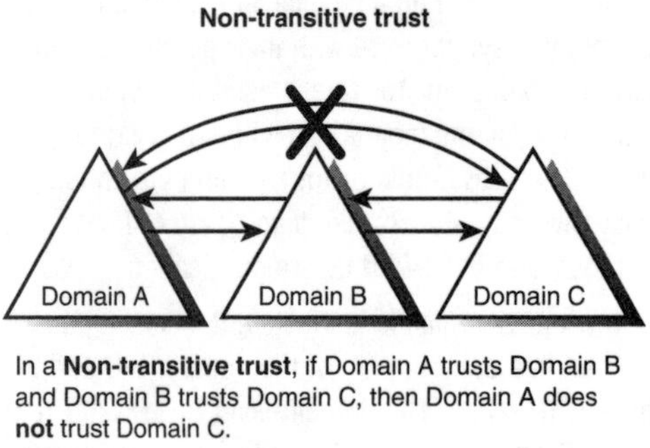

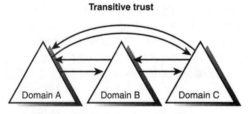

In a **Non-transitive trust**, if Domain A trusts Domain B and Domain B trusts Domain C, then Domain A does **not** trust Domain C.

Figure 3.2 Nontransitive trusts.

Transitive trust

In a **Transitive trust**, if Domain A trusts Domain B and Domain B trusts Domain C, then Domain A **also** trusts Domain C.

Figure 3.3 Transitive trusts.

Trusts in Windows NT domains were configured as separate one-way, non-transitive trusts. This means that if Domain A is established as trusting Domain B, then users within Domain B may be granted access to resources located in Domain A (see Figure 3.4).

In order to provide two-way access for users and resources, two one-way trusts had to be configured, one providing a trust for resources in Domain A to users in Domain B and the other providing trust for resources in Domain B to users in Domain A.

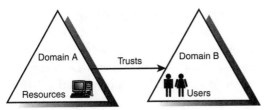

If Domain A trusts Domain B, the Users in Domain B may access resources in Domain A, but not the other way around.

Figure 3.4   One-way trust relationship.

Windows NT trusts are one-way and nontransitive, while Windows 2000 trusts are transitive and two-way by default. Windows 2000 trusts may be restricted to one-way nontransitive trusts.

By default, Windows 2000 creates two-way transitive trusts, allowing for users within any domain within a forest to be granted access to resources located within any other domain within the forest. In modern large-scale deployment scenarios, this is obviously much easier to maintain.

Figure 3.5 contrasts the differences in trust requirements in order to allow five domains to share full trust between Windows NT and Windows 2000.

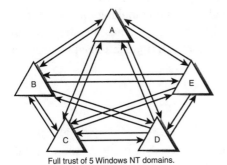

Full trust of 5 Windows NT domains.

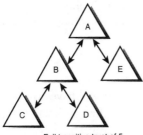

Full transitive trust of 5
Windows 2000 domains.

Figure 3.5   Comparison between Windows NT and Windows 2000 full trust within five domains.

Obviously, using Windows NT in larger enterprise deployments would magnify these issues significantly, adding management overhead and potential for access denial due to resource placement within the domain web. The use of two-way transitive trusts within the Windows 2000 Active Directory can turn a trust nightmare into a simple, easy, centralized administration issue.

Logical Structure

The Active Directory catalog is simply a distributed listing of all *objects* within the enterprise, along with the *attributes* assigned to each. An object might be a user, group, printer, or computer. Attributes are defined qualities for each, such as a user's name and login, or a printer's location and asset identification. The schema defines the available attributes for objects listed within the catalog as each is created.

 Schema changes should only be made after a thorough review by senior administrators. Typically, schema changes are only enacted by software installations such as the domain-prep and forest-prep procedures required for Exchange 2000 installations.

Searching for resources is made much simpler by this process. As an example, an administrator could search the global catalog looking for users with a last name of Jones in order to find a particular user—a much easier solution than searching through the user listings for each domain linked via trust in older versions of Windows.

Domains

The domain remains the primary organizational unit in Windows 2000. Those familiar with NT will recognize this level of organization and coordination. A domain contains various types of objects, including users, groups, printers, workstations, member servers, and domain controllers (see Figure 3.6).

Users

User logins provide access to resources. Each account will have an associated name, logon ID, and password as well as many other optional attribute values. User logons may be directly granted permissions allowing access or restricting access to various resources and administrative rights.

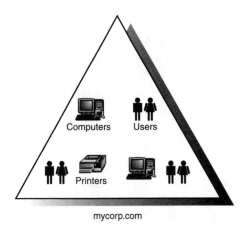

mycorp.com

Figure 3.6 Domains contain objects in a centralized administrative grouping.

Groups

Groups provide a simple method for the administration of large numbers of users. Although it may be simple to assign access rights and restrictions individually to a small number of users, this can rapidly become a significant administrative burden when 20,000 or more users are involved. Assigning access and administrative rights to groups, and making users members of these groups, allows users to inherit the access permissions assigned to those groups of which they are members.

For example, in order to change the access rights of a user promoted from Sales to an executive office, the administrator need do nothing more than make the user a member of the Executive group and remove her membership from the Sales group. Changing individually assigned permissions is no longer necessary, which eases the administrative burden in a large deployment.

Considerations for the use of groups in order to provide access and administrative rights inheritance are provided later in Chapter 6.

Objects

Other object accounts may be created within the catalog including printers, workstations, and servers. The Active Directory database may contain references to objects. Attributes assigned to these object references may allow them to be more easily located, accounted for, or organized in large deployment scenarios.

Member Servers

Member servers are computers running software designed to provide centralized services to distributed users and workstations, but which do not participate in login authentication as do domain controllers. Member servers have local user accounts and may be used when resource access is desired without the use of domain-level account permissions.

Organizational Units

Windows 2000 introduces a new subdomain grouping category: the *organizational unit (OU)*. Objects may be grouped into organizational units, and administrative rights over those objects may be granted to users or groups that do not require full domain administrative rights. Organizational units may also be grouped within one another, allowing many levels of administrative capability to be granted, each inclusive of those organizational units under its level of authority.

Organizational units may be created that more closely match the administrative structure of a business model. For example, an admin can group users, printers, and computers within the Sales department into one organizational unit. Users, printers, and computers within the Human Resources department may then be grouped into another organizational unit, with separate access rights appropriate to its separate requirements (see Figure 3.7).

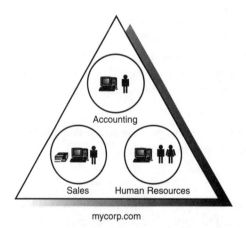

mycorp.com

Figure 3.7 Organizational units allow objects to be grouped to match a business model.

Unlike a Domain Administrator account, a user account granted administrative rights over the Sales organizational unit would have no inherent rights over the Human Resources organizational unit. If there were nested organizational units for the Conflict Management and Employee Retention subdepartments within the Human Resources organizational unit, the administrator over the Human Resources department would also have administrative rights over both nested organizational units as well. However, a user account granted administrative rights over the Employee Retention organizational unit would not have any inherent rights over the Conflict Management nor parent Human Resources organizational units.

Configuration settings and software deployment may also be enacted based on organizational unit membership using Group Policy Object (GPO) assignment, which will be discussed in detail in Chapter 7.

Trees

The Windows 2000 active directory allows for nested domains as well. Often, it is useful to separate domains based on separate business requirements such as internationally deployed corporate offices. In this case, the root (or top-level) domain might be **mycorp.com**, which has child domains of **europe.mycorp.com**, **asia.mycorp.com**, and **australia.mycorp.com**. Additional child domains may be created beneath existing domains, allowing extensible subordination of domain administration to whatever degree is required. In this way, the child domain **europe.mycorp.com** may function as the parent to the second-level child domains **germany.europe.mycorp.com** and **denmark.europe.mycorp.com**.

A hierarchical collection of parent/child domains with a contiguous namespace (one in which all child domains contain the full name of their parent domain) is referred to as a *tree*. Figure 3.8 illustrates a tree for the **mycorp.com** domain namespace.

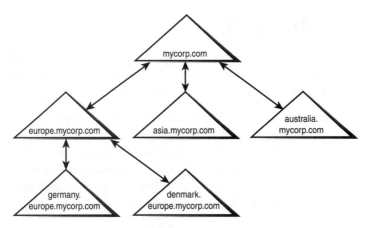

Figure 3.8 Tree diagram for **mycorp.com**.

The first domain installed will form the root domain for a tree. No parents may be added to existing domains, only children.

Forests

It is occasionally useful to link multiple trees into larger administrative groupings. This is often done when it is necessary to maintain separate legal holdings, or after a merger of two corporations has occurred and migration to a single tree has not yet been accomplished. Multiple trees joined by full two-way transitive trusts create a larger grouping called a *forest*.

Forests may be identified by the lack of a continuous namespace such as is found within a tree. A forest may contain the trees whose root domains are **mycorp.com** and **newcorp.com** (see Figure 3.9).

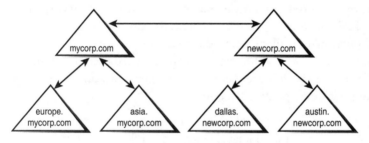

Figure 3.9 Forest diagram for trees **mycorp.com** and **newcorp.com**.

Physical Structure

When objects are located in widely distributed geographic areas, or in other cases when slow network connections link separate network subnets, it may be necessary to group computers and printers into separate *sites*.

Each site may contain one or more IP subnets, and will have one domain controller designated as a *bridgehead server*. This server is responsible for replicating changes to the global catalog between all local servers, and replicating all site-local changes with bridgehead servers located in other sites. The advantage of this configuration is that replication may be enacted only during off-peak hours, preventing swamping of low-bandwidth connections.

Practice Questions

Question 1

Which of the following are valid administrative groupings? [Check all correct answers]

❑ a. Domain

❑ b. Forest

❑ c. Organizational unit

❑ d. Site

❑ e. Tree

Answers a, b, c, and e are correct. The levels of administrative grouping are: organizational units, domains, trees, and forests. Organizational units may also be nested to provide finer granularity of administrative control. Answer d is incorrect because a site is a subgrouping of resources that reflects the physical structure rather than the logical structure. A site is one or more IP subnets connected to other sites via slower network links.

Question 2

Arrange the following in order of grouping from largest to smallest:

➤ Domain

➤ Forest

➤ Organizational unit

➤ Tree

The correct order is:

1 Forest

2 Tree

3 Domain

4 Organizational unit

Question 3

> Which of the following are valid FSMO roles? [Check all correct answers]
>
> ❑ a. Domain Naming Master
> ❑ b. Infrastructure Master
> ❑ c. Global Catalog Server
> ❑ d. PDC Emulator
> ❑ e. RID Master
> ❑ f. Schema Master

Answers a, b, d, e, and f are correct. Answer c is incorrect because it is not a single-master role. The global catalog is a distributed multimaster role shared equally by all global catalog servers.

Question 4

> The user **sjones** has been granted administrative rights over the **Marketing** organizational unit. Marketing contains two additional organizational units: **Media** and **Talent**.
>
> Will **sjones** be able to administer resources within the **Talent** organizational unit?
>
> ○ a. Yes
> ○ b. No

Answer a is correct. Administrative rights are inherited by lower-level organization unit groupings.

Question 5

> By default, Windows 2000 trusts are two-way and nontransitive.
>
> ○ a. True
> ○ b. False

Answer b is correct. By default, Windows 2000 Active Directory trusts are two-way and transitive.

Question 6

Which of the following groupings of linked domains would be a tree?

- ○ a. **mycorp.com** and **newcorp.com**
- ○ b. **mycorp.com** and **newsite.mycorp.com**
- ○ c. **Marketing and Talent**
- ○ d. Windows 2000 and Window NT

Answer b is correct. A tree contains domains in the same contiguous namespace. Answer a is incorrect because the two domains do not share a common root nor a parent/child relationship. Answer c is incorrect because **Marketing** and **Talent** are not domain names, but suited more to organizational unit naming. Answer d is incorrect because Windows 2000 and Windows NT are two operating systems.

Question 7

A user granted Domain Administrator access over the domain **dallas.mycorp. com** may administer which of the following groupings? [Check all correct answers]

- ❑ a. **mycorp.com** within the central USA site
- ❑ b. **dallas.mycorp.com** within the **mycorp.com** domain
- ❑ c. **austin.mycorp.com** within the **mycorp.com** domain
- ❑ d. **Sales** organizational unit within the **dallas.mycorp.com** domain
- ❑ e. **Managers** organizational unit within the dallas.mycorp.com **Sales** organizational unit

Answers b, d, and e are correct. A user granted administrative rights over a domain inherits administrative rights over all groupings contained therein. Answer a is incorrect because **mycorp.com** is the parent to **dallas.mycorp. com**. Answer c is incorrect because **austin.mycorp.com** is a sibling domain to **dallas.mycorp.com**.

Question 8

> Which of the FSMO roles should not be assigned to a global catalog server?
>
> ○ a. Domain Naming Master
> ○ b. Infrastructure Master
> ○ c. PDC Emulator
> ○ d. RID Master
> ○ e. Schema Master

Answer b is correct. The Infrastructure Master role should not be assigned to a global catalog server. Answers a, c, d, and e are incorrect because all other FSMO roles may be assigned as necessitated by enterprise requirements.

Question 9

> Which of the following groupings encompasses all of the others?
>
> ○ a. Domain
> ○ b. Forest
> ○ c. Organizational unit
> ○ d. Tree

Answer b is correct. A forest contains one or more trees. Answer a is incorrect because both forest and trees may contain one or more domains. Answer c is incorrect because a domain or organizational unit may contain one or more organizational units. Answer d is incorrect because one or more trees are contained in a forest.

Question 10

> The Schema Master server in the root domain is responsible for synchronizing the time through an enterprise.
>
> ○ a. True
> ○ b. False

Answer b is correct. The PDC Emulator in the root domain is responsible for time synchronization. The Schema Master role is assigned to the computer responsible for changes made to the enterprise schema.

Need to Know More?

 Stanek, William R.: *Microsoft Windows 2000 Administrator's Pocket Consultant*. Microsoft Press, Redmond, WA, 2000. ISBN 0-7356-0831-8. A helpful reference for network administrators to keep close at hand. The soft-cover trade-sized book is a condensed, easily carried version of many larger tomes of information.

 Willis, Will, David Watts, Tillman Strahan: *Windows 2000 System Administrator's Handbook*. Prentice Hall PTR. ISBN 0-1302-7010-5. A good reference for Active Directory deployment considerations.

 Microsoft Windows 2000 Server Resource Kit. Microsoft Press, Redmond, WA, 2000. ISBN 1-5723-1805-8. An exhaustive library covering detailed information on all aspects of Windows 2000 Server implementations. An invaluable reference for IT departments supporting Microsoft Windows 2000 networks.

 www.microsoft.com/windows2000/techinfo/proddoc/default. asp. *Windows 2000 Product Documentation Online*. A complete online copy of the documentation for all versions of the Windows 2000 operating system.

Name Resolution

Terms you'll need to understand:

✓ NetBIOS name
✓ FQDN host name
✓ Lightweight Directory Access Protocol (LDAP)
✓ WINS server
✓ **hosts** file
✓ DNS server
✓ **ipconfig**
✓ **nbtstat**
✓ **net**
✓ **nslookup**
✓ **ping**
✓ **tracert**

Techniques you'll need to master:

✓ Understanding the use and format of LMHOSTS and HOSTS files
✓ Recognizing the types of WINS static mappings and their uses
✓ Understanding the use of the cache-only, primary, and secondary DNS server types
✓ Using the name resolution command-line utilities **ipconfig**, **nbtstat**, **net**, **nslookup**, **ping**, and **tracert**

In Chapter 2, we briefly discussed identification of hosts within a TCP/IP network using name resolution. In this chapter, we will look more closely at the resolution of NetBIOS and FQDN naming using local caching, static lookup files, and the WINS and DNS services. Windows 2000 and Windows XP use DNS natively, but maintain NetBIOS name support for backwards compatibility with legacy software.

You should already be familiar with the terminology for name resolution presented in Chapter 2, and if you want to attempt to configure name resolution yourself, you should have a computer with Windows 2000 Server or Advanced Server loaded (make sure to apply all hotfixes and patches—discussed later in Chapter 10).

Overview

Name resolution is the process of converting easy-to-remember name identifiers to their host-identification IP equivalent. Two forms of name resolution will be discussed in this chapter: NetBIOS naming used by legacy software and applications, and *fully qualified domain name (FQDN)* resolution, which is native to Windows 2000 and Windows XP.

NetBIOS Naming

NetBIOS naming provides a flat-namespace method of identification, which was the native mode of name resolution in older versions of Windows. This method lacks scalability because all NetBIOS names may occur only once within a network and are limited to 16 characters in length. NetBIOS names are registered for a system and the services running on that system.

Restrictions to NetBIOS naming include:

➤ Limited to 16 characters in length (15 characters plus a 1-character identification for the particular service being registered)

➤ Must be unique within a network (i.e., there may only be one instance of WORKSTATION1)

➤ Limited to a flat namespace. Hierarchical naming requires FQDN naming

NetBIOS names are registered dynamically at system startup, when a service starts, and upon user login. NetBIOS names are broadcast for the network browser service, and may also be registered in a WINS service if one is defined for the local system. Configuration for WINS registration is covered later in this chapter.

FQDN Naming

Modern versions of Windows use FQDN host names in order to identify systems within a network. This system provides a scalable hierarchical system in which computers may be grouped as required by business model or legal requirement. Chapter 3 detailed domain, tree, and forest configurations.

FQDN host names may be registered dynamically at system startup, when a service starts, and upon user logon. A single IP address may be given several host names, allowing a single server to maintain many identities as required by naming convention. This is helpful when migrating from one domain-naming scheme to another and public identities are important, such as when building and maintaining the public Web site. FQDN host names may also be statically registered in a DNS server, or registered by DHCP proxy if using older versions of Windows that are unable to dynamically register themselves at startup. DHCP configuration will be covered in greater detail in Chapter 6.

Lightweight Directory Access Protocol (LDAP)

FQDN naming is integral to the Windows 2000 Active Directory structure, where resources are addresses using FQDN host names. These allow browsing the global catalog for resource records using the *Lightweight Directory Access Protocol (LDAP)*.

Each object within the catalog is stored so that it may be queried using LDAP, extracting the *distinguished name* for the target object. The portion of the distinguished name that is unique to the target object is called the *relative distinguished name*. This is basically just the first part of the distinguished name.

A typical distinguished name for a computer **myserver** in the organizational unit **accounting** within the domain **mycorp.com** would look like this:

```
CN=myserver,OU=accounting,DC=mycorp,DC=com
```

Table 4.1 details the elements of this LDAP distinguished name.

Table 4.1 LDAP name elements.	
Element	Description
CN=myserver	Relative distinguished name
CN	Common name—the name designating an object or group
OU	Organizational unit—the organizational unit containing the object or group
DC	Domain component—a portion of the domain naming scheme

Make sure you are able to recognize the common elements of a presented LDAP distinguished name.

NetBIOS Naming

NetBIOS naming is the more basic form of naming and is maintained in order to provide backwards compatibility to legacy applications and older versions of the Windows operating system. NetBIOS name resolution may be performed using any of the following:

➤ The local **NetBIOS** name cache

➤ The LMHOSTS file

➤ A **WINS** server

➤ A broadcast to the local subnet

In the event of failure of all of the above, Windows will attempt NetBIOS name resolution using the following (discussed later in this chapter):

➤ The HOSTS file

➤ A **DNS** server

The NetBIOS name of a computer is set at the time of system load, but may also be changed later by following these steps:

1. Right-click the My Computer icon and select Properties.

2. After the System Properties dialog box is visible, select the Network Identification tab and click the Properties button to open the Identification Changes dialog box (see Figure 4.1). The NetBIOS name is the same as the Computer Name box show here.

3. You may edit this name and click the OK button to save the changes.

 If the computer is joined to a domain already, this may result in unpredictable results such as the creation of a second Active Directory computer object with the new name, without removing the old name. Also, any remote access of resources located on the renamed system may be unavailable without redirecting the mappings to the new name. Chapter 8 includes details on resource management.

Figure 4.1 The Identification Changes dialog box opened by the Properties button of the Network Identification tab.

NetBIOS Name Cache

The computer maintains a listing in memory of the most recent NetBIOS names resolved, in order to speed up the process of resolution for future attempts to resolve the names of often-visited locations. This is referred to as the NetBIOS name cache, and it contains recently resolved NetBIOS names as well as those preloaded from the LMHOSTS file.

LMHOSTS File

If a computer is unable to resolve a NetBIOS name from its local NetBIOS name cache, it will attempt to resolve the name using its LMHOSTS file, which is located by default in this directory:

```
\\<systemroot>\system32\drivers\etc\
```

The LMHOSTS file lists a series of IP addresses and the NetBIOS names associated with each. A sample LMHOSTS file is included in a default Windows installation (**lmhosts.sam**) and looks like this:

```
# 102.54.94.97   rhino   #PRE #DOM:networking  #net group's DC
# 102.54.94.102  "appname  \0x14"  #special app server
# 102.54.94.123  popular  #PRE  #source server
# 102.54.94.117  localsrv  #PRE  #needed for the include
#
# #BEGIN_ALTERNATE
# #INCLUDE \\localsrv\public\lmhosts
# #INCLUDE \\rhino\public\lmhosts
# #END_ALTERNATE
```

Table 4.2 details the important keywords you should know the name of in an LMHOSTS file.

Table 4.2 Important LMHOSTS keywords.	
Keyword	**Description**
#BEGIN_ALTERNATE	Begins the definition of a *universal naming convention (UNC)* alternate path for the LMHOSTS file. This is often used when a single centrally located file is used for a distributed deployment.
#DOM:[<domain name>]	Associates the address with a particular domain. This is useful to direct domain-related actions such as logon authentication.
#END_ALTERNATE	Terminates the definition of an alternate path for the LMHOSTS file.
#INCLUDE	Specifies a file to be included as if a part of the local LMHOSTS file.
#PRE	Causes the computer to pre-load this entry into the local NetBIOS name cache by default.

Add #PRE entries last in the LMHOSTS file, because they will be loaded into the cache and so will never be resolved using the file. This places other, more often resolved names at the beginning of the LMHOSTS file, which will improve performance in name lookups.

WINS Resolution

A computer that cannot resolve a NetBIOS name locally may also query a NetBIOS name server, such as the WINS service which may be configured on a Windows 2000 server.

To configure a system to use a WINS server for NetBIOS name resolution, follow these steps:

1. Right-click on the My Network Places icon and select Properties.

2. Right-click on the desired interface and select Properties in order to open the *<connection_name>* Properties dialog box, where you will navigate to the Internet Protocol (TCP/IP) settings (see Figure 4.2).

3. Click the Properties button in order to open the Internet Protocol (TCP/IP) Properties dialog box.

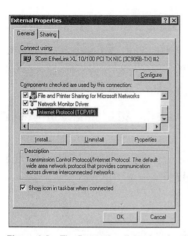

Figure 4.2   The Properties dialog box for the connection named External.

4. Select the Advanced button in order to open the Advanced TCP/IP Settings dialog box and select the WINS tab. Here, you may enter the address of one or more WINS servers to be used in NetBIOS name resolution. These should be arranged in the order they should be attempted, starting at the top. The order may be adjusted using the arrows just to the right of the WINS address box (see Figure 4.3).

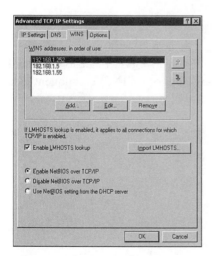

Figure 4.3   The WINS tab showing available WINS server addresses.

5. Click the OK button on each dialog box to apply the changes and close each dialog box.

WINS Service Configuration

A Windows 2000 server may be configured to provide WINS name resolution support by adding the WINS service by the following steps:

1. Select Start, then Settings, and then Control Panel.

2. From the Control Panel folder, double-click the Add/Remove Programs icon.

3. Click the Add/Remove Windows Components and navigate to the Networking Services icon (see Figure 4.4).

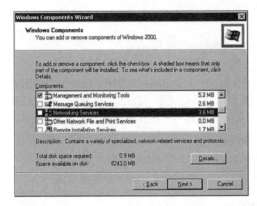

Figure 4.4 The Windows Component Wizard showing Networking Services highlighted.

4. Click Details in order to open the Network Services dialog box and select the Windows Internet Naming Service (WINS) component (see Figure 4.5).

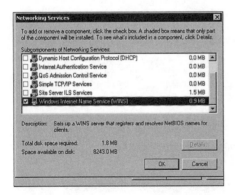

Figure 4.5 The Networking Services dialog box showing the WINS service highlighted.

5. Select the OK button and follow any further dialog boxes through until configuration is completed.

 You will need your Windows 2000 Server/Advanced Server CD in order to add new Windows components.

After the service has been configured on your server, make sure to reapply all necessary services packs and hotfixes (see Chapter 10 for details). You may then administer the WINS service using the *Microsoft Management Console (MMC)* snap-in for WINS management, which may be accessed by this path:

1. Select Start, then Settings, and then Control Panel.

2. From the Control Panel folder, double-click the Administrative Tools folder and then select the WINS MMC (see Figure 4.6).

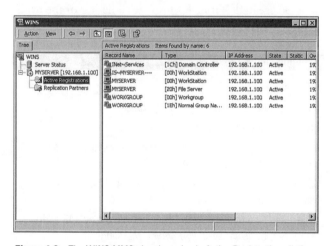

Figure 4.6   The WINS MMC showing a basic Active Registrations listing.

WINS Server Properties

After the MMC is open, you may fully administer the WINS service. Right-clicking the WINS icon allows you to add other WINS servers to this MMC, making management of multiple replication partners much easier.

Right-clicking on a server provides a pull-down menu with options that include manual triggering replication with any replication partners, backup of the WINS database, verification of database consistency, database scavenging (removal of expired registrations), and the properties for the server.

Selecting this option opens the Properties dialog box for the selected server. Here, you may configure the backup path, refresh cycle, extinction lifespan for registrations, database verification schedule, and logging settings.

Logging should only be used for diagnostic testing, as this will generate a large number of event log entries.

Static Mappings

Active Registrations provide a list of all current system and service NetBIOS registrations on this server. Right-clicking on this option will provide a pulldown listing with several options allowing the location of a current record, the addition of a new static mapping, and the ability to import records from an LMHOSTS file or export the current WINS database to an external file.

Selecting the option to create a new static mapping opens a dialog box in which a new record may be created. Table 4.3 provides a listing of the available types of static mappings that may be created.

Table 4.3 WINS static mapping types.	
Type	**Description**
Domain Name	Indicates a Windows NT domain controller.
Group	Creates a workgroup reference.
Internet Group	Creates a group of IP addresses that define a shared resource such as a group of print spoolers.
Multihomed	Specifies a single computer that has multiple IP addresses assigned to the same name.
Unique	Associates a computer's NetBIOS name with a single IP address for each of three services: File Server, Messenger, and Workstation.

Static Mappings do not expire and must be manually removed in order to remove them from the WINS database.

Replication Partners

The Replication Partners tab shows other servers configured to replicate WINS information with the current server. Right-clicking on this tab will allow the addition of a new replication partner.

Servers may be configured as push, pull, or push/pull replication partners. Table 4.4 defines each of these replication types.

Table 4.4	WINS replication partner types.
Type	**Description**
Push	This server pushes out changes in the WINS database to this partner.
Pull	This server pulls any WINS database changes from this partner.
Push/Pull	This server will push out any new changes and periodically pull changes from this partner.

Be familiar with the types of replication partner and consider the use of push- or pull-only replication partners in order to reduce network bandwidth utilization in a large enterprise deployment.

FQDN Host Naming

Resolution of the fully qualified domain name (FQDN) is the native name resolution method employed by modern versions of the Windows operating system. This hierarchical naming scheme provides scalability to include even the largest enterprise deployments. Host name resolution may be performed using any of the following:

➤ The local DNS cache

➤ The HOSTS file

➤ A DNS server

In the event of failure of all of the above, then Windows will attempt FQDN and NetBIOS name resolution using the following (discussed previously in this chapter):

➤ A broadcast to the local subnet

➤ The LMHOSTS file

➤ A WINS server

The FQDN host name of a computer is a combination of the machine name (the NetBIOS name, such as **myserver**) and the DNS suffix (such as **mycorp.com**). This name is set when the computer joins a domain, but may also be changed later. To change the FQDN host name of a computer, follow these steps:

1. Right-click the My Computer icon and select Properties.

2. Once the System Properties dialog box is visible, select the Network Identification tab and click the Properties button to open the Identification Changes dialog box. The host name is the same as the Computer Name box show here.

3. You may edit this name and click the OK button to save the changes.

 A domain controller must be demoted to a member server before the name can be changed. Chapter 9 details the promotion of member servers and the demotion of domain controllers.

Changing the domain in the Member Of selection changes the DNS suffix portion of the FQDN host name.

 Changing domain membership may only be done on workstations and member servers, and affects the ability of users to access resources located on the computer being moved. Chapter 8 explains resource management procedures.

DNS Cache

The computer maintains a listing in memory of the most recent FQDN host names resolved, in order to speed up the process of resolution for future attempts to resolve the names of often-visited locations.

HOSTS File

If a computer is unable to resolve a FQDN host name from its local DNS cache, it will attempt to resolve the name using its HOSTS file, which is located by default in this directory:

```
\\<systemroot>\system32\drivers\etc\
```

The HOSTS file lists a series of FQDN host names and the IP addresses associated with each. A sample HOSTS file is included in a default Windows installation (HOSTS) and looks like this:

```
127.0.0.1  localhost  # default local system loopback
```

Additional entries may be made for other static name resolution associations. This file does not need to be reloaded manually, as it is checked each time a name resolution attempt is unable to find an entry in the local DNS cache.

DNS Resolution

A computer that cannot resolve a FQDN host name locally may also query a DNS server, which may be configured on a Windows 2000 server.

 For client addresses to be registered dynamically, the DNS server must be a version that supports dynamic registration. Windows 2000 DNS service supports dynamic registration.

In order to configure a system to use a DNS server for name resolution, follow these steps:

1. Just as with the WINS service, right-click on the My Network Places icon and select Properties.

2. Right-click on the desired interface and select Properties in order to open the <connection_name> Properties dialog box, where you will navigate to the Internet Protocol (TCP/IP) settings.

3. Click the Properties button in order to open the Internet Protocol (TCP/IP) Properties dialog box. You may set the first two DNS server addresses here.

4. If more advanced lookup options are required, select the Advanced button in order to open the Advanced TCP/IP Settings dialog box and select the DNS tab. Here, you may enter the address of one or more DNS servers to be used in FQDN host name resolution. These should be arranged in the order they should be attempted, starting at the top. The order may be adjusted using the arrows just to the right of the DNS Server Addresses box (see Figure 4.7).

5. Configure DNS suffixes here, if you need to rapidly attempt to resolve names in integrated multiforest solutions which may have multiple non-contiguous domain namespaces. Click the OK button on each dialog box to apply the changes and close each dialog box.

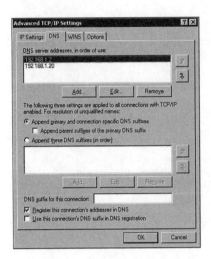

Figure 4.7 The DNS tab showing available server addresses and the option for dynamic registration of this address selected.

DNS Server Types

A Windows 2000 server may be configured to provide DNS name resolution support by adding the DNS service.

Table 4.5 lists the types of DNS service that may be created.

Table 4.5 DNS server types.	
Type	**Description**
Cache-Only	A caching DNS server is used to reduce network traffic for common local name-resolution. It does not have a copy of a DNS database, only *Forwarders* configured to allow queries to be passed to external DNS servers if the desired name is not already cached in its local DNS cache.
Primary	Primary DNS servers maintain a database containing a listing of static or dynamic name registrations for objects and services.
Secondary	Secondary DNS servers maintain a read-only copy of name registrations that is regularly synchronized with the primary DNS server.

Querying

A request to a DNS server for name resolution is referred to as a query. Two types of DNS queries exist:

. . . .

➤ *Iterative*—All registrations on the server are checked for a name or IP address match. If no local copy exists, then the server returns a failed lookup.

➤ *Recursive*—If the target DNS does not have a matching name or IP address, it will pass along the query to the servers listed in its Forwarder listing. If any of these returns the name resolution information, it will pass this back to the querying client. If the recursive attempt fails, it will report the failure back to the client.

A query resulting in the conversion of a FQDN host name to its IP address equivalent is referred to as *forward lookup*. An attempt to resolve a host name from a provided IP address is referred to as a *reverse lookup*.

Zones

A DNS *zone* is a domain namespace for which the server is authorized to resolve naming, such as **mycorp.com** or **dallas.mycorp.com**. There are several types of zones that may be created.

A single DNS server may support more than one zone, and multiple DNS servers may support a single zone. This provides the ability to distribute name resolution services as mandated by the particular network configuration in use.

Table 4.6 lists types of zones that may be created.

Table 4.6 DNS zone types.	
Type	**Description**
*Active Directory Integrated**	The database is integrated into the Active Directory, so that updates occur automatically as part of the normal Active Directory replication process. This is the recommended type of DNS zone to use in Windows 2000 Active Directory scenarios.
Reverse Lookup	A Reverse Lookup zone is used to resolve IP addresses to their FQDN host name counterparts. Just like standard Forward Lookup zones, Reverse Lookup zones may be Standard Primary, Standard Secondary, or Active Directory Integrated.
Standard Primary	An updateable DNS database contained in a locally stored text file.

(continued)

Table 4.6 DNS zone types *(continued)*	
Type	**Description**
Standard Secondary	A read-only copy of a standard primary DNS database contained in a locally stored text file. This type of deployment is often used to reduce network traffic to the primary name server by providing a "local" copy of the database for name resolution queries.

*Active Directory Integrated zones may only be created in DNS servers running on Windows 2000 domain controllers. These zones provide fault tolerance and scalability because all servers may accept dynamic registrations and serve DNS queries.

DNS Service Configuration

The DNS service may be installed on a Windows 2000 server by the following steps:

1. Just as with WINS service installation, select Start, then Settings, and then Control Panel.

2. From the Control Panel folder, double-click the Add/Remove Programs icon.

3. Click the Add/Remove Windows Components and navigate to the Networking Services icon.

4. Click Details in order to open the Network Services dialog box and select the Domain Name System (DNS) component.

5. Select the OK button and follow any further dialog boxes through until configuration is completed.

After installing all service packs and hotfixes, you may now administer the DNS service using the MMC snap-in for DNS management, which may be accessed by this path:

1. Select Start, then Settings, and then Control Panel.

2. From the Control Panel folder, double-click the Administrative Tools folder and then select the DNS MMC (see Figure 4.8).

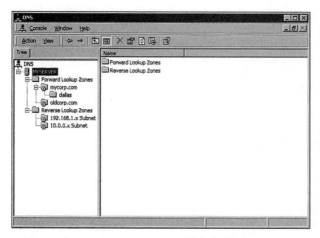

Figure 4.8 The DNS MMC showing a several Primary and Reverse Lookup zones configured for resolution.

DNS Server Properties

After the MMC is open, you may fully administer the DNS service. Right-clicking the DNS icon will allow you to connect to other DNS servers.

Right-clicking on the server will provide a pull-down menu with options that include adding a new zone, clearing the local cache, database scavenging, and the properties for the server.

Selecting this option will open the Properties dialog box for the selected server. Here, you may configure the IP addresses on which to listen for DNS queries (used if the server has multiple IP addresses bound to its network interface card or cards), list Forwarders to be used for recursive queries if local lookup fails, server options, lookup hints, logging, and monitoring. The Monitoring tab provides the ability to test the DNS server in its ability to perform lookup queries locally or recursively (see Figure 4.9).

Creating Zones

Right-clicking on the Forward Lookup Zones or Reverse Lookup Zones icons provide a a drop-down list that includes the option to add a new zone. Selecting this option opens the New Zone wizard in which a new zone may be created.

In order to create zones on non-domain controller servers, the administrator must be a member of the local Administrators group. For DNS servers running on domain controllers, the administrator must be a member of the DNS-, Domain-, or Enterprise Admins groups.

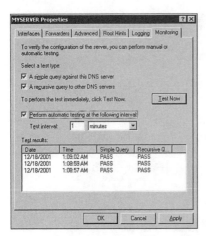

Figure 4.9 The Monitoring tab for the DNS server **myserver**.

A new Forward Lookup zone should be created for each host name zone over which the DNS server will provide authoritative name resolution. A new Reverse Lookup zone should be created for each IP subnet for which the DNS server will provide authoritative name resolution.

Child domains may be added to existing Forward Lookup zones by right-clicking the appropriate zone and selecting the option to add a new zone. Here, the child domain name (such as **dallas**) that will be prepended to the existing domain (**mycorp.com**) is specified, in order to provide authoritative name resolution capability over the child domain (**dallas.mycorp.com**).

Resource Records

A DNS database contains several types of resource records. These identify an object, domain, or service within the DNS zone.

Table 4.7 provides a listing of the available resource record types that may be found in a DNS zone.

Table 4.7 DNS resource record types.		
Designation	**Type**	**Description**
A	Host	Mapping of a host name to its associated IP address in a forward lookup zone. Also referred to as an Address record.
CNAME	Alias	An alternate name referring to an existing Host (A) record. Sometimes referred to as a Canonical name record. Often used in

(continued)

Designation	Type	Description
		Web deployments to allow names like **www.mycorp.com** to resolve to the Host (A) record for the primary Web server such as **myweb.mycorp.com**.
MX	Mail Exchange	A special-purpose alias that redirects email to a specified Host (A) record. This is often used to allow mail to be sent to a root domain (**<name>@mycorp.com**) or to an address based on the Web server's name (**<name>@www.mycorp.com**) and be redirected to the company mail server (**mymail.mycorp.com**). This does not redirect any other services from the original Host (A) record, only email redirection occurs.
NS	Name Server	Designates a DNS domain for which this DNS server provides authoritative name resolution services.
PTR	Pointer	Mapping of an IP address to its associated host name in a reverse lookup zone.
SOA	Start of Authority	The first record created in a zone. This record defines the primary authority for the zone, as well as other configuration parameters.
SRV	Service	Designates services published within the Active Directory.

Table 4.7   DNS resource record types *(continued)*

Zone Configuration

Right-clicking on any zone or record produces a drop-down menu from which several options may be selected, including the Properties dialog box.

The properties of a zone allow for the configuration of Zone Transfers, which act in Standard Primary and Standard Secondary zones (Forward and Reverse Lookup) just as the WINS replication partner setup did. However, rather than specifying a push/pull relationship, a server is designated as a primary master or secondary server. The primary master accepts updates and the secondary servers synchronize their copies of the DNS database with the master server. Only those records that have changed since the last update will be transferred during this process, reducing the impact on network bandwidth.

Active Directory Integrated zones do not require Zone Transfer configuration, as their updates occur within the normal Active Directory replication process.

Clicking the Notify button on the Zone Transfers tab will open the Notification dialog box, where the administrator may specify which servers are to be automatically notified to perform a zone transfer whenever a change occurs to the database. Obviously, this should be carefully planned in order to avoid swamping the network with zone transfer update requests.

If the administrator wants to manually cause an update to occur, they may do so by incrementing the Serial Number field on the Start Of Authority tab. When secondary servers check for updates, they compare the serial number on their copy of the database to this value. Any updates to the database will increment this value automatically, triggering an update in all secondary servers on the next update cycle.

The Security tab allows the administrator to specify the authorized servers that are to receive updates to zone changes. This may be to any server, only specified servers, or all servers listed on the Name Servers tab.

 A Standard Primary zone may be one-way converted to an Active Directory Integrated zone, but this process cannot be reversed.

Command-Line Utilities

Along with the WINS and DNS snap-in MMC utilities, Windows 2000 also includes a number of command-line tools that may be used in the troubleshooting of name resolution issues. These may be enacted by opening a command prompt by selecting Start, and then Run, and entering the command: **cmd** <Enter>. This will open a command-line terminal window, which may be closed using the **exit** command.

Table 4.8 provides a listing of some of the command-line name resolution utilities provided with Windows 2000.

Table 4.8	Name resolution command-line utilities.
Command	**Use**
ipconfig	Provides information on the current IP configuration data for the computer.
nbtstat	Used to display data or flush and reload the NEtBIOS name cache.
net	May display or modify network settings.
nslookup	Provides a lookup for host address in order to verify DNS server function and authority.
ping	Allows connectivity testing to a local or remote address.
tracert	Details the routing information between the local computer and a remote address. Often used to identify network bottlenecks, as this utility displays the time taken for each hop along the route.

ipconfig

The **ipconfig** utility displays information about the current IP settings for all adapters. It is most often used with the **/all** flag. For details on all possible options, type **ipconfig /?** at the command prompt. See Listing 4.1 for an example of the use of the **ipconfig** utility.

Listing 4.1	An example of the use of the ipconfig utility.

```
C:\>ipconfig /all
Windows 2000 IP Configuration
        Host Name . . . . . . . . . . . : myserver
        Primary DNS Suffix  . . . . . . : mycorp.com
        Node Type . . . . . . . . . . . : Hybrid
        IP Routing Enabled. . . . . . . : No
        WINS Proxy Enabled. . . . . . . : No
Ethernet adapter External:
        Connection-specific DNS Suffix  . :
        Description . . . . . . . . . . : 3Com EtherLink XL
        Physical Address. . . . . . . . : 00-11-22-33-44-55
        DHCP Enabled. . . . . . . . . . : No
        IP Address. . . . . . . . . . . : 192.168.1.102
        Subnet Mask . . . . . . . . . . : 255.255.255.0
        IP Address. . . . . . . . . . . : 192.168.1.101
        Subnet Mask . . . . . . . . . . : 255.255.255.0
        IP Address. . . . . . . . . . . : 192.168.1.100
        Subnet Mask . . . . . . . . . . : 255.255.255.0
        Default Gateway . . . . . . . . : 192.168.1.1
        DNS Servers . . . . . . . . . . : 192.168.1.2
                                          192.168.1.20
        Primary WINS Server . . . . . . : 192.168.1.252
        Secondary WINS Server . . . . . : 192.168.1.5
```

nbtstat

The **nbtstat** utility displays information about the current IP settings for all adapters. It is most often used with the **-c, -n, and -R** flags. For details on all possible options, type **nbtstat /?** at the command prompt.

Table 4.9 provides a list of the three most common flags for **nbtstat** and their uses, and Listing 4.2 shows an example of the use of the **nbtstat** utility.

Table 4.9	nbtstat flags.
Flag	**Use**
-c	Provides details from the NetBIOS name cache.
-n	Lists the NetBIOS information for the local system.
-R	Flushes the existing NetBIOS name cache and reloads any #PRE designated items from the LMHOSTS file.

Listing 4.2 An example of the use of the nbtstat utility.

```
C:\ >nbtstat -n
External:
Node IpAddress: [192.168.1.100] Scope Id: []
                NetBIOS Local Name Table
       Name                Type        Status
    - - - - - - - - - - - - - - - - - - - - - - - - - - - - - -
    INet~Services <1C> GROUP     Registered
    IS~MYSERVER....<00> UNIQUE   Registered
    MYSERVER      <00> UNIQUE    Registered
    WORKGROUP     <00> GROUP     Registered
    MYSERVER      <20> UNIQUE    Registered
    WORKGROUP     <1E> GROUP     Registered
```

net

The **net** utility provides a large number of options for command line administration of network configuration data. Its most common name resolution option is **net config workstation**, which provides details on the current domain and NetBIOS name of the local system. For details on all possible options, type **net /?** at the command prompt and then investigate each branch. Listing 4.3 shows an example of the use of the **net** utility.

Listing 4.3 An example of the use of the net utility.

```
C:\>net config workstation
Computer name                    \\MYSERVER
Full Computer name               myserver
User name                        MyAdmin
Software version                 Windows 2000
Workstation domain               MYCORP
Workstation Domain DNS Name      mycorp.com
Logon domain                     MYCORP
COM Open Timeout (sec)           0
COM Send Count (byte)            16
COM Send Timeout (msec)          250
```

nslookup

The **nslookup** utility verifies DNS lookup functionality in the form **nslookup <domain>**. Listing 4.4 shows an example of the use of the **nslookup** utility.

Listing 4.4   An example of the use of the nslookup utility.

```
C:\>nslookup myserver
Server:  mydns.mycorp.com
Address:  192.168.1.2
Name:    myserver.mycorp.com
Address:  192.168.1.100
```

ping

The **ping** utility verifies connectivity to a remote address. For details on all possible options, type **ping /?** at the command prompt. Listing 4.5 shows an example of the use of the **ping** utility.

Listing 4.5   An example of the use of the ping utility.

```
C:\>ping -a station1.mycorp.com
Pinging station1.mycorp.com [192.168.1.50] with 32 bytes of data:
Reply from 192.168.1.50: bytes=32 time<10ms TTL=128
Reply from 192.168.1.50: bytes=32 time<10ms TTL=128
Reply from 192.168.1.50: bytes=32 time<10ms TTL=128
Reply from 192.168.1.50: bytes=32 time<10ms TTL=128
Ping statistics for 192.168.1.50:
    Packets: Sent = 4, Received = 4, Lost = 0 (0% loss),
Approximate round trip times in milli-seconds:
    Minimum = 0ms, Maximum =  0ms, Average =  0ms
```

tracert

The **tracert** utility provides details of routing information between the local system and a remote address. For details on all possible options, type **tracert** at the command prompt. Listing 4.6 shows an example of the use of the **tracert** utility.

Listing 4.6 An example of the use of the tracert utility.

```
C:\>tracert www.mycorp.com
Tracing route to myweb.mycorp.com [192.168.2.90]
over a maximum of 30 hops:
  1   <10 ms    10 ms   <10 ms   router1.mycorp.com [192.168.1.1]
  2   <10 ms    10 ms   <10 ms   router2.mycorp.com [192.168.2.1]
  3    20 ms    10 ms    10 ms   myweb.mycorp.com [192.168.2.90]
Trace complete.
```

A strong familiarity with these utilities is essential for a network administrator. Make sure that you try these utilities and experiment with other functions of each.

Practice Questions

Question 1

> Which of the following are valid possible NetBIOS names? [Check all correct answers]
>
> ❑ a. COM
> ❑ b. MYCORP.COM
> ❑ c. MYFAVORITECOMPUTER
> ❑ d. MYSERVER
> ❑ e. MYSERVER.MYCORP.COM

Answers a and d are correct. Although COM might not be the best name for a computer, it is still a valid possible NetBIOS name, as is MYSERVER. Answers b and e are incorrect because they are hierarchical domain names suitable to FQDN name resolution. Answer c is incorrect because a NetBIOS name is limited to 16 characters in length.

Question 2

> Which of the following are valid name resolution options in Windows 2000? [Check all correct answers]
>
> ❑ a. DNS service
> ❑ b. HOSTS file
> ❑ c. LMHOSTS file
> ❑ d. WINS name cache
> ❑ e. WINS service
> ❑ f. Zone transfer

Answers a, b, c, d, and e are correct. All of these are valid name resolution options. FQDN host names may be resolved using a DNS service or a HOSTS file, while NetBIOS names may be resolved using an LMHOSTS file, querying the WINS name cache, or using a WINS server. Answer f is incorrect because a zone transfer is used to provide updates to DNS registration records between DNS servers and is not used for name resolution.

Question 3

> Arrange the following name elements into the proper order for a valid LDAP distinguished name:
>
> ➤ CN=rjones
> ➤ DC=com
> ➤ DC=mycorp
> ➤ OU=marketing

The correct answer is:

➤ CN=rjones

➤ OU=marketing

➤ DC=mycorp

➤ DC=com

The LDAP distinguished name is: CD=rjones,OU=marketing,DC=mycorp, DC=com.

Question 4

> You and your partner are given a static name resolution text file that has been misnamed by the head of IT to **_osts**. Rather than go back to the IT head to figure out which file this is, your partner decides to just rename it. You get a glimpse of a few lines and see the following:
>
> ```
> # 192.168.1.20    mydns      #PRE
> # 192.168.1.54    pdc01      #PRE #DOM:marketing
> ```
>
> Your partner concludes that this is an LMHOSTS file and renames it accordingly. Is your partner correct?
>
> ○ a. Yes
> ○ b. No

Answer a is correct. Your partner has chosen correctly. An LMHOSTS file includes NetBIOS names and their related IP addresses. The #PRE designation causes an entry to be loaded at startup or when the **nbtstat –R** command is given.

Question 5

> Which of the following type of replication is used if all updates to the local server are only to be sent to the replication partner?
>
> ○ a. Pull
>
> ○ b. Push
>
> ○ c. Push/pull

Answer b is correct. Data is to be pushed out to the replication partner. Answer a is incorrect because a pull replication would bring data from the replication partner to the local server. Answer c is incorrect because it is specified that this should be a push-only replication.

Question 6

> You have noticed that there is a significant network bottleneck in the subnet where your primary DNS server is located and analysis of the traffic indicates that name resolution for your ecommerce Web portal is impacting overall network performance. You decide to place two additional secondary DNS servers in another subnet and arrange for all three to be load balanced for external client name resolution. Will this help to correct the problem?
>
> ○ a. True
>
> ○ b. False

Answer a is correct. Provided that the analysis is correct and no other issues are affecting network performance, then setting up to secondary (read-only) name servers in another subnet will help to balance the load on your network and improve performance.

Question 7

> Three of the types of DNS zone are:
> ➤Active Directory Integrated
> ➤Standard Primary
> ➤Standard Secondary
>
> Match the following characteristics with the appropriate zone type: [Answers may be used more than once]
> ➤May only be created on DNS servers running on Windows 2000 domain controllers
> ➤Maintains an updateable database
> ➤Read-only copy of the database
> ➤Updates occur with normal domain replication.

The correct answers are:

➤ Active Directory Integrated

➤May only be created on DNS servers running on Windows 2000 domain controllers

➤Maintains an updatable database

➤Updates occur with normal domain replication.

➤ Standard Primary

➤Maintains an updatable database

➤ Standard Secondary

➤Read-only copy of the database

Question 8

You need to create resource records in order to direct all Web queries sent to **www.mycorp.com** to the old Web server **srvweb1.mycorp.com**, and all email sent to **<name>@mycorp.com** to the new email server **newmail.mycorp.com**.

You decide to create a CNAME of **www.mycorp.com** for the **newmail.mycorp.com** Host (A) record, and an MX record for **srvweb1.mycorp.com** that redirects email to **www.mycorp.com**. Will this have the desired effect?

○ a. Yes, both requirements will be met.

○ b. No, only the first requirement will be met.

○ c. No, only the second requirement will be met.

○ d. No, neither requirement will be met.

Answer d is correct. Neither requirement will be met. Answers a and b are incorrect because the CNAME for **www.mycorp.com** was created as an alias to the mail server, and not the Web server. Answers a and c are incorrect because you created an MX record for email sent to the web server to be redirected to the mail server, instead of creating an MX record for the domain **mycorp.com**.

Question 9

Which of the following command line utilities may be used to verify network connectivity to a remote address? [Check all correct answers]

❑ a. ipconfig

❑ b. nbtstat

❑ c. nslookup

❑ d. ping

❑ e. tracert

Answers d and e are correct. Both the **ping** and **tracert** utilities may be used to verify connectivity to a remote address. Answers a and b are incorrect because both **ipconfig** and **nbtstat** are used to provide local configuration information. Answer c is incorrect because **nslookup** is used to verify DNS name resolution function and does not provide information on whether the remote address is reachable.

Question 10

You are given this piece of code:

```
Reply from 192.168.1.50: bytes=32 time<10ms TTL=128
Reply from 192.168.1.50: bytes=32 time<10ms TTL=128
Reply from 192.168.1.50: bytes=32 time<10ms TTL=128
Reply from 192.168.1.50: bytes=32 time<10ms TTL=128
```

Which of the following utilities generated this output?

O a. ipconfig

O b. nbtstat

O c. nslookup

O d. ping

O e. tracert

Answer d is correct. The **ping** utility provides a round-trip connection time to a remote host repeatedly. Answers a and b are incorrect because both **ipconfig** and **nbtstat** are used to provide local configuration information, not connection time. Answer c is incorrect because **nslookup** is used to verify DNS name resolution function and does not provide information on connectivity. Answer e is incorrect because the **tracert** utility provides a per-hop time rather than a repeated test of the end-to-end connectivity.

Need to Know More?

 Stanek, William R.: *Microsoft Windows 2000 Administrator's Pocket Consultant.* Microsoft Press, Redmond, WA, 2000. ISBN 0-7356-0831-8. A helpful reference for network administrators to keep close at hand. The soft-cover trade-sized book is a condensed, easily carried version of many larger tomes of information.

 Microsoft Windows 2000 Server Resource Kit. Microsoft Press, Redmond, WA, 2000. ISBN 1-5723-1805-8. An exhaustive library covering detailed information on all aspects of Windows 2000 Server implementations. An invaluable reference for IT departments supporting Microsoft Windows 2000 networks.

 www.microsoft.com/windows2000/techinfo/proddoc/default.asp. *Windows 2000 Product Documentation Online.* A complete online copy of the documentation for all versions of the Windows 2000 operating system.

5

DHCP Configuration

. . . .

Terms you'll need to understand:

✓ Static addressing
✓ Dynamic addressing
✓ DHCPDISCOVERY
✓ DHCPOFFER
✓ DHCPREQUEST
✓ DHCPACK
✓ Lease duration
✓ Scope
✓ Client reservations

Techniques you'll need to master:

✓ Diagramming the four phases in a DHCP lease request and identifying which two are used in lease renewal
✓ Understanding the effect of using lease durations that are longer and shorter than the default
✓ Creating, activating, and configuring a DHCP scope
✓ Understanding the use of DHCP lease client reservations

Chapter 2 covered host addressing in an academic sense. However, the reality of host addressing can be an administrative headache when the number of machines exceeds a handful, or when computers are highly mobile. Each computer must have a unique IP address assigned, but doing this manually on each terminal can be difficult in large-enterprise deployment scenarios. Fortunately, Microsoft Windows offers an automated solution to this problem in the form of the *Dynamic Host Configuration Protocol (DHCP)* service.

This chapter covers the installation, authorization, and configuration of the DHCP service within the Windows 2000 networking environment. Any Windows 2000 server may host the DHCP service, including nondomain controllers. In order to initially authorize a DHCP server within a Windows 2000 Active Directory network, the administrator must be a member of the Enterprise Admins group.

Overview

Unique per-system IP addressing is necessary within modern networks in order to allow intersystem communication, file sharing, and all other functions that have become a part of the rapidly growing network deployment scenarios found in almost every type of business spanning the globe. Assignment of addressing manually can be a tedious matter, requiring access to the client system as well as time to change configuration details. In large-scale deployments, this task can rapidly become unmanageable.

Windows provides an automated IP address configuration utility called the *DHCP service.* Many other operating systems may also provide DHCP support, but we will focus on the Windows 2000 version of this service in support of distributed Windows clients.

Static Addressing

Static addressing is necessary for certain critical systems whose addresses must not change. Typically, these are systems providing remotely addressed centralized services such as print, Web, and database servers. In modern networks, most systems do not require a permanent, statically assigned IP address. In fact, in scenarios involving highly mobile users using laptops or wireless connectivity products (IEEE 802.11-compliant devices), the use of static addressing may impede performance or prevent connectivity altogether. Roaming users who move from one subnet to another may find themselves unable to connect when outside of their originally configured subnet when using statically assigned addressing. Imagine the calls you may receive when the Board of Directors find themselves unable to connect to the network using their laptops in the new boardroom.

Manual addressing of dozens, hundreds, or even thousands of machines also provides ample opportunities for human-introduced error in the form of incorrect settings, duplicate IP addressing, or typographic error during entry, any of which may result in a loss of connectivity for the user of the misconfigured client.

Dynamic Addressing

Automated deployment using DHCP simplifies this process immensely. The DHCP server dynamically provides an IP address to each computer from an available pool of IP addresses. This allows a smaller pool of addresses to be shared among a larger number of client systems that do not always require connectivity, provides centralized management, and simplifies large-scale modifications to network configuration. New configuration settings are updated on the client system each time it boots, when the current DHCP lease expires, or when manually requested by the user.

DHCP Leasing

Each IP address assigned by a DHCP service is given a limited-duration lease for the current client. When this lease reaches 50% of its lifetime, the client computer will automatically attempt to obtain a new lease for the same address. If a DHCP server can be reached, then the lease will be renewed, or replaced with a new lease if the network configuration has been changed. If a DHCP server is not immediately available, the DHCP client will continue using its existing lease information and wait until 85% of the lease period has expired before attempting again to renew its lease. If the DHCP server remains unavailable, the client will continue to use its current lease information until the lease expires. If a DHCP server cannot be reached at this point, the client will cease using the leased information, and begin attempting to locate another DHCP server.

When a system configured to use the DHCP client for addressing boots, it will attempt to use its previous DHCP leased information provided the lease has not yet expired. If the lease has expired, the former leased information will be dropped and the client will initiate the process for obtaining a new lease.

DHCP Lease Generation

A computer configured to use the DHCP client for addressing must request a new lease from an available DHCP server when it boots, when its lease is nearing expiration, or when the user requests a manual refresh of leased information. The complete process of lease generation involves four phases:

1. Discovery

2. Server Offer

3. Client Request

4. Server Acknowledgement

When a lease has reached 50% of its lifespan, or when a manual refresh has been requested, only the last two steps are enacted in order to renew a lease from the original DHCP server that granted the lease. If this server remains unavailable, then the process will begin with a new attempt at Discovery.

 A client with multiple NICs using DHCP addressing will perform this task for each of the NICs separately.

Discovery

The Discovery procedure is initiated when the DHCP-enabled client computer sends out a local subnet broadcast, requesting a DHCP lease. During this time, the client utilizes a temporary placeholder IP address of 0.0.0.0 and a subnet mask of 255.255.255.255.

The client broadcasts a DHCPDISCOVER message, which includes the name of the computer requesting the DHCP lease and the MAC address of its network card. This is sent out using a UDP broadcast using ports 67 and 68. Because broadcasts do not pass through most routers, it may be necessary to configure a DHCP Proxy server in order to reach a DHCP server located in another subnet. Setting up a DHCP Proxy server will be discussed in Chapter 13.

The client will wait for a lease offer for 1, 2, 4, and 8 seconds, and then will initialize the TCP/IP protocol using a default address within the address range of 169.254.0.1-169.254.255.254. This allows the client to continue requesting a lease every 5 minutes until a server becomes available. During this time, users of the client system will be unable to access network resources using the network configuration settings normally provided by the missing DHCP lease.

Offer

When the DHCPDISCOVER signal is sent, all DHCP servers authorized to provide leases within the subnet respond with an offer of a lease. The offered address will be temporarily reserved, pending the client's response, to prevent accidentally offering the same leased address to multiple clients at once.

Each authorized server responds with a DHCPOFFER message, which includes the name and MAC address of the requesting client, along with the offered IP address, subnet mask, and lifespan of the offered lease.

Request

The DHCP client will respond to the first offer it receives, sending back to the offering server a request for the offered lease. Systems attempting to renew an existing lease will initiate this process as the first step of renewal.

The client sends a DHCPREQUEST message back, indicating which server's offer it is requesting. This message causes all other servers that provided a lease offer to release the temporary reservation for the offered address and release the address back into their available pool.

Acknowledgement

The DHCP server indicated in the request message then sends back a DHCPACK message, acknowledging the successful grant or renewal of the IP address lease. This message also includes any configuration information provided by the lease, allowing the client to begin using the leased information in order to provide access to the network.

Hall Passes and Leases

An easy way to remember this process is to think of a student in school asking for a hall pass from their teacher. In this case, the student represents the DHCP client and the teacher represents the DHCP server. The hall pass is the requested IP address information provided by a DHCP lease.

1. The student raises his hand and says, "Teacher, I need the hall pass." (Discovery)

2. All teachers in the room identify the student by name and hold up hall passes taken from the basket of passes each has been given, asking, "Billy, do you want a hall pass?" (Offer)

3. The student agrees and reaches to be given the hall pass from the nearest teacher, saying, "Yes, please. Thank you, Mr. Jones." All other teachers in the room go back to their own students, putting their hall passes away again. (Request)

4. Mr. Jones hands the hall pass to the student, telling him, "This is good for one hour. Make sure to check back before then in case I need to write you a new pass. And make sure to leave through the lefthand door on your way out so the monitor will let you go by." (Acknowledgement)

In this example, the student requests the pass, is offered several, accepts the nearest one, and is given the pass along with instructions on its term and other information needed in order to let the student leave the classroom. This models the steps involved in the DHCP lease generation process. If the student checks back a half-hour later, he may be told the hall pass is still good or given a new one, just as an existing DHCP lease may be renewed.

DHCP Lease Duration

The default lifetime for a DHCP lease is eight days. This may be adjusted to shorter or longer periods of time, or even configured as unlimited in duration, requiring a manual removal of the lease before the address returns to the IP address pool.

Table 5.1 details some of the strengths and weaknesses of different lease durations.

Table 5.1 Lease duration changes.	
Change	**Effect**
Shorter	Decreased lease duration may be useful in scopes providing DHCP leases to highly mobile users. Addresses will be rapidly returned to the available IP address pool, allowing a small number of addresses to support a larger number of client computers and more rapid updates to changes in network configuration. This may be useful when preparing for network reconfiguration, so that client connectivity will be minimally affected. Server availability becomes more critical and network bandwidth utilization will be higher as lease duration is reduced.
Longer	Increasing lease duration allows clients to hold leases for longer periods of time. This may be useful when DHCP server availability is limited. Addresses are not returned to the address pool rapidly, which may result in new clients being unable to obtain a lease until an outstanding lease for a removed client finally expires. Changes in network configuration may also take longer. This solution is acceptable in scenarios involving desktop deployment and few mobile users in a fairly stable network environment. Longer duration leases minimize bandwidth utilization for lease renewal.

(continued)

Table 5.1 Lease duration changes *(continued)*	
Change	**Effect**
Unlimited*	An unlimited lease duration is generally going to be useful only in highly stable network environments or when client systems may have very extended periods without DHCP server accessibility. IP addresses are not returned to the IP address pool unless the leases are manually removed.

The New Scope wizard does not allow selection of unlimited duration leases. This must be configured later if desired.

DHCP Server Setup

If the DHCP service was not selected as an option during the initial server installation, it will be necessary to install this service. The DHCP service may be installed using the following steps:

1. Select Start, then Settings, and then Control Panel.

2. From the Control Panel folder, double-click the Add/Remove Programs icon.

3. Click the Add/Remove Windows Components and navigate to the Networking Services icon.

4. Click Details in order to open the Network Services dialog box and select the Dynamic Host Configuration Protocol (DHCP) component.

5. Select the OK button and follow any further dialog boxes through until configuration is completed.

You will need your Windows 2000 Server/Advanced Server CD in order to add new Windows components.

After the service has been installed on your server, make sure to reapply all necessary service packs and hotfixes (see Chapter 10 for details). You may then administer the DHCP service using the Microsoft Management Console (MMC) snap-in for DHCP management, which may be accessed here:

1. Select Start, then Settings, and then Control Panel.

2. From the Control Panel folder, double-click the Administrative Tools folder and then select the DHCP MMC (see Figure 5.1).

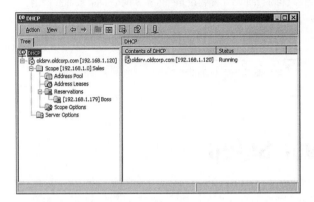

Figure 5.1 The DHCP MMC showing a basic Active Registrations listing.

Server Authorization

After the DHCP service has been installed, it must be *authorized* in order to be able to provide DHCP leases for your clients. This prevents unauthorized servers from providing conflicting lease information within a shared subnet, but only functions between Windows 2000 DHCP servers.

> Non-Windows 2000 DHCP servers may still provide DHCP lease information to clients located in the same subnet.

A member of the Enterprise Admins group may authorize a DHCP server in the following way:

1. Open the DHCP MMC and then right-click the DHCP icon to open the drop-down options menu.

2. Select Manage Authorized Servers from the drop-down menu in order to open the dialog box for server authorization (see Figure 5.2).

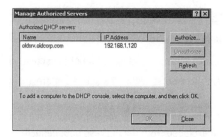

Figure 5.2   The Manage Authorized Servers dialog box showing one authorized server.

3. Click the Authorize button and specify the server to be authorized in the dialog box provided.

> ➤ You may also unauthorize a server to be removed here. Steps you must take before unauthorizing a server are covered later in this chapter, in the section called "Unauthorizing DHCP Servers."

4. Click the Yes button in order to authorize the specified server.

5. Click Close in order to return to the DHCP MMC.

Scope Configuration

After a DHCP server has been authorized to support clients within your forest, it is necessary to set up a *scope* for each subnet that will be supported. A scope defines the IP address pool to be used within a particular subnet, address reservations for specific clients, and any configured settings that will be provided in the DHCP leases.

 Each subnet requires a separate scope. Do not use the same addresses in more than one scope, in order to prevent potential conflict.

Scope Parameters

The parameters for each scope must be defined before it may be used. These specify the basic settings to be used for leases provided within the scope's range of IP addresses.

Table 5.2 lists the scope parameters that may be configured using the New Scope wizard.

Table 5.2 Scope parameters.	
Parameter	**Purpose**
Description (opt)	Provides a meaningful description of the scope.
End IP Address	The last IP address within the scope's address pool.
Exclusion Address Range (opt)	A list of any addresses or address ranges that will be excluded from the address pool defined by the start and end IP addresses for the scope.
Lease Duration	The lifespan of a lease, specified in days, hours, and minutes.
Name	An identifiable name for the scope. This should be meaningful and easily identifiable.
Subnet Mask*	The subnet mask assigned to DHCP clients within this scope, which may be entered as a number of bits, or as a numerical subnet mask value.
Start IP Address	The first IP address within the scope's address pool.

*All settings may be changed later except for the subnet mask. A scope must be deleted and recreated in order to change this setting.

Scope Creation

A new scope may be created using the New Scope wizard. This is accomplished by the following steps:

1. Open the DHCP MMC as detailed previously under Server Authorization.

2. Right-click on the desired authorized server's icon and select New Scope from the list of drop-down options.

   ►A *superscope* may also be created here. This is a container that allows many scopes to be referenced using a single identity.

3. Enter the name and description for the new scope when prompted. The scope name must be unique.

4. Enter the starting and ending IP addresses for the scope's address pool, along with the subnet mask to be used within this scope as either a number of bits or a subnet mask numerical value (see Figure 5.3).

5. Select Next once all values have been set.

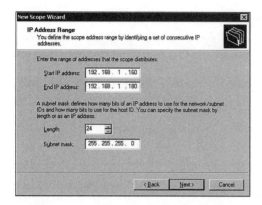

Figure 5.3   The New Scope wizard showing IP range and Subnet Mask configuration details.

6. Add any IP values within the scope's range to be excluded from the IP address pool, if desired, and Select Next.

7. Set the value of the lease duration in days, hours, and minutes and select Next.

8. You will be prompted to choose if you wish to configure any desired DHCP options at this time. Options will be discussed later in this section. Select Yes to configure options now, or No to create the scope now. Select Next and then Finish to close the wizard now.

Scope Activation

A newly created scope must be activated before it may be used to provide DHCP leases to clients. In order to activate a scope, follow these steps:

1. Open the DHCP MMC as detailed previously under Server Authorization.

2. Right-click on the desired scope and select Activate from the drop-down menu.

Scope Options

Scope options are additional configuration settings that will be included in the lease sent to the client. These settings may include information such as a default gateway (router) for the subnet or the IP addresses for DNS or WINS servers.

Scope options that may be configured within the New Scope wizard include:

➤ *DNS Server*—The IP addresses of DNS servers, arranged in the order they should be attempted.

➤ *Domain Name*—The domain name to be registered during client DNS registration.

➤ *Router (Default Gateway)*—The IP address or addresses of routers available within the scope's subnet.

➤ *WINS Server*—The IP addresses of WINS servers, arranged in the order they should be attempted.

These and other scope options may be configured later using the DHCP MMC.

1. Open the DHCP MMC as detailed previously under Server Authorization.

2. Right-click on the desired scope and then right-click on the Scope Options icon and select Configure Options from the drop-down menu to open the Scope Options dialog box (see Figure 5.4).

➤ The Advanced tab allows configuration of class-level scope options. This is discussed in the next part of this section.

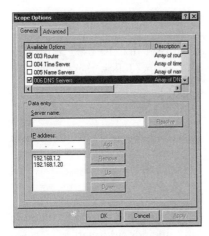

Figure 5.4 The Scope Options dialog box showing selected options.

3. Configure any options desired. Select Apply to apply the changes and OK to close the dialog box.

Scope Option Levels

Scope options may be applied at several levels, allowing ease in the administration of large networking deployment scenarios. IP configuration information may be provided by DHCP scope option settings at the server, scope, class, and reserved client levels, or defined statically in the local machine settings.

Each lower level of this architecture will override settings from the higher level, allowing generic values to be set, and then overridden with more customized values as the level is more closely refined, down to the machine itself.

Table 5.3 lists the levels at which scope options may be assigned.

Table 5.3	Scope assignment levels.	
Level	**Applied To**	**Overrides**
Server	The highest level. Settings here apply to all DCHP leases unless overridden at a lower level.	None
Scope	Settings here apply to all DHCP leases in the scope unless overridden at a lower level.	Server-level settings
Class	Settings here apply to machines that fall into a particular class, such as a Windows XP system.	Server-level and Scope-level settings.
Reserved Client	Settings here apply to a single reserved client lease.	Server-, Scope-, and Class-level settings.
Local System	Settings on the local machine itself, such as the DNS servers to be used.	Any DHCP-provided settings.

Remember that settings at a higher level are overridden by settings at a lower level.

Client Reservations

Sometimes, it is necessary to ensure that a particular computer always receives the same DHCP lease. This is often used rather than a true static assignment in networks that encounter routine network configuration changes, but which provide standard services such as a print or file server. In order to maintain connectivity for clients to access these services, each machine must receive the same IP address each time, while regular network changes dictate the need to update settings via DHCP lease.

Client reservation provides the best of both solutions, associating a specific MAC address with a standard IP address that is kept reserved from the normal IP address pool. This is also useful in high-utilization networks where a user must be guaranteed the ability to obtain a lease immediately, as the reserved IP address will never be returned to the IP address pool until the reservation has been removed.

Client reservations may be defined within the DHCP MMC.

1. Open the DHCP MMC as detailed previously under Server Authorization.

2. Right-click on the desired scope and then right-click on the Reservations icon and select New Reservation from the drop-down menu to open the New Reservation dialog box (see Figure 5.5).

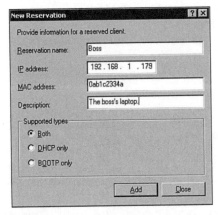

Figure 5.5 The New Reservations dialog box showing a reservation allowing the boss's computer to always have a lease reserved.

3. Enter a meaningful unique name for the reservation, the IP address to be assigned, the client's MAC address, and a meaningful description of the reservation.

4. Click Add in order to add the new reservation.

5. Continue entering lease reservations until done, and then click Close to return to the DHCP MMC.

Practice Questions

Question 1

> There are two forms of IP address assignment:
> ➤ Dynamic
> ➤ Static
>
> Match the following characteristics with the appropriate assignment type:
> ➤ All settings are fixed unless manually changed
> ➤ IP addresses are dynamically assigned from an available pool
> ➤ Settings may be applied based on scope, class, or MAC-level assignment
> ➤ Settings may be centrally managed

The correct answers are:

➤ Dynamic

   ➤IP addresses are dynamically assigned from an available pool

   ➤Settings may be applied based on scope, class, or MAC-level assignment

   ➤Settings may be centrally managed

➤ Static

   ➤All settings are fixed unless manually changed

Question 2

> DHCP clients wait until they are 85% of the way through the lifespan of their lease before attempting to renew the lease. True or false?
> ○ a. True
> ○ b. False

Answer b is correct. DHCP clients will first attempt to renew their lease when they reach 50% of the lease duration. If they are unable to contact a DHCP server at this time, they will try again at 85% of the lease duration, and again at the end of the lease if necessary, and then every 5 minutes until a server becomes available.

Question 3

> Arrange the four phases of DHCP lease generation into their proper order:
>   ➤ Client Request
>   ➤ Discovery
>   ➤ Server Acknowledgement
>   ➤ Server Offer

The correct answer is:

➤ Discovery

➤ Server Offer

➤ Client Request

➤ Server Acknowledgement

Question 4

> Which of the phases of DHCP lease generation are enacted during a successful lease renewal? [Check all correct answers]
>   ❑ a. Client Request
>   ❑ b. Discovery
>   ❑ c. Server Acknowledgement
>   ❑ d. Server Offer

Answers a and c are correct. In a successful lease renewal, only the Client Request and Server Acknowledgement will occur. Answer b is incorrect because the previous lease provides the client with the DHCP server's contact information and so no Discovery is required. Answer d is incorrect because the client already has a lease, which is simply renewed. No new IP addresses must be held in temporary reserve during this process.

Question 5

> Which change in lease duration would be best for remote salespersons that remain in the field without DHCP server connectivity for two weeks or more?
>
> ○ a. Shorter than default
>
> ○ b. Default
>
> ○ c. Longer than default
>
> ○ d. Unlimited

Answer d is correct, as it is the best answer for long-term client leases that may need to be retained even after lengthy periods without DHCP connectivity. Answers a and b are incorrect because the default least period is eight days, and anything shorter than that would also be less than the minimum stated length of two weeks. Answer c is potentially correct, as a very long-term lease could be configured, but in this case, it is not the "best" answer as requested in the question.

Question 6

> Arrange the steps involved in setting up a client reservation in order:
>
> ➤ Activate the scope
>
> ➤ Authorize the server
>
> ➤ Create a client reservation
>
> ➤ Define a scope
>
> ➤ Load the DHCP service using the Add/Remove Programs utility

The correct answer is:

➤ Load the DHCP service using the Add/Remove Programs utility

➤ Authorize the server

➤ Define a scope

➤ Activate the scope

➤ Create a client reservation

Question 7

When a DHCPDISCOVER message is received by several Windows 2000 DHCP servers, which will return a DHCPOFFER to the Windows 2000 client?

○ a. None. The server would send back a DHCPACK instead.

○ b. All authorized DHCP servers

○ c. The closest server to the client

○ d. The server with the most recent DHCP version

Answer b is correct. All authorized servers will send back a DHCPOFFER message, and temporarily reserve the offered IP address until the client returns a DHCPREQUEST message. Answer a is incorrect because the client must first request the lease before a server acknowledgement may be sent. Answers c and d are incorrect because all authorized servers within a subnet will respond to a discovery message.

Question 8

Arrange the scope option levels in the order from the broadest to the most specific:

➤ Class

➤ Local Machine

➤ Reserved Client

➤ Scope

➤ Server

The correct answer is:

➤ Server

➤ Scope

➤ Class

➤ Reserved Client

➤ Local Machine

The Local Machine settings are not technically part of the DHCP settings, as these are set directly on the machine, but are included here for completeness.

Question 9

> What is the default duration for a DHCP lease?
>
> O a. 1 hour
> O b. 1 day
> O c. 4 days
> O d. 8 days
> O e. 14 days
> O f. Unlimited

Answer d is correct. The default lease duration is eight days. Answers a, b, c, e, and f are incorrect as they are either shorter or longer than the default duration.

Question 10

> DHCP clients that are unable to renew their lease at the end of its duration will continue to use their current settings until a server becomes available. True or false?
>
> O a. True
> O b. False

Answer b is correct. DHCP clients that cannot renew their lease before the end of its duration will release their IP configuration settings and revert to an address within the 169.254.0.1-169.254.255.254 range, and will broadcast a DHCPDISCOVERY message every 5 minutes until a server becomes available.

Need to Know More?

 Lemon, Ted, and Ralph E. Droms: *The DHCP Handbook: Understanding, Deploying, and Managing Automated Configuration Services.* Pearson Higher Education, 1999. ISBN 1-5787-0137-6. A highly detailed coverage of the use and deployment issues surrounding the DHCP service. This is a great book to keep on your reference shelf.

 Microsoft Windows 2000 Server Resource Kit. Microsoft Press, Redmond, WA, 2000. ISBN 1-5723-1805-8. An exhaustive library covering detailed information on all aspects of Windows 2000 Server implementations. An invaluable reference for IT departments supporting Microsoft Windows 2000 networks.

 www.microsoft.com/windows2000/techinfo/proddoc/default. asp. *Windows 2000 Product Documentation Online.* A complete online copy of the documentation for all versions of the Windows 2000 operating system.

Active Directory Administration

. . . .

Terms you'll need to understand:

✓ Delegated administrative rights
✓ Full Control
✓ Implicit Denial
✓ Explicit Denial
✓ Inheritance
✓ Microsoft Management Console (MMC)
✓ Delegation of Control wizard
✓ Custom console
✓ MMC snap-ins
✓ Taskpad Creation wizard
✓ Task Creation wizard

Techniques you'll need to master:

✓ Understanding the strategies for assigning delegated access rights and permissions
✓ Recognizing the standard access permissions and their uses
✓ Resolving inherited and explicit access rights assignment and denial scenarios
✓ Creating a custom MMC and taskpad

Centralized administration in the enterprise environment is one of the major advantages of a domain-based system over a workgroup. This chapter covers the administration of Active Directory objects including user and computer accounts, access control over Active Directory objects, delegation of common administrative tasks to sub-Admin user accounts, and the tools used for administration. The reader should be familiar with the topics covered in Chapter 3, including user and group objects. Additional references are listed at the end of this chapter.

Overview

Administration of access rights and permissions is one of the most fundamental tasks required of a Windows 2000 network administrator. The process of efficiently organizing user and computer accounts, as well as group and organizational unit membership, may take a great deal of planning and coordination. Once completed, many of the more tedious tasks may be readily delegated to authorized users.

Delegated Permissions

Delegated user accounts do not require full Domain Admin or Enterprise Admin rights in order to perform these common tasks. Instead, the network administrator may grant authority over only the specific portions of the Active Directory structure required. For example, delegation of administrative rights over organizational units might be used in order to allow departmental managers to be able to perform routine tasks for users within their own departments, without exposing other resources such as would occur if the manager's user account was granted full Domain Admin rights.

Table 6.1 details the two basic strategies for assigning access permissions.

Table 6.1 Access permission strategies.	
Strategy	**Description**
All permissions	All permissions are granted within the specified organizational unit, including object creation, modification, and deletion.
Specific permission assignment	Only a specified permission is granted to a user or group.

Managing permissions at the organizational unit level is considered easier than tracking permissions at the object level.

Permissions

Access permissions may be granted or denied to a user or group, allowing rapid assignment of delegated permissions. Windows 2000 provides a number of permissions that may be assigned. These are already assigned to the default groups created during installation such as the Domain Admins group.

When assigning access permissions for Active Directory objects, several standard permissions are available (see Figure 6.1).

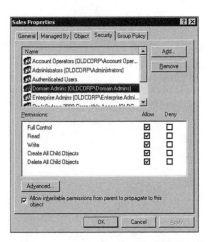

Figure 6.1 Standard access permissions assigned to the Domain Admins group for the Sales organizational unit.

Table 6.2 details the five standard access permissions.

Table 6.2 Standard access permission.	
Permission	**Description**
Create All Child Objects	Allows any type of child object (user, computer, group, child organizational unit) to be created within the organizational unit.
Delete All Child Objects	Allows the removal of any child object within the organizational unit.

(continued)

Table 6.2 Standard access permission *(continued)*	
Permission	**Description**
Full Control	Includes all other standard access permissions, as well as the permissions to change ownership and change permissions on objects within the organizational unit.
Read	May view objects, attributes, permissions, and current ownership.
Write	May modify object attributes.

In addition to the standard access permissions, delegation of control may be made at a very detailed level using the advanced access permissions option (see Figure 6.2).

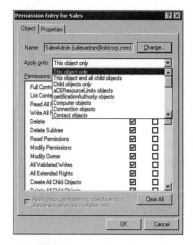

Figure 6.2   Advanced access permissions showing the application scope listing.

Access right assignment for specific attributes or objects may result in an inability to perform delegated tasks. It is best to avoid this level of assignment when possible.

Access Rights

Access rights, such as the ability to Create All Child Objects within a container, may be explicitly allowed or explicitly denied. By default, if not explicitly allowed, permissions are implicitly denied.

Resolving User and Group Permissions

User accounts inherit permissions allowed or denied to all of the groups of which they are members. The final set of access rights is determined by first determining the least restrictive combination of access rights, and then determining if any are explicitly denied. Permission evaluation involves the following considerations:

➤ If a user account is not explicitly allowed access rights over an object, then the rights are implicitly denied the user.

➤ If a user account is not explicitly allowed access rights, but a group of which it is a member is explicitly allowed access rights over an object, the user will inherit these rights.

➤ If a user is explicitly denied access rights over an object, then the user will be denied those rights even if granted directly or through membership in a group.

➤ If a user is explicitly granted access rights over an object, and a group of which she is a member is denied access rights, the user will continue to have access to the explicitly granted rights.

Explicit denial of access rights "wins" any time it is present, except if the denial is inherited and the user is explicitly granted access rights. It is best to assign access rights by assigning access permissions to groups and making users members of those groups.

Container Inheritance

By default, child objects inherit access rights assignments from their parent unless inheritance is specifically prevented by unchecking the box labeled Allow Inheritable Permissions From Parent To Propagate To This Object. The user will be presented with the option to copy or remove the inherited permissions.

Selecting to copy the permissions from the parent will maintain the existing rights assignments, but allow editing and removal of each. The option to remove inherited permissions does just that. Selecting this option will remove all access permissions to the child object, allowing an entirely new set of permissions to be employed.

Once permission inheritance is blocked, changes to the access rights of the parent object will not be propagated to the child. Any changes that must be made to both must be made to the parent and child objects separately.

Assignment

Access rights over an organizational unit are assigned and modified in the Active Directory Users And Computers Microsoft Management Console (MMC). Creating custom MMCs will be covered in greater detail later in this chapter.

To assign or modify permissions over an object, perform the following:

1. From the desktop, select Start | Settings | Control Panel | Administrative Tools | Active Directory Users And Computers.

> The Active Directory Users And Computers MMC component is installed on domain controllers during the configuration of Active Directory.

2. From the Menu bar, select View and click to enable Advanced Features.

3. Navigate to the desired object, right-click on it and select Properties.

4. In the Properties box, select the Security tab.

5. To remove an existing account or group, highlight the target and select the Remove button. In order to add a new account or group, select the Add button and locate the desired security principle to be added (see Figure 6.3).

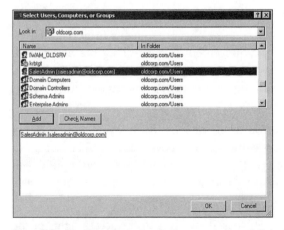

Figure 6.3 The Users, Computers, or Groups selection window showing the SalesAdmin account in oldcorp.com selected.

6. Once added, highlight the target user or group and select Allow or Deny checkboxes in the Permissions box as desired for the standard access permissions.

7. In order to assign special permissions, select the Advanced tab, then navigate to the appropriate group or user and select View/Edit in order to access a detailed listing of the special access rights which may be allowed or denied.

8. Once completed, select Apply and OK at each level in order to close all windows. New rights assignments will not become available until after the next login of the user.

Delegation of Authority

By distributing administrative control over organizational units to delegated user accounts responsible for each, the network admin may reduce the need for full administrator accounts while also handing off many of the more basic tasks to other users and making time for higher-level network administrative duties.

Control should be delegated at the lowest level possible as required by business rules. Delegation at the organizational unit level is typically the best solution for task delegation within a domain. Make sure to document all delegation actions, so that access control difficulties encountered later may be resolved more easily.

Delegation of Control Wizard

The Active Directory Users And Computers MMC includes the Delegation of Control wizard, which will assist in delegating control over objects, without requiring a detailed effort for each task delegation.

Table 6.3 details the six common tasks that may be delegated using this wizard.

Table 6.3 Common tasks that may be delegated.	
Task	**Description**
Create, delete and manage groups	Allows the creation, modification, and deletion of groups within the selected organizational unit.

(continued)

Table 6.3 Common tasks that may be delegated *(continued)*	
Task	**Description**
Create, delete, and manage user accounts	Grants the rights necessary to create, modify, and delete user accounts within the selected organizational unit.
Manage group policy links*	Allows the user permissions to manipulate the group policy links of the selected organizational unit.
Modify the membership of a group	Grants the right to manipulate membership of the groups within the selected organizational unit.
Read all user information	Allows read-only access to attributes of the objects within the organizational unit.
Reset passwords on a user account	Grants the permission to reset passwords on any user accounts within the selected organizational unit. This is the most often delegated task.

The use of group policies will be detailed in Chapter 7.

In order to perform a delegation of authority over an organizational unit, perform the following:

1. As detailed in the Assignment section above, open the Active Directory Users And Computers MMC, enable Advanced Features if necessary, and then select the Security tab.

2. Navigate to the desired object, right-click on it, and select Delegate Control.

3. Select Next to begin the wizard, and Cancel to go back to the MMC.

4. Now, you may add users or groups to be delegated rights over the selected object by clicking Add. The Remove button allows the removal of previously added delegates. Select Next after all selections are correct.

5. Select from the Common Tasks to be delegated or click on the option to Create A Custom Task To Delegate (see Figure 6.4) and select Next when done.

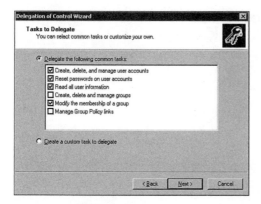

Figure 6.4   Standard task assignment in the Delegation of Control wizard.

6. If only common tasks were selected, then select Finish to complete the delegation process. In a custom permissions creation, you will be provided the opportunity to select whether the delegation of control will be for the selected object and all objects within it, or only over specific objects such as computer, group, printer, shared folder, or user objects. Select Next when ready.

7. You may select permissions to be granted from three categories of permissions: General, Property-Specific, and Creation/Deletion Of Specific Child Object Types (see Figure 6.5).

➤ General permissions include the same list as the common tasks earlier.

➤ Property-Specific permissions include attribute-specific rights such as the ability to edit Address information or the Managed By attribute.

➤ Creation/Deletion Of Specific Child Object permissions grant the ability to create a new object of the specified type, or to remove an existing object of the specified type.

8. Select Next when done and then Finish to complete the delegation process.

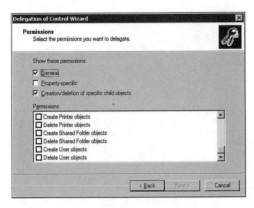

Figure 6.5 Custom permissions listing showing several items from the Creation/Deletion Of Specific Child Objects listing.

Management Tools

Once management task permissions have been successfully delegated, the controls necessary to perform the delegated tasks must be made available. The standardized user interface implemented in Microsoft Windows 2000 and later is called the MMC.

Custom Consoles

When opening any of the items from the Administrative Tools folder, the utilities will be presented in the MMC standardized format. Many of the tools might be contained within others, such as the Event Viewer, which is present as an icon of its own as well as within the Computer Management MMC. Users may create their own customized MMC by including all of the snap-ins needed for administrative tasks to be performed.

A custom MMC could be created containing all of the snap-ins needed for administrative tasks delegated to a particular group of users, and then distributed from a common network file share or by using a Group Policy. The recipient must have Read or better access to the MMC file and his computer must have a copy of the snap-ins included in the MMC.

NOTE

A custom MMC may also be distributed as an email attachment or via instant messenger. However, due to the number of attachment-based viruses, many businesses now strip some or all types of attachments. This method of distribution only works if your mail server and clients allow custom console (**.msc**) file attachments to pass.

MMC Snap-Ins

In order to deploy custom a custom MMC, the snap-ins used must be present on the administrator's computer. The Administrative Tools snap-ins may be installed using the Microsoft Installer package, **adminpak.msi.**

This package is located on the Windows 2000 Server/Advanced Server disk and may be installed on the local machine by performing the following:

1. From the desktop, select Start|Settings|Control Panel|Add/Remove Programs.

2. Select Add New Programs, click on the CD Or Floppy button, and select Next when prompted.

3. Browse to the drive containing the Windows 2000 Server/Advanced Server CD and open the I386 folder to locate the **adminpak.msi** file. Highlight this file and select Open to begin installing the Administrative Tools on the local system.

 If the Windows 2000 Server CD is unavailable, the **adminpak.msi** file may also be found in the **<*systemroot*>\WINNT\system32** folder on a system running Windows 2000 Server/Advanced Server.

4. Continue as prompted through the installation process. Once completed, the snap-ins for administration will be available for the deployed custom MMC.

Custom MMC Creation

Custom consoles may be created for many tasks, each saved individually as a Microsoft Stored Console (**.msc**) file, which may be distributed just as any other file type.

To create a custom MMC, perform the following:

1. From the desktop, select Start|Run. Type "MMC" and hit the Enter key.

2. After the new console opens, you may select Console from the Menu bar and then Add/Remove Snap-In.

3. Click the Add button in order to open the Add Standalone Snap-In dialog box (see Figure 6.6). The Remove button will remove a previously added snap-in, and the About button will provide information on a selected snap-in.

Figure 6.6 Listing of available MMC snap-ins.

4. Select the snap-in to be added and click the Add button. Some snap-ins will have additional configuration details to be specified (see Figure 6.7).

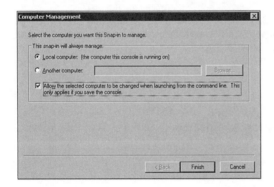

Figure 6.7 Configuration details for the Computer Management MMC snap-in.

5. Continue adding snap-ins until finished and then select Close.

6. Select OK to return to the newly configured console.

7. In the Menu bar, select Console and then Options. Here you may name the MMC, select an alternate icon if desired, and select Console Mode (see Figure 6.8).

➤ Author mode is used to create and modify a console file.

➤ User mode is used when you want to limit the ability of users to modify the console.

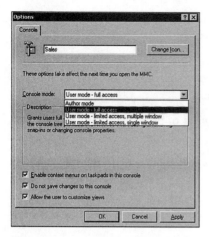

Figure 6.8   Console options showing the Console Mode listing.

Saved console files can be opened in Author mode even if saved in User mode by right-clicking on the file in your system browser and selecting Author from the list of available options. To prevent users from altering the console, you must remove the NTFS permission Write from the file.

8. Select Apply in order to apply the changes and OK to return to the console.

9. From the Menu bar, select Console and Save As, and then provide a name and location for the new console file. The default location is in the Administrative Tools folder.

Additional Customization

When creating administrative tools for delegated users who are not as skilled with the Windows 2000 MMC, you may provide additional assistance by creating a set of command and function shortcuts. These shortcuts are set up within a specialized view called a *taskpad*. Different taskpad views may be created in order to group shortcuts in a more useful configuration for each user.

To create a taskpad view using the Taskpad Creation wizard, open a console in Author mode and perform the following:

1. Highlight a task to be specified and from the header, select Action and then New Taskpad View.

2. Select Next when prompted, and then configure the desired taskpad view formatting. Select Next when ready.

   ➤ The Details Pane Style selections allow the creation of a Horizontal List, Vertical List, or a selection of icons only with No List for tasks that are not connected to list items.

   ➤ Task Descriptions may be configured to provide descriptions in Text, or as a pop-up Infotip.

3. Select whether the new taskpad view will apply only to the selected item or to all items from the same tree as the selected item. Select the option to change the default display to this taskpad to allow the taskpad to become the default page when the console is opened. Click the Next button when finished.

4. Provide a name and (optional) meaningful description for the new taskpad view and then select Next.

5. You may select Finish to finalize the new taskpad view. You may leave the option to Start New Task Wizard selected if you would like to begin adding tasks to the new view immediately.

6. In order to hide the normal tree view and leave only the taskpad, select from the header View and then Customize. Deselect the Console Tree option and click the OK button to exit.

7. Save your console to preserve the changes you have made.

To create a new task using the Task Creation wizard, open a console in Author mode and, perform the following:

1. With the Console tree view open, select an existing taskpad and from the header, select Action and then Edit Taskpad View.

2. Select the Tasks tab and click the New button to add a new task.

3. Select Next when prompted and then select from the task options to create a shortcut to a menu command, shell command, or a navigation shortcut.

   ➤ A *menu command* executes an MMC menu item

   ➤ A *shell command* might be used to open a URL or execute a file or custom script.

   ➤ A *navigation* shortcut can be used to move to another view listed in the favorites tab.

4. In a navigation task, select from the available list. For shell command tasks, enter the command along with any parameters. Menu commands are selected from the tasks detailed when highlighting an item from the tree listing.

5. Once selected, click Next and enter a name and (optional) meaningful description for the task; then select Next.

6. Select an icon to be used for the new task, preferably one that is topical or meaningful to the task, and then click the Next button.

7. Select the option to Run This Wizard Again in order to create another task, and click Finish.

8. If completed, select OK to return to the console (see Figure 6.9).

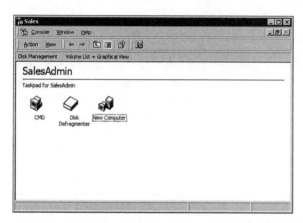

Figure 6.9 Taskpad for SalesAdmin. The New Computer shortcut allows creation of a new computer object only in the Sales organizational unit.

9. Hide the tree view and save your console to preserve the changes you have made.

Practice Questions

Question 1

> Which of the following are standard Active Directory access permissions?
> [Check all correct answers]
>
> ❏ a. Create All Child Objects
> ❏ b. Delete All Child Objects
> ❏ c. Edit
> ❏ d. Full Control
> ❏ e. Modify All Child Objects
> ❏ f. Read
> ❏ g. Write

Answers a, b, d, f, and g are correct. The five standard Active Directory access permissions are: Create All Child Objects, Delete All Child Objects, Full Control, Read, and Write. Answers c and e are incorrect because there are no standard access permissions for the modification of existing objects other than the Write permission.

Question 2

> Three types of rights assignment are possible:
> ➤Explicitly Allowed
> ➤Explicitly Denied
> ➤Implicitly Denied
>
> Arrange these in order of resolution if no group membership is present.

The correct answer is:

1. Implicitly Denied (default)

2. Explicitly Allowed (overrides all Implicit Denials)

3. Explicitly Denied (overrides all Allow permissions when applied directly)

Question 3

An object must inherit the access permissions of all objects it is contained within. True or false?

○ a. True

○ b. False

Answer b is correct. By default, an object will automatically inherit the access rights of its parent, but this option may be disabled and the parent's access rights copied to or removed from the child.

Question 4

What is the level at which rights assignment is recommended?

○ a. Domain

○ b. Enterprise

○ c. Organizational unit

○ d. Trust

○ e. User

Answer c is correct. The recommended level of rights assignment and delegation is over the organizational unit level. Answer a is incorrect because a Domain Administrator account may have overly broad rights present. Answer b is incorrect because the rights of an Enterprise Admin are even broader than those of a Domain Admin. Answer d is incorrect because rights are not assigned to trusts, which are simply connectors that connect domains. Answer e is incorrect because the assignment of rights at the user level is complex, difficult to alter rapidly to support large-scale changes, and may override OU-based security restrictions.

Question 5

There are only six tasks that may be delegated using the Delegation of Control wizard. True or false?

○ a. True

○ b. False

Answer b is correct. There are six common tasks that may be delegated using the Delegation of Control wizard, but many additional tasks may be assigned by creating a custom task assignment.

Question 6

Which is the most often delegated common task?

○ a. Create, delete, and manage groups

○ b. Create, delete, and manage user accounts

○ c. Manage group policy links

○ d. Modify the membership of a group

○ e. Read all user information

○ f. Reset passwords on a user account

Answer f is correct. User support tasks, such as the resetting of forgotten passwords, are often delegated to trusted human resources in each department or office in order to reduce administrative overhead and improve response time to user requests.

Question 7

Which of the following are examples of custom consoles? [Check all correct answers]

❑ a. Active Directory Sites And Services

❑ b. Active Directory Users And Computers

❑ c. Computer Management

❑ d. DHCP

❑ e. DNS

❑ f. Local Computer Control

❑ g. Sales Administration

❑ h. WINS

Answers f and g are correct. Local Computer Control and Sales Administration would be custom consoles. Answers a, b, c, d, e, and h are incorrect because all of these are standard Windows 2000 Administrative Tools snap-ins for the MMC.

Question 8

Which console mode allows the addition of a task to an existing taskpad?

○ a.   Author mode

○ b.   None; it is impossible to add new tasks once saved

○ c.   User mode

Answer a is correct. Opening a custom console in author mode allows editing of the console, including the addition of a new task. Answer b is incorrect because a console may be edited after being saved. Answer c is incorrect because user mode is meant for general use and restricts the ability to make changes to the console interface.

Question 9

Which of the following are valid ways to distribute a custom **.msc** file? [Check all correct answers]

❏ a.   CD-ROM

❏ b.   Email

❏ c.   Instant Messenger

❏ d.   Network file share

❏ e.   Using a Group Policy

Answers a, b, c, d, and e are all correct. A custom **.msc** file may be distributed in all of the same ways any other form of file may be. Although not specifically mentioned in the chapter, answer a is correct because a CD-ROM is a standard method of deployment for files.

Question 10

A taskpad is a customized form of console that hides the raw MMC functionality behind a series of shortcuts. True or false?

○ a.   True

○ b.   False

Answer a is correct. A taskpad is simply another view that may be created within a custom console. In order to be more user-friendly, it utilizes shortcuts to access common MMC tasks, commands, and other functions.

Need to Know More?

 Stanek, William R.: *Microsoft Windows 2000 Administrator's Pocket Consultant.* Microsoft Press, Redmond, WA, 2000. ISBN 0-7356-0831-8. A helpful reference for network administrators to keep close at hand. The soft-cover trade-sized book is a condensed, easily carried version of many larger tomes of information.

 Microsoft Windows 2000 Server Resource Kit. Microsoft Press, Redmond, WA, 2000. ISBN 1-5723-1805-8. An exhaustive library covering detailed information on all aspects of Windows 2000 Server implementations. An invaluable reference for IT departments supporting Microsoft Windows 2000 networks.

 www.microsoft.com/windows2000/techinfo/proddoc/default. asp. *Windows 2000 Product Documentation Online* is a complete online copy of the documentation for all versions of the Windows 2000 operating system.

Group Policy

Terms you'll need to understand:

✓ Group policy objects
✓ Administrative templates
✓ Block Inheritance
✓ No Override
✓ Filtering
✓ Linking group policy objects
✓ Slow network connections
✓ Folder redirection
✓ Software lifecycle

Techniques you'll need to master:

✓ Understanding the differences between Computer and User group policies and when they are processed
✓ Resolving final permissions based on inheritance from higher-level containers
✓ Modifying default inheritance using Block Inheritance, No Override, and access permission filtering
✓ Creating and applying linked and unlinked group policy objects
✓ Performing administration and software package deployment using group policies
✓ Understanding the role group policies play in the phases of the software lifecycle

This chapter covers the use of group policy to simplify and centralize administration over large-enterprise deployments of Windows 2000 Active Directory. Group policy inheritance within the Active Directory will be discussed, along with solutions for software deployment and desktop management using group policy. Additional references are listed at the end of this chapter.

Overview of Group Policies

Group policies are collections of configuration settings and details, which are assigned to computer and user accounts to customize the user environment and automate administration of settings and software. Group policies may be linked at the site, domain, organizational unit, and local computer level. In a Windows 2000 Active Directory domain, local settings are automatically overridden by Active Directory group policy settings. Windows 2000 Domain Controllers do not have local settings.

Group Policy Structure

Group policies are created as *group policy objects*, which define specified settings for users or computers. These group policy objects are then linked to Active Directory containers at the site, domain, or organizational unit level. A single group policy object may be linked to one or many containers, and a single container may have one or many group policy objects linked to it. The order of linked group policy objects is important, as conflict resolution depends on order to determine the final settings assigned. Conflict resolution is discussed in greater detail later in this chapter.

 Group policy association of linked remote group policy objects relies on a functioning trust between domains and may be affected by network conditions.

Stand-alone machines in a workgroup configuration also have a local group policy object, which defines settings for local users and the local system, but local policies are automatically overridden by higher-level policies when a system is a member of a Windows 2000 Active Directory-integrated domain.

Group policy objects have two parts: the group policy container and the group policy template, both of which are required for group policy function. Each group policy object is assigned a *globally unique identification (GUID)*, allowing group policies from one domain to be linked to objects in another domain without fear of identification confusion.

Group Policy Container

The group policy container is an Active Directory object that provides attributes allowing domain controllers to check for more recent versions of the group policy objects and to replicate changes if required. Additional attributes provide information allowing computers to locate the associated group policy template.

The group policy container may be viewed within the Active Directory Users And Computers MMC snap-in by selecting View|Advanced Features from the header. The group policy containers may be viewed within the Policies child container of the System node (see Figure 7.1).

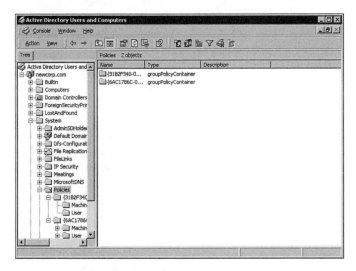

Figure 7.1 Active Directory Users And Computers MMC snap-in showing the System node and Policies containers.

Group Policy Template

Each group policy object has an associated group policy template, which is a folder hierarchy containing settings for the group policy. Each group policy template is stored on Windows 2000 Active Directory Domain Controllers as a folder structure designated by the group policy object's globally unique identifier, within the **%SystemRoot%\WINNT\SYSVOL\sysvol\ <domain>\Policies** directory and accessible through the public share **\\<server>\SYSVOL\<domain>\Policies**.

Group Policy Scope

Group policies are linked to Active Directory containers at the site, domain, and organizational unit and provide settings and configuration details for users and computers within the appropriate container.

Group policies define seven types of settings for users and computers within the containers to which they are linked. Table 7.1 details the seven types of settings.

Table 7.1 Group policy settings.	
Setting	**Description**
Administrative Templates	Registry-based configuration settings granting or restricting access to MMC components, applications, offline files, and Control Panel options within the user desktop environment. Administrative template settings may be applied to both users and computers.
Folder Redirection	Configures virtual links to server-based storage of user profiles, as an alternative to the more network-intensive roaming profile type. These links function as if the folders were located locally on the user's computer, but allow access to files regardless of which computer the user logs onto. Folder redirection settings may be applied to user accounts only.
Internet Explorer Maintenance	Configures customized settings for the Internet Explorer browser interface. These settings may be applied to user accounts only.
Remote Installation Services	Configures user options available within the Client Installation Wizard settings for use by the Remote Installation Services (RIS). These settings may be applied to user accounts only.
Scripts	This group of settings allows the specification of scripts, which will be enacted when prompted by certain events. Logon and Logoff script settings may be applied to user accounts, whereas Startup and Shutdown script settings may be applied to computer accounts.
Security Settings	Configures user, computer, and network access restrictions and settings. Security settings may be applied to both users and computers.

(continued)

Table 7.1 Group policy settings *(continued)*	
Setting	**Description**
Software Installation	Allows the assignment of Windows Installer (.wsi) packages for remote deployment, update, or removal of software. Software installation settings may be assigned to both users and computers.

Group policies are applied at the time of account initialization and at regular intervals thereafter. Domain Controllers refresh every five minutes to ensure that new settings, such as password policy changes, are rapidly replicated. By default, Windows 2000 and later systems that are not Domain Controllers will refresh group policy settings at a random interval between 30 and 90 minutes. This can be changed to a different random interval, but a specific time cannot be set. You can thus avoid having multiple machines attempting to refresh at the same time, alleviating potential network bottlenecks.

 Software installation and folder redirection settings are applied only at logon or startup and are not refreshed until the next system reboot or user logon. If users complain that new software installation options or folder redirections are not being applied, a logoff or reboot may be required to initialize these settings.

There are two files that provide registry settings for computer and user accounts. These files are both named Registry.pol and are located in the %SystemRoot%\WINNT\SYSVOL\sysvol\<*domain*>\Policies\ <*GPO_guid*>\ folder in either the \User or \Machine subfolders.

 Accounts must have the necessary permissions to access the Registry.pol files within the %SystemRoot%\WINNT\SYSVOL\sysvol\<*domain*>\Policies\ <*GPO_guid*>\ Machine\ and %SystemRoot%\WINNT\SYSVOL\sysvol\<*domain*>\ Policies\<*GPO_ guid*>\User\ folders to apply group policy object settings successfully. If settings are not being applied, log in as the user and attempt to access these files on the domain controller.

Computer policies are applied at startup, during the refresh cycle, and at shutdown. Computer group policy settings are applied in order before the logon screen is displayed. Adding more computer group policies to be evaluated will slow the time from power on to the display of the logon screen.

User policies are only applied at logon, during the refresh cycle while the user is logged onto the machine, and at logoff. After a user logs off a machine, only the computer settings remain until the next user logon. User settings are applied in order before the desktop appears. Adding more user group policies to be evaluated will slow the time from logon to the display of the desktop.

 When conflicts between user and computer settings occur, computer settings will override user settings in most cases. For example, if conflicting Control Panel settings were encountered when resolving UserA's logon to Workstation1, then the computer settings assigned to Workstation1 would be used where there is a conflict.

Group Policy Application

Group policies are linked to Active Directory containers at the site, domain, and organizational unit. Each group policy object may be linked to one or more containers, and each container may have one or more group policy objects assigned. When conflicts occur, the order in which the group policy objects are evaluated will affect the final settings applied.

Group policy settings for each container are inherited from the highest level to the lowest, with each lower level's settings overriding conflicting settings from higher levels unless higher-level settings have been configured for No Override, which will be discussed later in this section.

Site-Level Settings

Settings applied to sites affect all users and computers within a site, regardless of domain and organizational unit membership. These settings may be used to specify enterprise-level settings such as password complexity requirements. There is no higher level that encompasses all sites in an enterprise. Site-level group policies intended to apply to all sites must be created for one site and then linked to each of the others. Site-level settings are evaluated first.

Site-level settings are created and linked using the Active Directory Sites And Services MMC snap-in and may be edited there, or within the Group Policy MMC snap-in if the Group Policy MMC snap-in is customized to access the specific group policy.

Domain-Level Settings

Settings applied to a domain affect all objects within that domain. These settings are applied after site-level group policies. Conflicts with site-level specifications will result in the domain-level settings being applied unless the site-level group policy has been configured for No Override.

Domain-level group policies are created and linked using the Active Directory Users And Computers MMC snap-in, and may be edited there or within the Group Policy MMC snap-in if the Group Policy MMC snap-in is customized to access the specific group policy.

Organizational Unit Settings

Group policies may be linked to specific organizational units as well, allowing detailed desktop settings and customized application availability for users according to job requirements. These settings are applied last, with parent-level group policies applied before child nested-level settings, each level resolving conflicts with higher-level settings by applying the more specific settings unless a higher-level group policy is set for No Override.

Organizational unit-level group policies are created and linked using the Active Directory Users And Computers MMC snap-in, and may be edited there or within the Group Policy MMC snap-in if the Group Policy MMC snap-in is customized to access the specific group policy.

Same-Container Settings

Because multiple group policies may be linked to a specific container, conflicting settings are resolved by applying the group policies in the order they are arranged within the Group Policy settings in the Properties of the appropriate container (see Figure 7.2).

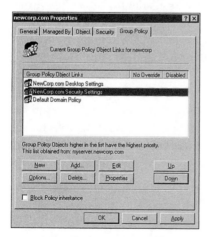

Figure 7.2   Group policies for the newcorp.com domain showing the order of multiple linked group policy objects.

Group policies linked to the same container are evaluated in order from the bottom to the top, so that the highest items in the list are those evaluated last and assigned in case of conflict with lower-placed group policies.

Remember that Group Policy settings are evaluated at the Site, then Domain, and then OU level. Same-container conflicts are resolved in list-order from bottom to top.

Modifying Default Inheritance

By default, group policies are applied in order from the site, through domain, organizational unit, and any nested organizational units below. It is important to remember the following when working with group policies:

➤ Group policy settings conflicts are resolved by applying the lowest-level linked group policy settings: domain group policy settings override site-level settings, organizational unit settings override domain and site, and nested organizational unit settings override settings inherited from parent organizational units, domain, or site.

➤ Within each container, conflicts arising between settings of multiple linked group policy objects are resolved by evaluating the group policies in order from the bottom to the top of the list. Settings from groups with a higher placement in the list will override conflicting settings from groups lower in the list.

Due to business rules, some settings such as password policies must be inherited by all containers, regardless of whether local administrators link group policy objects with different settings to lower-level containers. Other times, it is desirable to block the inheritance of default group policy settings for accounts placed within a particular container.

Block Inheritance

Windows 2000 Active Directory group policy containers may be configured to Block Policy Inheritance on the Group Policy tab of the Properties for the appropriate container. This option is not present at the site level, because there is no higher level at which a group policy may be linked.

The option to block inheritance affects the container and all children, preventing the inheritance of all higher-level policies with the exception of settings from higher-level group policy objects configured for No Override. There is no by-group policy option for this setting. It prevents the inheritance of all higher-level group policy settings equally.

No Override

Individual group policies may be configured to prevent lower-level group policies from overriding their settings by right-clicking the appropriate group policy link on the Group Policy tab of the Properties for the appropriate container and then selecting No Override.

Because a single group policy may be linked to multiple containers, this setting applies to the specific link and not to all assignments of the group policy object. It prevents any lower-level group policy from overriding the defined settings.

> If new group policy settings do not take effect on accounts within a container, check all parent containers to ensure that no higher-level group policy settings are conflicting and set to No Override.

Filtering Using Access Permissions

Individual group policies may be further limited from application to particular users or groups by restricting the access permissions granted them to the particular group policy link. This is done by opening the Properties of the desired container, selecting the Group Properties tab, right-clicking on the group policy link to be edited, and selecting Properties for the group policy link. Go to the Security tab to edit access permissions for the group policy link (see Figure 7.3).

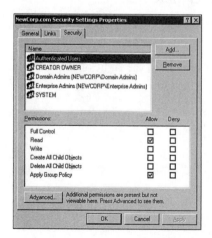

Figure 7.3   Access permissions for the newcorp.com domain-level Security Settings group policy link.

This method of limitation allows much greater control over group policy inheritance than the Block Inheritance and No Override settings, because it may be applied to any account or group uniquely. An account must be allowed both the Read and Apply Group Policy permissions on the group policy link in order for the settings defined in the group policy object to be applied.

When troubleshooting group policy failure for an account, make sure that the account and the groups of which it is a member do not have Deny set for either the Read or Apply Group Policy permissions, as Deny will override other Allow assignments.

Creating and Linking Group Policy Objects

By default, group policy objects may be created by members of the Enterprise Admins, Domain Admins, and Group Policy Creators groups. Enterprise Admins and Domain Admins group members have the ability to link group policies to domains and organizational units, whereas only members of the Enterprise Admins group may link them to sites.

Creating Unlinked Group Policy Objects

Some IT offices may delegate the creation of new group policy objects to one group of administrators, while a different group approves and links them. The following creates an unlinked group policy object:

1. Open an existing custom MMC console or create a new one as detailed in Chapter 6 and add the Group Policy MMC snap-in.

2. When prompted to Select Group Policy Object, click the Browse button.

3. On the All tab, click the new button located to the right of the Look In box (see Figure 7.4).

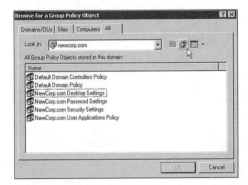

Figure 7.4 New group policy object selection for creating an unlinked group policy object.

4. Provide a meaningful name and click the OK button.

5. Click the Finish button to return to the MMC console to edit the new group policy object.

Linking Existing Group Policy Objects

Existing group policy objects may be linked to one or more containers. Administrators with the necessary permissions may link group policy objects at the site level using the Active Directory Sites And Services MMC snap-in and may link group policy objects at the domain or organizational unit level using the Active Directory Users And Computers MMC snap-in. Both procedures are functionally the same otherwise, and may be performed in the following manner:

1. Open the proper MMC snap-in and navigate to the appropriate container.

2. Right-click on the container and select Properties and then the Group Policy tab.

3. Select Add and then navigate to the existing group policy object from the listings for Domains/OUs and Sites. A group policy created at one level may be linked at any other level as desired, but changes to the policy's settings will affect all containers it is linked to.

4. Highlight the desired group policy object and select OK.

5. If needed, select Properties in order to edit the properties assigned to this link to the group policy object. Additional settings include:

➤ The Links tab can be useful here to see which other containers are linked to the same group policy object.

➤ You may disable/enable either the User or Computer settings on the General tab. This improves performance during evaluation because only those group policies linked with the remaining enabled account type (User or Computer) are processed during evaluation.

➤ Configure Security settings here to filter group policy assignment based on account and group membership.

6. If needed, you may disable/enable the new link using the Options button. Disabled policies are not processed during group policy evaluation.

7. Select Apply to allow the changes to take effect and OK to exit the Properties interface.

New group policy settings will take effect at the next user logon or computer startup.

Creating Linked Group Policy Objects

Group policy objects may be created and linked at the same time within the appropriate MMC snap-in for the required container type. Both procedures are functionally the same, and may be performed in the following manner:

1. Open the proper MMC snap-in and navigate to the appropriate container.

2. Right-click on the container and select Properties and then the Group Policy tab.

3. Select New and then provide a meaningful name for the new group policy object.

4. Configure any necessary details for the link using the Options or Properties buttons.

5. Select Apply to complete the creation of the new group policy object.

The new group policy object is created and linked to the designated container. It may then be linked to other containers as desired.

Editing Group Policy Objects

Group policy object settings may be edited using a custom Group Policy MMC console, created using the following steps:

1. Open an existing custom MMC console or create a new one (as detailed in Chapter 6) and add the Group Policy MMC snap-in.

2. When prompted to Select Group Policy Object, click the Browse button.

3. Navigate to the appropriate group policy object and select OK.

4. Click the Finish button and OK to close the Add interface and return to the MMC console to edit the selected group policy object. Remember to save the MMC console if desired for later use.

5. Edit any desired group policy object settings as desired (see Figure 7.5).

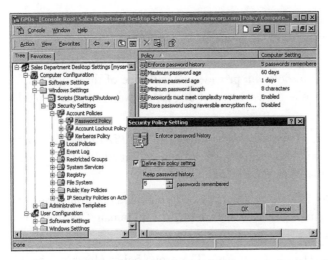

Figure 7.5 Custom MMC using the Group Policy snap-in to edit Password History requirements.

6. Close the MMC when editing is completed.

Highlighting the appropriate group policy object in a container's Properties Group Policy tab and then clicking the Edit button may also enact group policy setting changes. Make any desired changes and then close the temporary MMC window when done.

Removing Group Policy Objects
Highlighting the target group policy link in a container's Properties Group Policy tab and then clicking the Delete button may remove links to group policy objects or delete the objects themselves. When prompted, you may select to remove the link or to remove the link and delete the group policy object. Select the proper choice and click the OK button to remove the link or group policy object.

 Remember that deleting the group policy object will affect all containers and sub-containers to which it was linked. Do this only after careful consideration. Disable the group policy for a time first, to see if any complaints arise from users.

Specifying the Domain Controller

By default, group policy objects are created on the server hosting the PDC Emulator FSMO role. This may be altered if desired, so that changes are initially made on a different Windows 2000 Active Directory Domain

Controller than the default. You change the default by using the Group Policy MMC snap-in within a custom MMC console.

Highlight the desired group policy and select View | DC Options from the header. The pop up window will provide you with one of three options for which Domain Controller to use when editing group policy objects using the MMC snap-in:

➤ *The One With The Operations Master Token For The PDC Emulator*—This option is the default. All changes will take place initially on the Domain Controller designated as the PDC emulator.

➤ *The One Used By The Active Directory Snap-Ins*—This option allows the MMC snap-in's current focus to determine which Domain Controller will be initially edited.

➤ *Use Any Available Domain Controller*—The group policy object will be initially edited on any available Domain Controller, typically one within the same site as the user.

It is preferable to use the default to avoid having multiple administrators editing the same group policy on different machines, which may lead to potential replication conflicts.

Slow Network Connections

By default, group policy deployment can detect slow network connections and limit the changes and settings applied. This allows mobile users to complete the logon process without waiting while very large packages are sent over modems, or when network connectivity is limited. By default, group policy defines a slow network connection as one under 500Kbps. By default, when a slow network connection is detected, group policy will only evaluate Administrative Template, Security, and Encrypted File System (EFS) settings.

Administration Using Group Policy

Group policies are collections of configuration settings applied to user and computer accounts. These settings may be used to limit user access to selected components, to enforce standard settings, to ensure that users maintain access to their files and applications, or to secure the user environment. This last is especially useful for configurations such as public terminals, which must be restricted to Internet Explorer browsing only, for example.

The seven basic types of settings Microsoft identifies are: Administrative Templates, Folder Redirection, Internet Explorer Maintenance, Remote Installation Services, Scripts, Security Settings, and Software Installation.

Administrative Templates

Microsoft provides administrative template files (.adm) for user and computer settings. Opening the appropriate MMC snap-in and selecting the target group policy object to be altered will provide access to the administrative templates.

Types of Administrative Templates

Administrative templates provide control over user desktop settings, access to network resources, and the availability of operating system administrative tools. Table 7.2 details the seven types of administrative templates.

Table 7.2 Administrative template types.	
Type	**Description**
Control Panel	Controls access to utilities including the Display settings, the Printers folder, and the Add/Remove Programs Wizard. Only User templates of this type are provided.
Desktop	Provides control over desktop settings including the availability of Active Desktop settings and accessibility for the My Documents folder. Only User templates of this type are provided.
Network	Provides control over network and dial-up connection settings. Both User and Computer templates of this type are provided.
Printers	Controls Active Directory publication and Web sharing of printer resources. Only Computer templates of this type are provided.
Start Menu & Taskbar	Provides control over the appearance and accessible options within the Start Menu and the Windows taskbar. Only User templates of this type are provided.
System	Provides control over group policy application and the refresh interval, as well as user settings such as those used for profile, logon/logoff, and disk quotas. Both User and Computer templates of this type are provided.
Windows Components	Controls access to various Windows 2000 tools and components, including the MMC. Both User and Computer templates of this type are provided.

Application of Administrative Templates

Administrative templates may be selected and configured within the appropriate Group Policy MMC snap-in by navigating to the desired item within the appropriate Administrative Template container within either the User or Computer nodes of the group policy object. Right-clicking on any setting allows configuration.

Group Policy Settings

Settings within group policy objects may be configured in one of three states:

➤ *Disabled*—The setting is considered during group policy evaluation, and this setting is disabled unless overridden and enabled at a lower level.

➤ *Enabled*—The setting is considered during group policy evaluation, and this setting is enabled unless overridden and disabled at a lower level.

➤ *Not configured*—The setting is ignored during group policy evaluation. If enabled or disabled at a lower level, those settings will be evaluated.

Group Policy Scripting

Scripts may be assigned to computer startup and shutdown events, as well as user logon and logoff events. Scripts allow multiple actions to be automatically performed during the appropriate process, such as configuring custom network share mappings during logon, or emptying temporary storage during logoff.

 Logon scripts may also be assigned to a specific user account using the Properties of the account within the Active Directory Users And Computers MMC snap-in; however, these are not as easily managed for large enterprise organizations.

By default, scripts are run synchronously, requiring that the script must finish or time out before the next one starts. The default timeout setting for scripts is 10 minutes. Additional scripts defined in the user account's Properties will execute after group policy-deployed scripts.

Copying Scripts

To make scripts available for group policy deployment, the script files must be copied into the appropriate directory, as shown in Listings 7.1 and 7.2.

> **Listing 7.1   Directories for User group policy scripts.**

```
%SystemRoot%\WINNT\SYSVOL\sysvol\<domain>\Policies\<GPO_guid>\User\Scripts\Logon\
%SystemRoot%\WINNT\SYSVOL\sysvol\<domain>\Policies\<GPO_guid>\User\Scripts\Logoff\
```

> **Listing 7.2   Directories for Computer group policy scripts.**

```
%SystemRoot%\WINNT\SYSVOL\sysvol\<domain>\Policies\<GPO_guid>\Machine\Scripts\Startup\
%SystemRoot%\WINNT\SYSVOL\sysvol\<domain>\Policies\<GPO_guid>\Machines\Scripts\Shutdown\
```

Adding Scripts to the Group Policy Object

You must add scripts to group policy objects when they are copied into the proper group policy templates directory. You do so using the appropriate Group Policy MMC snap-in by first expanding the account type I Windows Settings I Scripts. Then right-click the desired script type and select Properties.

You can view a listing of available scripts by clicking the Show Files button, and you can assign new scripts by using the Add button and then selecting the appropriate script and setting any necessary parameters before clicking OK to add the script. By default, scripts in the list are processed from the top down.

Folder Redirection

Local profiles have the disadvantage of remaining on the computer on which they were created. Users who work on multiple computers will find their files, desktops, and settings different on each. You can set roaming profiles to provide roaming users with access to their files wherever they log on by copying all profile files and settings to the local computer at logon, and then synchronizing these with a copy stored on a central server at logoff. This process can be very network-intensive if the user's files, such as those in the My Documents folder, are large.

A better option in many cases is to use a group policy object to redirect folders to a central file server. The virtual link appears local to the computer, but all files remain on the central file server. This improves security by not leaving copies of files on local computers, decreases the network impact caused by roaming profile transfer, and allows for a centralized backup and storage solution on the file server.

Redirected Folders

Windows 2000 group policies may redirect five folders: Application Data, Desktop, My Documents, My Pictures, and Start Menu. These folders provide users with the same interface and settings regardless of the workstation they use to logon, while leaving the files on the central file server.

Folder redirection can be made to a standard shared location, enabling all users in the Marketing department to be provided with the same My Pictures folder, for example. Shared folders may also be directed to specific folders based on the logon ID of the current user by using the **%username%** variable.

The following code is an example of a mapped share to a specific user's folder in the UserFiles share on the network file server filesrv.newcorp.com:

```
\\filesrv.newcorp.com\UserFiles\%username%
```

Redirecting Folders

Folders can be redirected to a single location for each user (which may be a standard or customized location) using the **%username%** variable in Basic mode, or may be customized to allow redirection based on group membership using the Advanced mode. To redirect folders, open the appropriate Group Policy MMC snap-in and expand Users | Windows Settings | Folder Redirection. Then right-click the desired folder type and select Properties.

 My Pictures is a subfolder within My Documents.

The Setting option on the Target tab allows you to select one of three scopes of application for folder redirection:

➤ *No Administrative Policy Specified*—The default setting in which folders remain in their original locations and are not redirected.

➤ *Basic*—Redirects all users' folders to the same share, although customized folder selection may be accomplished using the **%username%** variable.

➤ *Advanced* Allows redirection to different shares based on group membership.

After selecting the appropriate scope and defining redirection target shares, the Settings tab provides additional configuration options that affect the location of existing folders and files when the redirection occurs:

➤ *Grant The User Exclusive Rights To* <folder>—Selected by default. This grants access rights to the new folder only to the user and System account. If not selected, the folder will retain its original access permissions.

➤ *Move The Contents Of* <folder> *To The New Location*—Selected by default. If not selected, files in the applicable user folder will remain in their old location and will not be available to the user unless copied to the new location.

Two configuration options are available for group policy removal. When a group policy is removed, one of these two options will apply:

➤ Leave the folder in the new location when policy is removed.

➤ Redirect the folder back to the local user profile location when policy is removed.

Software Deployment Using Group Policy

Software may be distributed, updated, or removed using group policies. Microsoft specifies two technologies that support software management using group policy:

➤ *Windows Installer*—The Windows Installer used packaged installation files (.msi) to perform installations and updates. Packages may be obtained from third-party sources or created for almost any purpose using products such as the Veritas WinInstall package, a limited edition of which is included on the Windows 2000 Server/Advanced Server CD. Versions of Windows Installer are available for Windows 95 and later operating systems.

➤ *Windows 2000 Software Installation and Maintenance Technology*—Allows the automatic deployment of Windows Installer packages using group policy. This only works on Windows 2000 and later operating systems. Using this technology, administrators can deploy, update, and remove applications automatically using group policies.

Software Lifecycle

All software packages pass through four distinct phases during the cycle extending from the preparation of a new package through its final removal. The four phases of the software life-cycle using Windows 2000 Group Policy are as follows, in order:

➤ *Preparation*—Windows Installer packages are created or acquired.

➤ *Deployment*—Packages are deployed using group policies.

➤ *Maintenance*—Updates are automatically applied using group policies.

➤ *Removal*—Packages are removed using group policies.

Preparation

Windows Installer packages (.msi) may be provided by vendors or created using third-party software utilities. Custom-on-install modifications to these use a file designation of .mst. These files allow you to be more specific about which components of software to install for each user or group.

Deployment

Distribution of software using group policy may take one of two forms:

➤ *Assignment*—Assigned User applications are advertised on the desktop and within the Start menu, and file associations are created. Double-clicking the icon or opening a document associated with the application initiates the installation process installation. Assignment of computer software packages causes installation to begin after the next startup. You may also force the installation of the new user package by specifying this during package assignment within the Group Policy MMC snap-in. Assigning packages allows users to only install packages that they need, saving disk space.

 Automated installation when opening an associated document type is referred to as *document invocation.*

➤ *Publication*—Published applications may be installed using document invocation or through the Add/Remove Software Wizard located within the Control Panel. They are not advertised in the Start menu or on the desktop.

Maintenance

After a package is installed, regular maintenance may include updates, hot-fixes, or upgrades to a newer version. Because group policies use versioning to determine if new settings should be applied (including software package delivery) updating the appropriate group policy can allow publication or assignment of upgrades to existing applications.

Removal

When a package is no longer in use or no longer necessary, group policy can automatically remove products installed using the Windows Installer on systems running Windows 2000 or later. Removal may take one of two forms:

➤ *Forced* Forced removal automatically deletes the software from a computer and removes icons and related file associations.

➤ *Optional* Optional removal removes the assignment advertisements and published applications from the Add/Remove Software Wizard but does not force the removal of existing installations of the package. A user may continue using such a package on computers in which it is already installed but will be unable to install it on other systems.

Group Policy Software Management

You can add software packages to group policy objects by using the appropriate Group Policy MMC snap-in. Expand the account type, Computer Configuration, and Software Settings. Then right-click Software Installation | New | Package.

When prompted for the proper file, navigate to the Windows Installer package and click Open. The file must be located on a network share to which the users have proper access permissions in order to access the deployment package. You may then select to publish or assign the package and select OK. An additional option of Advanced Published Or Assigned allows the administrator to set the Properties for the package deployment.

 Software is assigned to users when the same applications must be available to a user regardless of which machine she uses to log on. Software is assigned to computers when the same applications must be available for all users who log on to that machine.

Upgrading Packages with New Version

The Properties tab of the package allows configuration of upgrades by allowing the specification of the target package, any specific packages the new package will upgrade, and whether the package is a required upgrade for existing packages. If the Required option is selected, then a mandatory upgrade will occur. Clearing this checkbox allows an optional upgrade to be distributed.

Mandatory upgrades may cause problems for users if they have additional files dependent on the old version of the application. Be careful when using mandatory upgrades. If an optional upgrade was enacted and then a file associated with the new version is opened, the upgrade will proceed through document invocation.

Redeployment of Existing Packages

Software patches and updates may be redeployed by right-clicking on the package within the Group Policy MMC snap-in and selecting All Tasks | Redeploy Application, and then select Yes when prompted. Updated patches will be redeployed using the same method by which they were originally distributed.

Removing Packages

Applications may be removed by right-clicking on the package within the Group Policy MMC snap-in and selecting All Tasks | Remove. You will be prompted to select one of two options for removal:

➤ *Immediately Uninstall Software From Users And Computers*—A mandatory removal of software that will occur during the next reboot or logon.

➤ *Allow Users To Continue To Use The Software But Prevent New Installations*— An optional removal, allowing current users to continue using the application but removing installation advertisements.

Selecting OK will assign the package removal to the group policy, to be applied during the next computer startup or user logon.

Practice Questions

Question 1

> Which of the following are portions of a group policy object? [Check all correct answers]
>
> ❏ a. Group policy container
> ❏ b. Group policy inheritance
> ❏ c. Group policy linking
> ❏ d. Group policy settings
> ❏ e. Group policy template

Answers a and e are correct. A group policy object is made up of the group policy container and the group policy template. Answer b is incorrect because inheritance involves the evaluation of settings applied to parent containers. Answer c is incorrect because linking is the process of assigning a group policy object to a container. Answer d is incorrect because a group policy template contains all user and computer settings.

Question 2

> Group policy objects may be linked at the following levels:
> ➤ Domain
> ➤ Organizational unit
> ➤ Site
>
> Match the following tools with the appropriate levels:
> ➤ Active Directory Sites And Services
> ➤ Active Directory Users And Computers

The correct answers are:
➤ Domain
    ➤ Active Directory Users And Computers
➤ Organizational unit
    ➤ Active Directory Users And Computers
➤ Site
    ➤ Active Directory Sites And Services

Question 3

Which of the following is the file used to store a group policy's registry settings?

○ a. Registry.bat

○ b. Registry.msi

○ c. Registry.mst

○ d. Registry.pol

Answer d is correct. Registry settings are stored in the Registry.pol file in the \Machine and the \User subfolders. Answer a is incorrect because a .bat file would be a batch file. Answer b and c are incorrect because .msi files are Windows Installer files and .mst files are used for at-install customization of Installer packages.

Question 4

Setting conflicts within multiple group policies assigned to the same container are resolved by evaluating the group policies in the order they appear in the list from the top down. True or false?

○ a. True

○ b. False

Answer b is correct. Group policies assigned to the same container are evaluated from the bottom up.

Question 5

Which of the following options to modify default inheritance prevents lower-level settings from being used in place of higher-level settings?

○ a. Block Inheritance

○ b. Filtering

○ c. Master Settings

○ d. No Override

Answer d is correct. The No Override setting prevents lower-level settings from overriding higher-level settings. Answer a is incorrect because the Block Inheritance option prevents higher-level settings from propagating to lower-level containers unless set with the No Override option. Answer b is incorrect because filtering using access permissions allows assignment of group policies based on account and group membership. Answer c is incorrect because there are no master group policy settings.

Question 6

There are two actions involved in assigning a group policy object's settings to a container:

➤ Creation

➤ Linking

Match the following groups with the action for which they have the appropriate permissions:

➤ Group Policy Creators

➤ Domain Admins

➤ Enterprise Admins

The correct answers are:

➤ Creation

    ➤ Domain Admins

    ➤ Enterprise Admins

    ➤ Group Policy Creators

➤ Linking

    ➤ Domain Admins

    ➤ Enterprise Admins

Question 7

Adding multiple group policy objects will slow down computer startup or user logon. True or false?

○ a. True
○ b. False

Answer a is correct. The more group policies that must be evaluated, the slower the initialization process will be.

Question 8

By default, a slow network connection is one detected as being:

○ a. Inactive
○ b. Less than 28.8Kbps
○ c. Less than 56Kbps
○ d. Less than 64Kbps
○ e. Less than 128.8Kbps
○ f. Less than 500Kbps
○ g. Less than 1.54Mbps
○ h. Less than 10MBps

Answer f is correct. By default, a slow network connection is one that is detected as being less than 500Kbps. Answers a, b, c, d, e, g, and h are all incorrect because they specify incorrect values.

Question 9

Administrative templates are provided for:
- Computers
- Users

Match the following Administrative template types with the groups for which they are provided:
- Control Panel
- Desktop
- Network
- Printers
- Start Menu & Taskbar
- System
- Windows Components

The correct answers are:

- Computers

    - Network

    - Printers

    - System

    - Windows Components

- Users

    - Control Panel

    - Desktop

    - Network

    - Start Menu & Taskbar

    - System

    - Windows Components

Question 10

Arrange the four phases of the software lifecycle in order:
- ➤ Deployment
- ➤ Maintenance
- ➤ Preparation
- ➤ Removal

The correct answers are:

➤ Preparation

➤ Deployment

➤ Maintenance

➤ Removal

Need to Know More?

 Stanek, William R. *Microsoft Windows 2000 Administrator's Pocket Consultant*. Microsoft Press, Redmond, WA, 2000. ISBN 0-7356-0831-8. This is a helpful reference for network administrators to keep close at hand. The soft-cover trade-sized book is a condensed, easily carried version of many larger tomes of information.

 Microsoft Windows 2000 Server Resource Kit. Microsoft Press, Redmond, WA, 2000. ISBN 1-5723-1805-8. This exhaustive library covers detailed information on all aspects of Windows 2000 Server implementations. It is an invaluable reference for IT departments supporting Microsoft Windows 2000 networks.

 msdn.microsoft.com/scripting/. *Windows Scripting Host* provides documentation for scripting within the Windows environment. Many useful samples and solutions to everyday tasks may be found here.

 www.microsoft.com/windows2000/techinfo/proddoc/default. asp. *Windows 2000 Product Documentation Online* is a complete online copy of the documentation for all versions of the Windows 2000 operating system.

Resource Management

. . . .

Terms you'll need to understand:

✓ Publishing resources

✓ Orphan pruning

✓ Classless Inter-Domain Routing (CIDR)

✓ Universal Naming Convention (UNC)

✓ Administrative shares

✓ Shares

✓ Sessions

✓ Console message

Techniques you'll need to master:

✓ Understanding the purpose of Active Directory resource publication

✓ Recognizing a correct printer location specification

✓ Publishing shared folder and printer resources to the Active Directory

✓ Resolving final access permissions based on reference, share, and NTFS permissions

This chapter covers the procedures involved in making shared resources available to users by publishing references to the shared resources within the Active Directory. Specific details will be provided for implementing and monitoring shared folder usage, as well as publishing printer object references. You should be familiar with the basics of Active Directory nomenclature, discussed in Chapter 3. Additional references are listed at the end of this chapter.

Overview

In large-enterprise deployment scenarios, the number of possible resources that users may need to access becomes overwhelming quite easily. If a user wants to find a printer located near the Sales office, searching through a huge listing of all printers to find the right one may be daunting. The logical next step: Call the IT manager and waste some of her time finding the right item. But there are other options.

Sharing Resources

In order to simplify the task of locating shared resources, such as remote folders and printer objects, and so minimize the number of such calls, the wise network administrator might prefer to take advantage of the Windows 2000 Active Directory. Shared folders, printers, and other objects may be published in the Active Directory listing, creating a reference to the shared resource that may contain additional location-based information, making it easier to search for and locate the desired resource.

Publication of a Resource

Publishing a resource creates a reference to the object that is independent from the object itself. Both may be independently managed, and permissions to locate the published reference are separate from permissions to access or manage the referenced object. Each has its own *discretionary access control list (DACL)*, which specifies its associated access permissions.

 A user account must have at least Read permission on a published object reference in order to see it in a search of the Active Directory.

Multiple references may be created for a particular resource, and the published object references grouped into different organizational units in order to simplify access permission assignments.

Automatic Publication

Windows 2000 and later operating systems that are members of a domain will automatically publish shared resources to the Active Directory unless the option to List In The Directory checkbox is deselected in the object's Sharing properties. Resources accessed on systems running older versions of the Windows operating system must be published manually within the Active Directory.

An Administrator account is necessary in order to manually publish a shared resource to the Active Directory.

References to published resources will be verified every eight hours by the Windows 2000 domain controllers. Published resources failing to be verified three times will be removed from the Active Directory listing by a process known as *orphan pruning*. When a share is removed from a folder or printer object on a system running Windows 2000 or later version of Windows, published references will also be removed from the Active Directory.

Publication of printers may be configured using the Automatically Publish New Printers In Active Directory Group Policy setting in the Computer Configuration node under Administrative Templates I Printers. The automatic publication of printers may be enabled or disabled here. The default, if not specified, is to automatically publish shared printer resources to the Active Directory.

Location References

If a Windows 2000 domain involves a site with more than one IP subnet (discussed in Chapter 2), each subnet may be associated with a particular location. Through this procedure, a user may search for published printer objects in their own location more easily. This only works if the IP subnet configuration follows physical or geographic deployment, such as when each subnet is only used for systems within a particular city or building.

CIDR Subnet Identification

Active Directory location references use another form of IP addressing than those listed previously. The *Classless Inter-Domain Routing (CIDR)* addressing scheme used is considered a more easily extensible addressing method than earlier class-based subnetting schemes.

In CIDR subnet definitions, the address is made up of the Network Address address, followed by the number of bits in the network ID (for example, 192.168.20.0/24). This eliminates the need to specify lengthy subnet masks, which for the same subnet would have been (192.168.20.0/255.255.255.0). The subnet is not functionally different; only the addressing format is different.

Location Specification

Location naming conventions for shared resources must be standardized throughout the enterprise in order to provide maximum accessibility for users searching the Active Directory. Location naming should always be from most generic to most precise in the format:

```
general name/less general name/more precise name/...
```

The maximum length of a specified location is 260 characters, while each name may not exceed 32 characters in length.

Location may be specified for subnet on the Location tab of the subnet's Properties dialog box accessed within the Active Directory Sites And Services MMC snap-in. The location for a published printer may be specified on a Windows 2000 system or later on the General tab of its Sharing dialog box (see Figure 8.1).

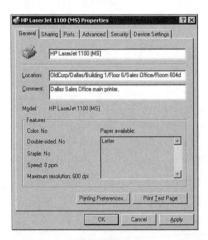

Figure 8.1   Sharing dialog box for the Dallas Sales office printer showing its Location specification.

File Sharing

File shares allow access to resources located on remote systems. By locating files physically according to issues such as network bandwidth, storage capacity, and backup strategy, the network administrator can provide enhanced user access to these files.

Shared Folders

In order to provide file access to users on remote workstations, folders must be shared and permissions assigned to user accounts allowing this access. A review of access permissions in Chapter 6 may be helpful.

Creating a Shared Folder

Folders may be shared within the Windows Explorer browser, which is found on most Windows 2000 and later systems by performing the following:

1. Select the My Computer icon on the desktop to open the Windows Explorer browser and then navigate to the proper location, creating the desired folder if it does not already exist.

2. Right-click on the folder to be shared and select Sharing to open the Sharing tab of the Properties dialog box for the folder (see Figure 8.2).

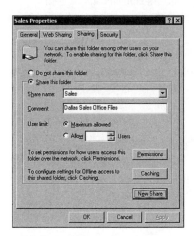

Figure 8.2   Sharing tab of the Properties dialog box for the Sales folder.

3. Select the New Share button and provide a Share Name, (optional) Comment, and a maximum number of concurrent connections (see Figure 8.3).

Figure 8.3 New Share dialog box for the New Sales share. A maximum of 10 concurrent connections has been specified for this share.

4. Select the Permissions button in order to edit access permissions for the new share. By default, the Everyone group has Full Control access granted.

5. Apply any changes and select OK to close the dialog boxes.

Table 8.1 details the three shared folder access permissions.

Table 8.1	Shared folder access permissions.
Permission	**Description**
Change	Allows deletion or modification files and folders within this share, provided the user's NTFS permissions allow.
Full Control	Includes all other permissions as well as the ability to modify share attribute values.
Read	Allows directory listing of the share's contents and read-only access to files and folders within the share, provided the user's NTFS permissions allow.

Shares may be browsed in the Windows Explorer using the *Universal Naming Convention (UNC)* format:

```
\\server\share
```

Browsing the server alone will reveal any open shares available. In order to hide a share from simple browsing, an *administrative share* is created by adding the dollar sign ($) to the end of a share. In order to view the contents of this share, it is necessary to specify the share explicitly:

```
\\server\share$
```

A number of administrative shares are created by default during system installation, including a default share for each logical drive on a system (i.e., c$ for the C: drive and d$ for the D: drive). In order to provide better security, it is often best to remove these shares or modify the default access permissions on each.

Publishing a Shared Folder

After a share has been created, it may be published to the Active Directory. Published file shares may be relocated physically without impacting a user's ability to locate the published resource, provided that the reference information published to the Active Directory is updated after the relocation has been completed.

Shared folders may be published in the Active Directory Users And Computers MMC snap-in by performing the following:

1. Open the MMC and right-click on the organizational unit in which the new reference should be published. Select New within the drop-down list and Shared Folder.

2. Provide a name and complete UNC reference to the desired shared folder (*server**share*).

3. When done, click the OK button to publish the shared folder.

4. Navigate to the proper organizational unit containing the published shared folder reference, if necessary, and right-click on the shared folder to access its properties.

If the shared folder reference was published in the wrong location, you may use the Move option here to move it to another existing organizational unit.

5. Enter a meaningful description of the share and provide useful keywords for searching the Active Directory by selecting the Keywords button and entering each in the dialog box provided.

6. Access permissions for the published reference to the share may be modified by selecting the Security tab. Custom permission assignment may be made via the options provided by the Advanced button.

7. When done, click on Apply to apply the changes and select OK to close the dialog box.

Users without the Read permission on the published share reference will not be able to locate the item when searching the Active Directory.

Managing Shared Folders

Windows 2000 provides a simple interface for management and administration of files shares, the Shared Folders MMC snap-in, which is also included within the Computer Management MMC snap-in.

 Power Users may only use this snap-in on a local system, while Administrators and Server Operators may select Action and Connect To Another Computer from the Menu bar and specify a remote system to manage.

This snap-in provides the ability to view all existing shares on a server, both normal and administrative, as well as the number of users currently connected to each by selecting the Shares node (see Figure 8.4). Selecting New Share from Actions in the Menu bar may create additional shares. Right-clicking on a share allows editing of its Properties as well as the option to Stop Sharing, which should only be done if no users are accessing the shares currently.

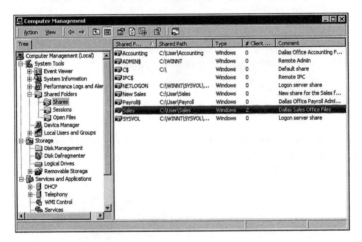

Figure 8.4 Shares listing for the local server.

The Sessions node shows all current connections to shared folders (see Figure 8.5). Selecting Disconnect All Sessions from Actions in the Menu bar may terminate all current connections. Right-clicking on a share allows the closing of a single session.

The Open Files node shows all currently open files in the shared folders. Selecting Disconnect All Open Files from Actions in the Menu bar may terminate all current connections. Right-clicking on an open file allows the closing of a single file connection.

Figure 8.5 Sessions listing for the local server.

Data loss may occur if files are in use when a session is terminated or a file dis-connected.

In order to view changes in shared folders management information listed in any of these nodes, select Refresh from Actions in the Menu bar.

Users may reestablish disconnected sessions, or a Windows-based system may attempt to automatically reconnect. In order to prevent access to forcibly disconnected sessions, it is necessary to change the access permissions on the share. Changes in access permissions are applied at the next attempt to connect to a shared resource.

Sending Console Messages

Before disconnecting sessions or open files, it is best to notify users using a console message. This option is available within the Shares node, by selecting All Tasks from Actions in the Menu bar, and then selecting Send Console Message.

The Send Console Message dialog box allows a message to be sent to selected recipients (see Figure 8.6). The message may also be sent to systems not currently connected to the local system by using the Add Recipient function.

Recipient systems will display the message to any currently connected user (see Figure 8.7).

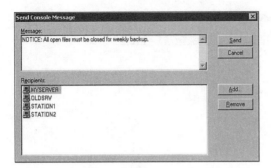

Figure 8.6 Send Console Message dialog box.

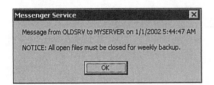

Figure 8.7 Messenger Service display.

Permissions Resolution

In order to locate published resources when searching the Active Directory, users must have at least the Read permission on the published reference. Access permissions to the resource must also be configured before access is possible. It is generally best to restrict the Read permission on the published reference to only those able to access the resource, limiting listings to only what the users may utilize and minimizing calls to the IT office about Access Denied messages.

When accessing shared folders, a combination of Share permissions and NTFS permissions is used in order to determine the final level of access granted to a user. All inherited and granted share permissions are compared first, in order to determine the access permissions for the share itself. All inherited and granted permissions are then compared in order to determine the access permissions for files and folders within the shared folder. In each comparison, the most favorable combination of access permissions is used, unless a Denial is present.

Share and NTFS permissions are then compared in order to determine the final level of access granted to the user for resources located within the shared folder. Here, the least favorable combination of access is used. As an example, a user who is able to modify and update files directly on the server may have read-only access from a remote system if the appropriate permissions on the share allow Read and not Change.

 The most favorable combination is used for NTFS and Share access permission resolution, and the least favorable combination for both when determining final access rights.

Printer Sharing

Systems that provide spooling for printers may publish shared printer references to the Active Directory in much the same way that shared folders may be published. Windows 2000 and later systems automatically publish their shared printers. For older systems, it is necessary to manually publish printer references using the Active Directory Users And Computers MMC snap-in.

In order to publish a printer within the Active Directory Users And Computers MMC, perform the following:

1. Open the MMC snap-in and select Users, Groups, And Computers As Containers from View in the Menu bar.

2. Right-click on the organizational unit in which the new reference should be published. Select New within the drop-down list and Printer.

3. Provide the UNC for the printer and proceed to publish the printer reference.

After a printer has been published, its properties may be edited by right-clicking on the published printer reference and selecting from the available options. Table 8.2 lists some useful options here.

Table 8.2 Printer reference options.	
Option	**Description**
Connect	Performs an installation of the printer on a computer.
Move	Allows the published reference to be moved to another organizational unit.
Open	Allows management of jobs in the current print queue.
Properties	Allows changes to the print queue configuration and available drivers.

Windows 95/98 and later systems may automatically obtain updated printer drivers when they connect to a shared printer resource. It is necessary to add additional drivers for systems older than Windows 2000, which may be accomplished by editing the printer's Properties, selecting the Sharing tab, and then selecting the Additional Drivers button. This will open a listing of additional drivers that may be stored on the server for legacy operating system clients (see Figure 8.8).

Figure 8.8   Additional Drivers listing.

After installing any required additional drivers, client systems connecting will be able to automatically obtain their own version of the printer drivers when they connect to the shared resource. For systems older than Windows 95/98, it will be necessary to manually install the appropriate printer driver on the client.

Unix and Macintosh workstations which need to access Windows-based file and print services will also require the installation of additional subcomponents from the Other Network File And Print Services option available in the Add/Remove Programs|Add/Remove Windows Components utility found within the Control Panel.

Practice Questions

Question 1

> Which of the following must be published to the Active Directory? [Check all correct answers]
>
> ❏ a. Computers
> ❏ b. Groups
> ❏ c. Printers
> ❏ d. Shared Folders
> ❏ e. Users

Answers c and d are correct. Objects that are not already listed in the Active Directory must be published, including shared printer and folder resources. Answers a, b, and e are incorrect because Computers, Groups, And Users are already organized as objects within the Active Directory and do not need to be published.

Question 2

> By default, Windows 2000 systems will automatically publish shared printers to the Active Directory. True or false?
>
> ○ a. True
> ○ b. False

Answer a is correct. Shared printers on systems running older versions of Windows must be manually published, but Windows 2000 systems will automatically publish their own shared printers. There are no servers responsible for this task, as each system is responsible for publishing its own resources.

Question 3

The automatic removal of a published printer that cannot be contacted is called orphan _____ and occurs after _____ failed attempts to verify availability.

- ○ a. pruning; two
- ○ b. pruning; three
- ○ c. pruning; eight
- ○ d. trimming; two
- ○ e. trimming; three
- ○ f. trimming; eight

Answer b is correct. The automatic removal of an orphaned printer share published in the Active Directory is referred to as orphan pruning and occurs after three failed attempts to verify availability eight hours apart. Answers a, c, d, and f are incorrect because the number of attempts is three before removal. Answers d, e, and f are also incorrect because the term is not orphan trimming, but orphan pruning.

Question 4

In order to relocate published resource references to a different organizational unit, they must be removed and added to the new destination. True or false?

- ○ a. True
- ○ b. False

Answer b is correct. Published resources may be relocated to a different organizational unit by using the Move option within the Active Directory Users And Computers MMC snap-in.

Question 5

> Several types of specifications are involved in resource publication:
> - Administrative Share
> - CIDR Subnet
> - Location
> - Universal Naming Convention (UNC) path
>
> Match the following examples with the appropriate type:
> - \\myserver.mycorp.com\myfiles
> - 128.194.1.0/24
> - Austin\Sales\Office 211
> - payroll$

The correct answers are:

➤ Administrative Share

  ➤payroll$

➤ CIDR Subnet

  ➤128.194.1.0/24

➤ Location

  ➤Austin\Sales\Office 211

➤ Universal Naming Convention (UNC) path

  ➤\\myserver.mycorp.com\myfiles

Question 6

> Which of the following is the best example of Location naming for a printer located in the Sales department's front office in Austin?
> - a. Austin\Office 211\Sales
> - b. Austin\Sales\Office 211
> - c. Office 211\ Sales\Austin
> - d. Sales\Austin\Office 211

Answer b is correct. Location naming should be from the most general to the most precise. In this case, Austin is the most general, Sales is the intermediate grouping, and Office 211 is the most precise. Answers a, c, and d are incorrect because they do not follow this convention.

Question 7

Which of the following default groups may use the Shared Folders MMC snap-in to manage shared folders on a remote system? [Check all correct answers]

☐ a. Administrators

☐ b. Domain Users

☐ c. Everyone

☐ d. Power Users

☐ e. Server Operators

Answers a and e are correct. Members of the Administrators and Server Operators groups may manage remote systems using the Shared Folders MMC snap-in. Answers b and c are incorrect because the Domain Users and Everyone groups are not able to use this snap-in by default. Answer d is incorrect because members of the Power Users group may only manage the shared folder resources of the local system.

Question 8

An option to Send Console Message is available in the Actions within the Sessions node of the Shared Folders MMC snap-in. True or false?

○ a. True

○ b. False

Answer b is correct. The Send Console Message option is available in the Actions of the Shares node.

Question 9

Several types of permissions comparisons are necessary when accessing shared resources:

> ➤ Direct and Inherited NTFS permissions
> ➤ Direct and Inherited Share permissions
> ➤ Share and NTFS permissions

Match the following qualities with the appropriate type:

> ➤ Uses the least restrictive combination
> ➤ Uses the most restrictive combination

The correct answers are:

➤ Direct and Inherited NTFS permissions

> ➤ Uses the least restrictive combination

➤ Direct and Inherited Share permissions

> ➤ Uses the least restrictive combination

➤ Share and NTFS permissions

> ➤ Uses the most restrictive combination

Question 10

By default, Windows 2000 systems will automatically load all printer drivers necessary for Windows 95/98 and later, but must have earlier versions of drivers added manually. True or false?

○ a. True
○ b. False

Answer b is correct. It is necessary to add printer drivers for systems running versions of Windows earlier than Windows 2000. Systems earlier than Windows 95/98 cannot automatically update their drivers when connecting to a shared printer and must be manually configured.

Need to Know More?

 Stanek, William R.: *Microsoft Windows 2000 Administrator's Pocket Consultant*. Microsoft Press, Redmond, WA, 2000. ISBN 0-7356-0831-8. A helpful reference for network administrators to keep close at hand. The soft-cover trade-sized book is a condensed, easily carried version of many larger tomes of information.

 Microsoft Windows 2000 Server Resource Kit. Microsoft Press, Redmond, WA, 2000. ISBN 1-5723-1805-8. An exhaustive library covering detailed information on all aspects of Windows 2000 Server implementations. An invaluable reference for IT departments supporting Microsoft Windows 2000 networks.

 www.microsoft.com/windows2000/techinfo/proddoc/default. asp. *Windows 2000 Product Documentation Online*. A complete online copy of the documentation for all versions of the Windows 2000 operating system.

System Configuration

Terms you'll need to understand:

- ✓ Terminal services
- ✓ Basic and dynamic disks
- ✓ Primary and extended partitions
- ✓ Spanned volumes
- ✓ Striped volumes
- ✓ Mirrored volumes
- ✓ Redundant Array of Independent Disks (RAID)
- ✓ Fault tolerance
- ✓ Mixed mode
- ✓ Native mode
- ✓ Nesting

Techniques you'll need to master:

- ✓ Adding new Windows Components after installation has been completed on a Windows 2000 system
- ✓ Configuring dynamic volumes to provide fault tolerant file storage
- ✓ Understanding the details and use of the three main RAID configurations used in Windows 2000
- ✓ Identifying the requirements for changing from a mixed-mode to a native-mode domain

This chapter will provide an overview of some issues surrounding system configuration and domain membership. It is important that a prospective network administrator have actual experience with the installation process itself. Limited-duration evaluation versions of the software are available through many channels, and you are strongly urged to obtain a copy of Windows 2000 Server/Advanced Server and Professional in order to practice this process a few times to be familiar with the steps involved. Additional references are listed at the end of this chapter.

Overview

After the initial installation of an operating system and all necessary service packs and updates, it may be necessary to perform further configuration of the system including the addition of Windows components not selected during the initial installation, configuration of storage media, establishing domain membership, forming trusts, and the creation of user accounts and the organizational units in which to place them.

Adding Windows Components

Windows components may be added or removed after initial system installation through the Add/Remove Windows components option within the Add/Remove Programs wizard found in the Control Panel. This will open the Windows Component wizard (see Figure 9.1)

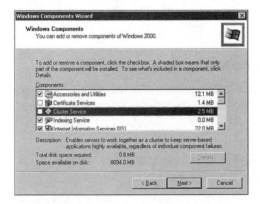

Figure 9.1   The Windows Component wizard.

Simply mark any new components to be added and unmark any to be removed and then continue through the configuration process for each new component.

Terminal Services Configuration

One exceptionally useful component that should be noted is the Terminal Services component, which allows remote users to access a *virtual desktop* on a server running Terminal Services. Windows 2000 Server/Advanced Server and Windows XP systems may support some form of this type of connection. This service allows legacy systems to create a virtual session to a Windows 2000 Server and perform any tasks as if present on that system (see Figure 9.2).

Figure 9.2   Local desktop showing a Terminal Services session to another system.

Client access to the virtual desktop creates a window that is similar to the one seen if sitting directly at a terminal on the server; only several Terminal Services connections may occur at the same time. In this way, a central server may be loaded and configured with application software, which is then accessed from client terminals that do not require the software to be loaded on each.

Client Access License (CAL) requirements must be met for any applications shared in this manner, and a Terminal Services Licensing service must be properly configured for the Application Server mode to be used. However, a limited version of this tool is available, which allows up to two concurrent connections to be made in the Remote Administration mode. This allows direct management of remote servers without requiring physical proximity, provided the server is operational and a network connection to port 3389 may be established.

The Terminal Services mode is selected during configuration of the Terminal Services Windows component at the time of installation on the server.

Terminal Services Client

Installation disks may be created for clients using the *Terminal Services Client Creator*, which is found within Control Panel|Administrative Tools. A Terminal Services client establishes a connection to a server running the Terminal Services service, and is loaded on the workstation.

Microsoft has also released an ActiveX-based Web client that may be loaded on a server running Microsoft's Internet Information Service (IIS), eliminating the need to load a separate client on each workstation, provided the system's Internet browser supports ActiveX components.

Details on the use of the Web-based *Terminal Services Advanced Client (TSAC)* may be found here: **msdn.microsoft.com/library/default.asp?url=/library/en-us/ termserv/tsovr_4uic.asp**.

Storage

Once the initial installation is completed, additional drive space may be configured in order to offer additional storage capacity, improved access efficiency, and fault tolerance against loss of data caused by a failure in the physical media.

Drive Configuration

Configuration of disk drive storage may be accomplished using the Disk Management node within the Computer Management MMC snap-in (see Figure 9.3).

Details about each partition (or logical section of a drive) are listed here, along with drive type and current condition of the partition.

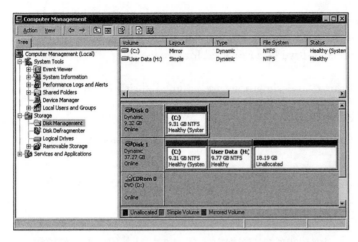

Figure 9.3   Disk Management showing multiple partitions on two physical drives.

Basic and Dynamic Disks

Windows 2000 provides two disk types: *basic* and *dynamic*. When upgrading an existing NT4 system, all disks will remain of the basic type and will maintain fault-tolerant configurations from the NT4 settings. In order to configure fault-tolerant features on new partitions in Windows 2000, disks must first be upgraded to dynamic.

Changes to disk type may be performed here by selecting the proper change from the All Tasks listing, which may be found within Actions in the header.

 A basic disk may be converted to a dynamic disk without additional preparation, but all dynamic volumes must be deleted before a dynamic disk may be reverted to the basic disk type.

Partitions and Logical Drives

Physical drives may be divided up into smaller sections, called *partitions*, which may be used for different purposes. Windows 2000 utilizes two partition types: primary and extended. They can be described as follows:

➤ *Primary* partitions may be accessed directly and given a drive letter for unique access. There may be up to four primary partitions on each physical disk in a Windows 2000 system.

➤ On each physical drive, one *extended* partition may also be configured, containing one or more *logical drives*. This allows more than four virtual drive assignments to be made on a single physical drive. A logical drive is a reference to a portion of an extended partition that is given a drive letter and may be used for file storage. An extended partition cannot be directly assigned a drive letter or used for storage.

Several special partition designations are assigned during installation:

> The *active* partition is the one in which the computer starts.

> The *boot* partition contains the operating system and its files required in order to start.

> The *system* partition contains hardware-specific files necessary to the boot process.

 The system partition may not be located on a volume that is striped or spanned, or one that is a member in a RAID-5 volume.

Each partition may be formatted as either FAT32 or NTFS, although to enable the advanced access capabilities of Windows 2000, NTFS must be used.

Dynamic Volumes

Windows 2000 also allows the creation of volumes, which are similar to partitions and may be directly addressed for file storage. Unlike partitions, a volume may be extended to include additional unused disk storage space or configured as a member of a volume set. A volume set allows space on multiple disks to be combined as a single storage space, or in order to provide fault tolerant storage solutions.

Spanned Volumes

Simple or spanned NTFS volumes that are not part of a mirrored or striped volume may be extended to include additional space on up to 32 physical disks. This allows the aggregation of unused space into a single spanned volume.

The downside to a *spanned volume* is that the loss of any drive containing a member of the volume set will cause the loss of all data within the volume. There is no fault tolerance in a spanned volume.

Striped Volumes

Striped volumes are similar to spanned volumes. They store information in two or more volumes located on separate drives. Information is broken into segments called *stripes* and stored in sequential order across all drives in the set. This improves disk read/write access time, but does not provide fault tolerance against the loss of a physical drive.

If any drive participating in a striped volume is lost, this will cause the loss of all data in the striped volume. A striped volume is also called a RAID-0 configuration.

Redundant Array of Independent Disks (RAID)

In order to provide options for fault tolerance, or the ability to recover data after the loss of physical drive media, a technology known as RAID was implemented.

 RAID stands for a *Redundant Array of Independent Disks*, or a *Redundant Array of Inexpensive Disks*. Both terms are used interchangeably, and generally just spoken of as a RAID configuration.

Different RAID configurations are possible, allowing greater access time or greater levels of fault tolerance, depending on available resources and business mandates. Table 9.1 provides a listing of the most common RAID types used in Windows 2000

Table 9.1	Common RAID configurations.			
RAID Level	**Type**	**Description**	**Advantages**	**Disadvantages**
0	Striping	Volumes on two or more physical disks are combined into a stripe set onto which data is written sequentially.	Performance is improved by allowing multiple read/write operations to occur simultaneously on multiple stripes.	Loss of any disk in the set will cause a loss of all data. No fault tolerance.

(continued)

Table 9.1	Common RAID configurations *(continued)*			
RAID Level	Type	Description	Advantages	Disadvantages
1	Mirroring	Two volumes located on separate disks are written to simultaneously, creating two copies of all data.	Faster than RAID-5 and complete redundancy. If one drive is lost, the other continues to provide file access.	Inefficient storage, because both volumes must be of the same size and both contain the same information, only 50% of the total space is available in the mirrored volume.
5	Striping with parity	Volumes on three or more physical disks are combined into a stripe set which also includes additional error-checking information that allows for the regeneration of lost data from the remaining disks.	More efficient than mirroring, while still allowing for data recovery in the event of a single drive's loss.	Slower than other forms of RAID storage because each write operation involves the calculation and storage of the parity error checking information.

In order to optimize performance in a RAID configuration, it is best to separate mirrored drives on separate controller channels and to utilize striped drives only for the RAID volumes, to prevent slowed overall response caused by ongoing access to data located on other partitions on the same drives.

Partitions, logical drives, and volumes may all be created and manipulated using the Disk Management node within the Computer Management MMC snap-in (see Figure 9.4).

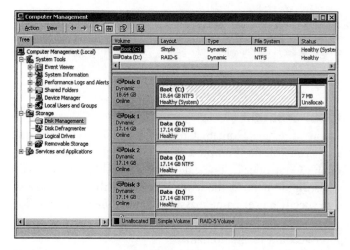

Figure 9.4   Disk Management showing a RAID-5 volume on three physical drives.

Domain Configuration

Peer-to-peer networking is acceptable for very small groups of computers that may share resources very infrequently. However, modern network scenarios mandate the use of a domain membership-based network. If you remain unclear on the meaning of terms such as domain, tree, forest, and organizational unit, please review Chapter 6.

Server Configuration

Servers that are to participate in Active Directory support are configured as Domain Controllers. Stand-alone servers are those that are not members of any domain, while member servers are non-Domain Controller servers that have been made members of a domain. At least one Domain Controller must be present for each Active Directory domain. A second Domain Controller is usually considered important as well, in order to provide fault tolerance against the loss of a server.

A server may be configured as a Domain Controller during its initial setup. A member server or stand-alone server may also be converted to a Domain Controller after being loaded and updated. This process is called *promotion*, and is accomplished using the **dcpromo** command-line utility.

The **dcpromo** command is also used to demote an existing Domain Controller to a simple member server, once all FSMO roles have been transferred to another Domain Controller in the domain.

Domain Controller Creation

During configuration of a new Domain Controller, or after enacting the **dcpromo** command, you will be prompted to specify whether the server is to be the first Domain Controller in a new domain or an additional Domain Controller in an existing domain. If the latter is selected, the administrator will be prompted to specify a user name, password, and domain information for an account with the permissions necessary to add a new Domain Controller computer account to the domain.

When creating a new domain, the administrator will then be prompted to specify whether the domain is to become a member of an existing forest, or the first domain in a new forest of trees. If selected as the root domain of a new forest of trees, the administrator will be prompted to enter the full DNS name and NetBIOS name of the new domain, as well as to specify the location of the domain database logs and select whether the domain information may be read by Windows 2000 servers only, or by legacy servers as well.

When adding a domain as a child within an existing forest, the administrator will be prompted to specify the parent domain, along with the necessary login information for a user account with permissions to create a child domain within that tree. The new child domain is specified, as a child of the existing domain, and information detailed for database log location and information access permissions.

Once completed, the new server will be configured as a Windows 2000 Active Directory Domain Controller.

If a DNS server is not available for the new domain during this process, the administrator will be prompted to install the DNS service on the local server. Active Directory requires the use of a DNS server in order to locate resources.

Domain Mode

A Windows 2000 Active Directory domain is configured as a *mixed-mode* domain by default. In a mixed-mode domain, the PDC Emulator must be a Windows 2000 Domain Controller, and other Domain Controllers may be either Windows 2000 Domain Controllers or NT 4.0 Backup Domain Controllers.

When no NT 4.0 Backup Domain Controllers will be used, and all Domain Controllers are running only Windows 2000, a domain may be converted to *native mode*. Native-mode domains allow the use of additional Active Directory integrated features, such as the use of *universal* groups discussed later in this chapter.

 Member servers may be Windows 2000 or NT 4.0 in both native-mode and mixed-mode domains. A domain must remain mixed-mode only if NT 4.0 Backup Domain Controllers are present.

A domain may be converted from mixed-mode to native-mode operation, but not the other way around. This is a one-way operation that cannot be undone once begun. All NT 4.0 Backup Domain Controllers must have been upgraded to Windows 2000 or removed before making this change, and administrators must be certain that they will not be needed again.

Conversion of a domain to native-mode operation is performed within the Active Directory Domains And Trusts MMC snap-in by opening Properties for the target domain and clicking the Change Mode button on the General tab. After acknowledging the warning prompt, the domain will be altered to native mode. There is no way back from this.

Establishing Trusts

Two domains, trees, or forests may be connected using a domain *trust*. Details of the types of trusts possible may be found in Chapter 3. The Active Directory Domains And Trusts MMC snap-in is used to configure a trust between two domains. An administrator for each domain must perform this procedure before the trust will be completed.

After opening the Active Directory Domains And Trusts snap-in and opening the Properties for the desired domain, an administrator may select the Trusts tab to see any existing trusts or in order to create a new trust. Trusts must be specified in each direction, specifying domains *trusted* to access resources within the current domain, and specifying *trusting* domains that allow the current domain to access resources located within their domain.

When creating a trust, a password is used. The same password must be agreed upon and entered at both trusting and trusted ends of the new connector.

Account Management

The most comprehensive effort involved in creating a new domain is the planning and creation of computer and user accounts, and the organizational units into which they will be placed.

Computer Accounts

Computer accounts are used to allow member computers to register with their Domain Controllers and publish any shared resources. The Domain Controller automatically changes computer account passwords every 30 days.

A user account that has been granted creative administrative rights over an organizational unit may create new computer accounts in that container. A user that has been granted the Add Workstations To Domain right may add up to 10 workstation accounts without having specific permissions over a particular container.

By default, all new Computer objects are created in the Computers container of the appropriate domain. These objects may be moved to a different organizational unit by opening the Active Directory Users And Computers MMC snap-in, right-clicking on the target computer account, selecting Move from the drop-down listing, and navigating to the desired target organizational unit.

Computer accounts may also be pre-created manually in the desired organizational unit by right-clicking the desired organizational unit and selecting New | Computer. Specify a name for the system to be added in the New Object - Computer dialog box, as well as a user account or group to be granted the right to join a system with this name to the domain (see Figure 9.5).

Figure 9.5 New Object - Computer dialog box showing the details for preloading a computer account named Station4 in the Dallas Sales office in the oldcorp.com domain.

Systems running Windows 95/98 or NT 4.0 must use an Active Directory client in order to access shared Windows 2000 Active Directory resources.

New User Accounts

User accounts allow user login, identification, location, and additional configuration information. The Properties page of a user account provides access to many tabs of information and configuration options. Network administrators will find that a lot of time may be spent in entering all of the required information into the fields as new users are added to domains.

Creating a new user account may be performed within the Active Directory Users And Computers MMC snap-in by right-clicking on the desired organizational unit and selecting New and User. The New Object - User dialog box allows entry of the name, initials, login name and home domain specification (see Figure 9.6).

Figure 9.6 New Object - User dialog box showing the details for creating a user account for John Q. Public.

Once this information has been entered, the administrator will be prompted for the password to be assigned to the user account and may specify whether the account is initially disabled, whether the user may change their own password, and if the password must be changed during the first successful login or if it never expires.

After creating the account, its properties may be edited by right-clicking on the target user account and selecting Properties. The administrator may also choose to move the account to another organizational unit, reset the password, disable or enable the account, and change its group membership from this drop down listing.

The Properties page provides a wide range of configuration options, allowing the specification of contact information, logon restrictions, account expiration date, location of user profile storage, Terminal Services configuration settings, remote access permissions, access permissions for modifications to the user account, and group membership (see Figure 9.7).

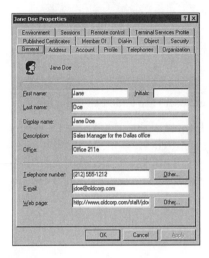

Figure 9.7 User account properties for user Jane Doe.

In order to simplify the creation of accounts that are nearly identical to existing ones, the wise network administrator will simply copy an existing user account by right-clicking on the target source account and selecting Copy to open a dialog box identical to that seen in a new computer account creation. After creation of the copy, the administrator may then make any required modifications to the copied account's properties. This is a quick way to create a new account with group membership and location information preconfigured from a standard template account.

Organizational Units

Creation of a new organizational unit container object may be accomplished using the Active Directory Users And Computers MMC snap-in by right-clicking on the desired container for the organizational unit and selecting New and Organizational Unit from the drop-down listing and specifying a name for the new organizational unit.

Organizational units may be placed inside of other organizational units, which is called *nesting*. Permissions assigned to the highest-level container will be inherited by all nested child containers unless specifically blocked from inheritance, as discussed in Chapter 8. Organizational units may be moved in the same way that user and computer accounts are.

Practice Questions

Question 1

Terminal Services may be used to provide virtual desktop connections to many client systems using the Remote Administrator mode of installation. True or false?

○ a. True

○ b. False

Answer b is correct. The Remote Administrator mode has a maximum of two concurrent connections and is designed to allow for remote access and support of a server. In order to support multiple client systems, Terminal Services must be installed in Application Server mode and the Terminal Services Licensing service must be properly configured.

Question 2

Which of the following are valid disk types in Windows 2000? [Check all correct answers]

❑ a. Basic

❑ b. Dynamic

❑ c. Extended

❑ d. Mirrored

❑ e. System

Answers a and b are correct. The valid disk types used in Windows 2000 are basic disks and dynamic disks. Answer c is incorrect because extended is a type of partition able to contain multiple logical disks. Answer d is incorrect because a mirrored volume creates identical copies of data on two physical disks. Answer e is incorrect because the system partition contains hardware-specific information necessary for system boot-up.

Question 3

> Which of the following volume types provide fault tolerance against the loss of a physical drive? [Check all correct answers]
>
> ❑ a. Mirrored (RAID-1)
>
> ❑ b. Spanned
>
> ❑ c. Striped (RAID-0)
>
> ❑ d. Striped with parity (RAID-5)

Answers a and d are correct. Mirrored and RAID-5 volume sets are considered to be fault tolerant, because the loss of a physical drive does not cause the loss of data stored on these volume types. Answers b and c are incorrect because the loss of a drive in either a Spanned or RAID-0 volume set will prevent later access to data stored in the volume.

Question 4

> Three RAID levels are considered the standard types used in Windows 2000:
>
> ➤ RAID-0
>
> ➤ RAID-1
>
> ➤ RAID-5
>
> Match the following characteristics with the appropriate level:
>
> ➤ Fastest access performance
>
> ➤ Fault tolerant
>
> ➤ Lowest storage efficiency
>
> ➤ Provides complete redundancy
>
> ➤ Slowest access performance

The correct answers are:

➤ RAID-0

   ➤ Fastest access performance

➤ RAID-1

   ➤ Fault tolerant

   ➤ Lowest storage efficiency

   ➤ Provides complete redundancy

➤ RAID-5

   ➤ Fault tolerant

   ➤ Slowest access performance

Question 5

Which of the following MMC snap-ins are used to create new volumes and new computer accounts?

○ a. Active Directory Management and Active Directory Users And Computers

○ b. Computer Management and Active Directory Domains And Trusts

○ c. Computer Management and Active Directory Users And Computers

○ d. Drive Management and Active Directory Users And Computers

---

Answer c is correct. New volumes may be created in the Disk Management node within the Computer Management MMC snap-in, while new computer accounts may be created in the appropriate organizational unit within the Active Directory Users And Computers MMC snap-in. Answer a is incorrect because there is no Active Directory Management MMC snap-in. Answer b is incorrect because the Active Directory Domains And Trusts MMC snap-in is used to modify domain properties and manage trusts. Answer d is incorrect because there is no Drive Management MMC snap-in.

Question 6

During drive configuration planning, there are several types of storage definitions that may be created:

➤ Disks

➤ Extended partitions

➤ Logical drives

➤ Primary Partitions

➤ Volumes

Match the following characteristics with the appropriate type:

➤ Exist on extended partitions

➤ Have a maximum of four on a single physical disk

➤ May be basic or dynamic

➤ May be configured to be fault tolerant

➤ May be directly accessed and assigned a drive letter

The correct answers are:

➤ Disks

   ➤ May be basic or dynamic

➤ Extended partitions

➤ Logical drives

   ➤ Exist on extended partitions

   ➤ May be directly accessed and assigned a drive letter

➤ Primary Partitions

   ➤ Have a maximum of four on a single physical disk

   ➤ May be directly accessed and assigned a drive letter

➤ Volumes

   ➤ May be configured to be fault tolerant

   ➤ May be directly accessed and assigned a drive letter

Question 7

> The commands used to promote and demote a Windows 2000 Domain
> Controller are **dcpromo** and **dcdemo**. True or false?
>
> ○ a. True
> ○ b. False

Answer b is correct. The **dcpromo** command is used both to promote member servers to become Domain Controllers, and to demote existing Domain Controllers to member server status.

Question 8

> Which of the following conditions *must* be met in order to be able to change a
> domain from mixed-mode to native-mode operation?
>
> ○ a. All Windows 2000 Domain Controllers must be made PDC Emulators.
> ○ b. All Windows NT 4.0 Backup Domain Controllers must be upgraded or
>   removed.
> ○ c. All Windows NT 4.0 Domain Controllers must be made Backup Domain
>   Controllers only.
> ○ d. The Windows 2000 PDC Emulator must assume all FSMO roles.

Answer b is correct. All remaining Domain Controllers must be running Windows 2000. Answer a is incorrect because only one Domain Controller per domain may hold the PDC Emulator role. Answer c is incorrect because all NT 4.0 Domain Controllers must have been upgraded to Windows 2000 or removed. Answer d is incorrect because the location of the FSMO roles will not prevent the change from mixed-mode to native-mode operation.

Question 9

> The _____ domain allows accounts within the _____ domain to access its
> resources.
>
> ○ a. trusting; trusted
> ○ b. trusted; trusting

Answer a is correct. The trusting domain allows accounts within the trusted domain to access its resources.

Question 10

The creation of an organizational unit within another organizational unit is called
_____.

- ○ a. Copying
- ○ b. Inheritance
- ○ c. Looping
- ○ d. Nesting

Answer d is correct. Nesting is the process of creating one organizational unit within another. Answer a is incorrect because organizational units are not copied. Answer b is incorrect because inheritance is the process by which access permissions to a parent container are allowed to apply to all child containers as well, unless blocked. Answer c is incorrect because containers may only contain other objects, preventing referential loops from arising.

Need to Know More?

 Knight, Natasha: *MCSE Windows 2000 Server Exam Cram*. The Coriolis Group, 2000. ISBN 1-57610-713-2. A helpful cram reference for the procedures involved in setting up and configuring Windows 2000 servers.

 Holme, Dan, Todd Logan, Laurie Salmon, and Dan Balter: *MCSE Windows 2000 Professional Exam Cram*. The Coriolis Group, 2000. ISBN 1-57610-712-4. A good cram reference for the procedures involved in setting up and configuring a Windows 2000 Professional system.

 Microsoft Windows 2000 Server Resource Kit. Microsoft Press, Redmond, WA, 2000. ISBN 1-5723-1805-8. An exhaustive library covering detailed information on all aspects of Windows 2000 Server implementations. An invaluable reference for IT departments supporting Microsoft Windows 2000 networks.

 www.microsoft.com/windows2000/techinfo/proddoc/default. asp. *Windows 2000 Product Documentation Online*. A complete online copy of the documentation for all versions of the Windows 2000 operating system.

Internet Information Services (IIS)

Terms you'll need to understand:

✓ Internet
✓ Intranet
✓ Site
✓ Virtual folder
✓ Web Distributed Authoring And Versioning (WebDAV)
✓ Anonymous authentication
✓ General Web permissions
✓ Execute Web permission
✓ Host header
✓ Web folder

Techniques you'll need to master:

✓ Understanding the use and application of the three methods of virtual site identification
✓ Understanding the purpose and use of the four authentication methods used by the Internet Information Service (IIS)
✓ Combining Authentication, Web permissions, and NTFS permissions to restrict access to IIS resources
✓ Creating virtual sites and virtual directories within the Internet Services Manager MMC snap-in

Chapters 7 and 8 discuss sharing resources within an Active Directory-integrated network using folder and share-level access. The Internet is a popular option for making resources more readily available to users. Files shared to the Web may be accessed using a client interface known as a *browser*. Microsoft's browser is Internet Explorer.

Windows 2000 provides a very popular Internet server, the Internet Information Service (IIS). This service provides support for the File Transfer Protocol (FTP)and the World Wide Web (WWW) using the Hypertext Transport Protocol (HTTP), as well as the Simple Mail Transfer Protocol (SMTP) and Network News Transfer Protocol (NNTP). This chapter discusses the configuration of Windows 2000 IIS.

IIS Overview

Before the advent of the graphical user interface (GUI), file sharing was accomplished by command-line actions alone. After a graphical interface was created, it became possible to publish files, graphics, and textual information for access by any client that supports HTTP. Access to these resources may be easily navigated using both private intranet and public Internet connections. Using the simple browser client, Web sites can distribute resources for personal and business topics almost anywhere in the world.

Intranets, Extranets, and the Internet

The Internet is a term coined to include all resources available through the global TCP/IP network. Often, the media use this term to refer in particular to resources that are available via HTTP and FTP and which are accessed using a browser. Resources distributed using these transfer protocols for external public use may be made available to authenticated users or to anyone who attempts to access them by way of anonymous authentication. Internet services allow businesses to establish an easy-to-access informational site and even an e-commerce site so that users may purchase items or conduct business entirely online from anywhere in the world.

A configuration allowing distribution of resources within an organization for its own use is referred to as an *intranet*. Intranets are typically restricted to prevent access by unauthorized users. Intranet configurations that are accessible to authenticated users remotely through the Web are often referred to as *extranets*. Intranets are very useful when providing a centralized store of information that each user can easily accessed from his browser interface, allowing the rapid distribution of updated information necessary for business.

Terminology

You need to understand several important terms when planning an IIS deployment. Table 10.1 lists some of the more important terms.

Table 10.1 IIS terminology.	
Term	**Description**
Site	A site is a uniquely identified FTP or Web location. A single server may host thousands of separate sites, each of which may have its own unique set of files, folders, authentication methods, and access rights.
Site Master	Each server may be preconfigured with settings to be applied to all sites of the appropriate type (FTP or WWW). Changes made to the master properties apply to all sites of that type, unless specified otherwise in an individual site. Master properties are overridden automatically by lower-level specifications.
Virtual site	Each site on a server, beyond the default site, is referred to as a virtual site. It must have an identifier that differentiates it from the host machine on which it resides.
Virtual folder	A virtual link to folders located in locations other than a site's root folder may be created. Users accessing a site use these virtual folders as if they were physically located within the site. This allows a Web-server to provide access to directories and files located in other areas or on other servers, improving security and file storage capacity capabilities.
WebDAV	Web Distributed Authoring And Versioning (WebDAV) is an industry standard that gives clients accessing folders with Internet Explorer the ability to use IIS as both a Web and file server. In Internet Explorer select Open|Open As Web folder to open an IIS site.

Site Identification

Each FTP or Web site must be uniquely identified on a server, so that client connections may be properly connected to the desired resources. The same site identification may be used on one FTP and one Web site, because they are differentiated automatically. By default, FTP connections use port 21, whereas Web connections use HTTP port 80.

The default sites are identified using the IP address or FQDN name of the host server, unless configured otherwise.

To uniquely identify sites other than the default site on a server, IIS provides three options: multiple IP addresses for one site, single IP address with a custom port, or single IP address with host headers. The three methods of virtual site identification are as follows:

➤ Multiple IP addresses—Each site may be assigned one or more IP addresses, allowing different addresses to reach a common site. This is useful when mergers bring together two discontinuous namespaces but require a common public access location. For example, a company may need both **http://www.newcorp.com/** and **http://www.oldcorp.com/** to direct customers to a single public Web site.

➤ Single IP with custom port—A port other than port 80 may be specified, allowing for improved security against automated port-scanning, as well as providing a method of sharing a single IP address between several sites. To access a site using a port other than the default for Web connections, users must specify the port in the uniform resource locator (URL) reference and the port must be open through any firewalls or proxy servers between the client and the server. A connection to the IP addresses assigned to **www.newcorp.com** using the custom port 8080 would look like this: **http://www.newcorp.com:8080/**.

➤ Single IP with host header—A host header is a unique name, registered as an alias for an IP address, which allows a single IP address to be uniquely connected to multiple sites. If an IP address is assigned multiple aliases (examples: sales.newcorp.com and humanresources.newcorp.com), then the one IP address may be assigned to both sites, and the host header configured to look for attempts to connect via a browser to the specific name, such as sales.newcorp.com. This greatly reduces the number of IP addresses required for a public server by allowing the same address to provide access to many sites located on the server.

Be very familiar with each of the methods of addressing described in Table 10.2. You may see them in many of the exam questions.

Multiple identification methods may be applied to a site. Each site may have one or more unique IP addresses, one or more IP addresses with custom port association, one or more IP addresses with host header, or a combination of any of these.

IIS Installation

By default, the IIS is installed on Windows 2000 Server/Advanced Server machines to support Web, but not FTP, connections. It may also be installed on Windows 2000 Professional systems, although this version is restricted to a maximum of 10 concurrent connections.

Components of the IIS may be added or removed via the Add/Remove Programs utility found within the Control Panel by this route: Start | Settings | Control Panel | Add/Remove Programs. You can view a list of components by selecting Add/Remove Windows Components and then navigating to the Internet Information Service option and selecting the Details button, which will open the IIS Components dialog box (see Figure 10.1).

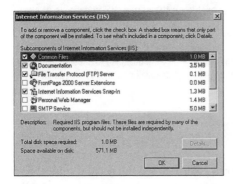

Figure 10.1   Internet Information Service components dialog box.

The Windows 2000 IIS is installed with several options selected by default. You can add others, and you may want to remove some to provide greater security to production environment servers. Table 10.2 describes a few of the more important components.

Table 10.2 Some important IIS components.	
Component	**Description**
Documentation	Includes topic information for Web and FTP site configuration, as well as Active Server Page (ASP) documentation and samples.
File Transfer Protocol (FTP) Server	Installs the FTP server service, which may host multiple FTP sites on a single machine.
FrontPage 2000 Server Extensions	Provides integrated support for FrontPage, Microsoft's Office Suite Web site application.

(continued)

Table 10.2 Some important IIS components *(continued)*	
Component	**Description**
Internet Information Services (IIS) snap-In	Installs the Internet Services Manager MMC snap-in.
Internet Services Manager	Installs HTML scripts, providing management of the site from a remote browser.
NNTP Service	Installs the NNTP server service, which provides newsgroup content support.
SMTP Service	Installs the SMTP server service, providing basic mail transfer functionality.
World Wide Web Server	Installs the server service responsible for hosting Web sites. Provided that sufficient resources are available on the server, IIS is capable of supporting thousands of sites.

Some components of IIS may be exploited to provide unauthorized access to resources on the server. Sample ASP scripts are a good example of this, because they are designed to show functionality and were not written with security as a focus. Often, it is best to install only those components necessary to the server's function.

Server Configuration

During the installation of the Windows 2000 IIS, several related folders and user accounts are created on the server. The two user accounts are IUSR_ *<computername>*, which is used for Anonymous authentication, and IWAM_ *<computername>*, which is used to start and run certain Web-deployed applications. Table 10.3 lists some important file locations created by IIS.

Table 10.3 IIS folders.	
Location	**Use**
%SystemDrive%\InetPub\	Default location of all Web (%SystemDrive%\ InetPub\ wwwroot\) and FTP (%SystemDrive%\ InetPub\ftproot\) files. In production servers, these files should be relocated to a different partition from the one used for system files.
%SystemDrive%\WINNT\IISHelp	Location of the Internet Information Services Documentation, if installed.
%SystemDrive%\WINNT\ System32\InetSrv\	Location of all DLLs and IIS executables, as well as the remote administration scripts, if installed (%SystemDrive%\WINNT\System32\InetSrv\IISAdmin\).

Folders and files for new sites should be located on a nonsystem partition to provide improved performance and security.

User Authentication

Authentication is the process by which the Web server determines if a particular user may access resources via the Web. Authentication is separate from applying access permissions, because it specifically deals with the ability of a user to connect to published sites or folders via their browser. Only after authentication allows a user to connect will access permissions then be checked for folder or file level access capabilities. A combination of both authentication and access permissions will determine if a particular file or folder is available to a user, and to what degree the user may access it.

Web Authentication Methods

Windows 2000 provides four types of authentication within its IIS: Anonymous, Basic, Digest, and Integrated Windows authentication. Authentication may be defined at the site, folder, or file level, with lower-level assignments overriding higher-level inheritance when defined.

 IIS can also support the government high-security standard called *Fortezza*.

The four authentication methods are as follows:

➤ *Anonymous*—Anonymous authentication provides users with access to public resources without requiring any form of access token, such as a login and password combination. When accessing resources through an anonymous connection, a special machine account is used automatically by IIS: **IUSR_<computername>**. This account is automatically created on each computer when IIS is installed. NTFS restrictions placed on this account will affect all users accessing resources via anonymous authentication.

➤ *Basic*—In Basic authentication, users are prompted for a login and password, which is then used for Web authentication. If the login credentials are rejected, the user will be prompted to reenter them. Basic authentication over an unsecured connection may expose user credentials to interception because they are sent in an unencrypted form.

➤ *Digest*—Digest authentication is identical to Basic authentication except that the login credentials are encrypted using a hashed value, which is then extracted by the server and used for authentication. This provides additional security over unsecured connections, but will only function if the IIS server is a member of a Windows 2000 Active Directory domain and the user is using Internet Explorer 5 or higher. As a result, this is not a good choice for resources that may be accessed by users of browser clients such as Netscape.

➤ *Integrated Windows*—Integrated Windows authentication uses the currently logged-on user's Windows 2000 account credentials to perform authentication to Web resources. This method is useful for intranets, because users will log in to client computers using their domain accounts. Integrated Windows authentication will use either Kerberos or NTLM Challenge/Response to establish the user credentials, just as in normal user login authentication to the domain. The drawback to this authentication method is that it does not work well in deployments in which many users using a standard account may access shared-access computers. It functions only with Internet Explorer browsers and will not work through HTTP proxy connections.

Only Anonymous and Basic authentication may be used for FTP sites, but all four may be used for WWW Web site authentication.

Combining Authentication Types

Multiple types of authentication may be enabled for a site, folder, or file using the Internet Services Manager MMC snap-in (see Figure 10.2).

Figure 10.2 Authentication modes available within the Internet Services Manager MMC snap-in's Web site properties dialog box.

Just as with NTFS access permissions, authentication modes are inherited from parent objects. However, Web authentication specifications made at lower levels will automatically override inherited authentication specifications.

When combining authentication methods, remember that the Web server will always attempt Anonymous authentication first if that method is enabled and that Basic authentication will always be attempted last if any other methods are enabled. If Anonymous authentication is combined with other methods, the others will be used if NTFS permissions prevent the IUSR_*<computername>* account or Internet Guests from accessing the desired resources.

When you change the properties of an object, you will be prompted to select which of its lower-level objects should also be updated.

Access Permissions

To access a Web resource, the user must be successfully authenticated to connect to a site. Then Web permissions are evaluated to determine if the user may access the resources within a site. Next, NTFS permissions are evaluated to determine the access permissions and restrictions placed on a particular object. Only then, after successfully passing these levels of verification, may a user be given access to the shared folder or file. Just as with share permissions within an Active Directory domain, the least restrictive set of inherited and assigned permissions will be granted at each level, and then the most restrictive combination of all will be applied for the final access granted to a user.

You can manipulate the Web and NTFS permissions as needed to provide or prevent access to WebDAV folders by users using Internet Explorer.

Web Permissions

Web-based access permissions are grouped into two categories: General and Execute permissions. General permissions are set at the site, folder, or file level and affect access permissions to read and modify static files. Execute permissions are set only at the site and folder level and control the ability of programs and scripts to execute on the server.

Figure 10.3 shows the Web permissions from a Web site's Properties page with the Execute Permissions drop-down menu exposed.

General permissions do not affect access to executable files and scripts, nor the other way around. Care should be taken to assign the correct General and Execute permissions required by the particular needs for the site. Table 10.4 details the four general Web permissions.

Figure 10.3 Web access permissions for the Sales Web site.

Table 10.4	General Web permissions.
Permission	**Description**
Directory Browsing	If a site's default document is not present, the server will return an error to the client's browser unless this permission is granted. If Directory Browsing is enabled, the user will be shown a listing of the current folder's contents, provided the default document is not present. This permission must be enabled for WebDAV folder access.
Read	This permission allows users to access non-executable files within a Web site. This is a read-only permission and does not grant the ability to edit or insert new files during WebDAV access. If this permission is not enabled, users cannot view files or contents of Web folders.
Script Source Access	This permission allows users with the proper Read and Write permissions to view or modify scripts on the Web site. Be careful with this permission, because users could potentially view password and account information contained in ASP pages. This permission must be enabled to access WebDAV folders to upload or download scripts.
Write	When enabled, users may insert or modify files using WebDAV folder access.

Table 10.5 describes the three Execute Web permissions.

Table 10.5   Execute Web permissions.

Permission	Description
None	If this option is chosen, no executables or scripts will be allowed to run in the specified site or folder. This does not affect static file access, such as .htm files.
Scripts Only	This setting allows scripts such as .asp files to be executed, but not executable .dll or .exe files.
Scripts And Executables	This setting allows all scripts and executable files to run in the specified site or folder. Be very careful with this permission, because a user with Write general permissions may upload any file desired and execute it on the server.

Permissions Wizard

To ease the application of basic permissions, Windows 2000 IIS provides the Permissions Wizard utility. This wizard should not be used for highly complex permissions assignments, but it does provide a simple method of applying basic Web and NTFS permissions to sites by using available templates or by selecting to inherit all security settings from the parent container.

You access the Permissions Wizard from within the Information Services Management MMC snap-in. First, navigate to the desired FTP or Web site, right-click on the appropriate item and select All Tasks | Permissions Wizard. After you choose to inherit the parent object's permissions or to use a specified template, you will be prompted to replace all current permissions or to add the required permissions in addition to any current specifications. After this, permissions are assigned accordingly. The available default templates are described in Table 10.6.

Table 10.6   Default IIS Permissions Wizard templates.

Template	Description
Public Web Site	Configures a Web site to allow all users to access Web resources. This is suitable for nonsensitive public Internet sites.
Secure Web Site	Configures a Web site for Windows Integrated access for Web resources. This is suitable for more restricted intranet sites.

You can create additional templates using the IIS Permissions Wizard Template Maker utility from the Windows 2000 Resource Kit.

The Permissions Wizard is a useful way to quickly assign permission changes from a parent object to child site or folder. Because lower-level assignments override inherited ones, this utility allows an administrator to propagate a new set of top-level permissions to lower-level objects.

Site Creation

This portion of the chapter will take you through creating FTP sites, Web sites and virtual directories, and Web-sharing of folders on the server using the Windows Explorer. You should practice these tasks several times in varying combinations, as they will be fundamental to a number of questions in the exam.

Secure site access capability may be established by installing a security certificate on the IIS server, associating the certificate with the appropriate site, and enabling the site for secure socket layer (SSL) connections. Secured site access would be required when obtaining personal information from a visitor, such as a credit card number. Connections to secure Web sites use the **https** preface instead of the default **http** preface, and secure Web connections occur using port 443 instead of the default port 80.

Master Properties

Every server has a set of properties assigned as the masters for the FTP and Web services. The administrator should configure default settings for all sites of the appropriate type (FTP or Web) in Master Properties. Master properties are overridden by settings made at the site, folder, or file level, allowing for greater levels of security to be applied to specific resources without affecting all other sites on the server.

 A single server can host thousands of sites, provided it has adequate storage, CPU, RAM, and network resources. Microsoft has successfully tested servers supporting more than 5,000 sites.

After the Internet Services Manager MMC snap-in has been opened, the master properties may be edited by performing the following steps:

1. Right-click on the Web server and select Properties.

2. Select WWW Service or FTP Service in the Master Properties box and click the Edit button. You may also enable Bandwidth Throttling here.

This allows the administrator to prevent a single user from using up all available bandwidth to a server by restricting the maximum data rate (in kb/s) each connection may use.

3. Modify any settings as desired within the pages of the Properties dialog box (see Figure 10.4).

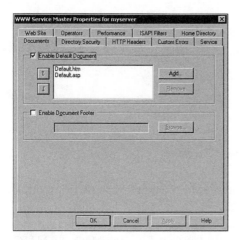

Figure 10.4   Master site properties showing the default document settings.

 When a user connects to a site without specifying which file or folder to open, the server will search for the first document in the site's root folder matching the list of default documents. To change the search order to a custom default document, move the desired default document entry to the top of the list.

4. When done, click the Apply button to save your changes and then the OK button to close the Properties interface.

Creating a Site

You can create a virtual site on the server after the master properties have been configured on a server, any necessary IP addresses have been added to the TCP/IP properties of its NIC (see Figure 10.5), and any DNS host naming have been configured for these IP addresses in the appropriate name servers.

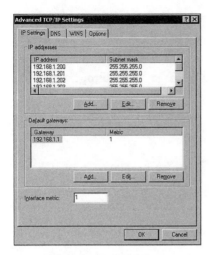

Figure 10.5 TCP/IP configuration showing multiple IP addresses.

It is best to locate the root folder and files for new sites on a partition other than the system drive. When this folder has been created and any desired initial files moved there, set all applicable NTFS permissions. After this is done, perform the following steps within the Internet Services Manager MMC snap-in to create a new site:

1. Right-click on the Web server; then select New and the appropriate type of site to be created (FTP, WWW, or SMTP).

2. Provide a meaningful description for the site, which will be the name shown for the site in the Internet Services Manager MMC snap-in (see Figure 10.6). Select Next to continue the site creation.

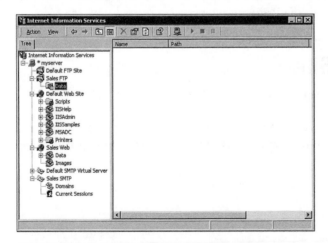

Figure 10.6 Internet Services Manager MMC snap-in showing several sites.

3. Select the first IP address and a custom port or appropriate host header to be used for the new site (see Figure 10.7); then click Next.

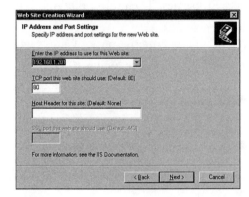

Figure 10.7 New site identification specification.

4. Specify the already-created folder or remote share to be used as the home directory for the new site, select whether Anonymous access is allowed, and then click Next.

5. Select the Web access permissions desired for the new site (see Figure 10.8); then click Next and Finish to create the site.

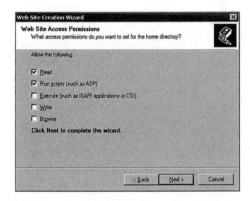

Figure 10.8 Web access permissions specification.

Web sites can use multiple IP addresses, custom ports, and host headers for identification. FTP sites can use only a single IP address and port combination. FTP sites do not support host headers. Also, remember that FTP sites support only Anonymous and Basic forms of authentication.

To add a new identifier or multiple IP addresses to the site, perform the following steps:

1. Right-click on the site and select Properties. Then select the Web Site tab.

2. Click on the Advanced button to the right of the IP Address box to open the Multiple Web Site Configuration interface (see Figure 10.9).

Figure 10.9 Multiple Web Site Configuration interface showing multiple addresses assigned to the Sales Web site.

3. Click on the Add button and specify the additional IP address and a custom port or appropriate host header if required.

4. Click OK to assign the new identifier.

5. After all new identifiers have been added, click OK to return to the Properties interface and click OK again to return to the MMC.

6. To apply the changes, right-click on the site and select Stop. Then right-click on the site again and select Start.

 If you do not restart the site, the changes made will not go into effect.

Creating a Virtual Folder

After a site has been created, you can add more virtual directories. These will appear to the client as if located within the home directory of the site, but they may be located elsewhere on the server itself or on a remote share.

To create a virtual folder within an existing FTP or Web site, perform the following steps within the Internet Services Manager MMC snap-in:

1. Right-click on the site and select New I Virtual Directory.

2. Provide the virtual directory with a meaningful name (this does not affect the name of the folder itself) and click Next.

3. Specify the target folder or share and click Next.

4. Select the Web access permissions desired for the new virtual folder. Click Next and Finish to create the virtual directory.

5. Edit any properties necessary and restart the site to make the new changes available to users.

Folder Web Sharing

After a site has been created, additional folders located on the server may be shared easily using the Windows Explorer interface by performing the following:

1. Right-click on the folder and select Sharing. Click on the Web Sharing tab.

2. Select the site in which to share the folder and select Share This Folder.

3. In the pop-up interface that appears, set the appropriate general access and execute permissions (see Figure 10.10). Click OK.

Figure 10.10   WebDAV Web folder opened within Windows Explorer.

4. Continue Adding additional Web shares to any other sites, if necessary. Click OK to close the Properties interface.

5. Restart the applicable site or sites so that your changes will take effect.

Accessing Web Sites

After a site has been created, the information may be accessed via several means. Web access using the HTTP protocol provides graphical and textual information presentation in a format that can be interlinked using an associated redirection called a hyperlink. FTP access provides a high-speed method of transferring files to and from a server.

Newer techniques allow for WebDAV access to shared Web folders, allowing IIS to perform as a central file server using port 80, as well as allowing the use of Microsoft's Office Suite Web site editing tool, FrontPage, to dynamically update site content on the Web server from a remote workstation.

Establishing a Connection

The primary client access utility for IIS-based connectivity is the browser. Internet Explorer is provided with the Windows operating systems and allows integrated access to Internet and intranet sites. The browser may be used in order to establish Web, FTP, and WebDAV connections to IIS resources.

Web Site Access

To open a connection to a Web site, enter the address of the proper site in the Address box within Internet Explorer. The address should be prefixed with the designation **http://** to specify the use of an HTTP connection on port 80 to the target server:

```
http://myserver.newcorp.com/
```

FTP Site Access

To open a connection to an FTP site, enter the address of the proper site in the Address box within Internet Explorer just as you would a Web site address, but prefixed with the designation **ftp://** to specify the use of an FTP connection on port 21 to the target server:

```
ftp://myserver.newcorp.com/
```

You can specify a login and password for the FTP connection by adding them before the server's address like this:

```
ftp://SalesAdmin:mypassword@myserver.newcorp.com/
```

The FTP service is often used to update information on a Web site by linking the same folders used in the Web site into the FTP site. FTP is used for large file transfers because it is faster than WebDAV connections using HTTP connectivity.

WebDAV

To open a WebDAV connection to a Web folder using Internet Explorer, enter the address of the proper site in the Address box just as you would for a Web site connection, including the **http://** prefix. To open the site as a Web folder, the user must select Open from the Internet Explorer header, enter the desired address, and select the Open As A Web Folder option. The folder will then be opened in the Internet Explorer browser, just as a normal share is opened in the Windows Browser. Figure 10.11 shows a WebDAV connection to the sales.newcorp.com site opened as a Web folder.

Figure 10.11   WebDAV Web folder opened within Internet Explorer.

Web folder connections can also be configured within the Add Network Place Wizard, found by opening the My Network Places icon on the desktop of Windows 2000 and later systems. The following steps will create a Web folder shortcut:

1. Double-click the Add Network Place shortcut.

2. Enter the desired Web folder's address (for example, **http://sales. newcorp.com/images/**) in the location. Click Next.

3. Enter a meaningful name for the shortcut and click Finish to create the new shortcut (see Figure 10.12).

Clicking on the shortcut in the My Network Places folder will open the Web folder. This shortcut may be copied elsewhere to distribute a simple connection to the Web folder.

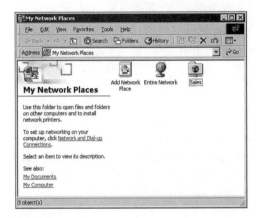

Figure 10.12 Shortcut to the Sales Web folder in the My Network Places folder.

Configuring Internet Explorer to Use a Proxy Server

Some networks are configured to use a proxy server for connectivity to external subnets. When routing through a proxy server, such as Microsoft's Proxy Server or Internet Security And Acceleration Server, Internet Explorer must be configured to forward its requests for HTTP connections through the proxy.

To do so within Internet Explorer, select Tools | Internet Options. Clicking the Connections tab and then selecting the LAN Settings button will open the interface (see Figure 10.13).

Figure 10.13 LAN Settings interface showing the proxy server setting.

It is often necessary to select the option to bypass Proxy Server For Local Addresses to allow connectivity with intranet servers located in the LAN. Otherwise, requests for these will be routed out through the proxy server, which may or may not have access to the internal resources being sought.

IIS Maintenance

Hackers wishing to gain entry into a server often target IIS. Many recent worms and viruses take advantage of known IIS exploits in order to spread themselves without the need for operator intervention. Because of this, it is important to maintain IIS in the most recent version and patch level. This process is discussed in greater detail in Chapter 11.

A regular backup of the IIS metabase is important. This backup will allow an administrator to rapidly recover from an accidental site deletion or an incorrect change across many sites. The metabase is unique to its home server and cannot be copied to another machine. It may be backed up by copying the %SystemDrive%\WINNT\System32\Inetsrv\Metabase.bin file elsewhere, or by using the Backup option within the Internet Services Manager. Right-clicking the server and selecting Backup/Restore Configuration will access this option.

Practice Questions

Question 1

> Which of the following terms refers to a link to a folder located in a different location than the home directory or to a share on a remote server, but appears to users as if located within the home directory?
>
> ○ a. Host header
>
> ○ b. Site
>
> ○ c. Virtual folder
>
> ○ d. Virtual site

Answer c is correct. A virtual folder is a link to another location which appears to users as if it were located within the site's home directory. Answer a is incorrect because a host header is a DNS alias used to allow a single IP address to uniquely identify multiple sites. Answer b is incorrect because a site is a uniquely identified connection to an FTP or Web server (which may contain virtual folders). Answer d is incorrect because a virtual site is simply a site other than the default site on a server.

Question 2

> There are two types of Web permissions:
>
> ➤ General Access
>
> ➤ Execute
>
> Match the following Web permissions with the proper type:
>
> ➤ Directory Browsing
>
> ➤ Read
>
> ➤ Scripts only
>
> ➤ Scripts and Executable
>
> ➤ Script Source Access
>
> ➤ Write

The correct answers are:

➤ General Access

    ➤ Directory Browsing

    ➤ Read

    ➤ Script Source Access

    ➤ Write

➤ Execute

    ➤ Scripts only

    ➤ Scripts and Executable

Question 3

Which of the following ports are used for default FTP and HTTP connections, respectively?

○ a. 20; 81

○ b. 21; 80

○ c. 23; 80

○ d. 80; 8080

Answer b is correct. By default, FTP connections are made using port 21, and HTTP connections are made using port 80. Answers a, c, and d are incorrect because they do not specify the correct ports for FTP and HTTP connections. Port 20 is used by the host monitoring protocol (HMP), port 23 is used for telnet connections, and port 8080 is an undefined port available for use.

Question 4

Which of the following are IIS components? [Check all correct answers]

❑ a. Documentation

❑ b. FTP

❑ c. NNTP Service

❑ d. SMTP Service

❑ e. WWW Server

Answers a, b, c, d, and e are all correct. Additional IIS components include the FrontPage 2000 Server Extensions and the IIS snap-in, which is listed in Administrative Tools as the Internet Service Manager snap-in.

Question 5

In order to provide Anonymous access to the files in a new Web site on the computer newserver.newcorp.com, you have decided to configure the NTFS access permissions for the files to include the IUSR_myserver account for both Read and Write permissions. Will this have the desired effect?

○ a. Yes

○ b. No

Answer b is correct. The name of the user account utilized in Anonymous authentication is the IUSR_<*computername*> account for the host server. Because the server is named newserver.newcorp.com, the proper account would be IUSR_newserver.

Question 6

The Permissions Wizard can set both Web and NTFS permissions. True or false?

○ a. True

○ b. False

Answer a is correct. The Permissions Wizard provides a simple way to set basic configurations of both Web and NTFS permissions on a site or folder.

Question 7

Which of the following must be evaluated to allow a user to access files using an intranet? [Check all correct answers]

❑ a. FTP permissions

❑ b. NTFS permissions

❑ c. User authentication

❑ d. Web permissions

❑ e. WWW permissions

Answers b, c, and d are correct. A user must be authenticated, Web permissions must allow access to the site, and NTFS permissions must allow the authenticated account to access the desired resources. Answers a and e are incorrect because there are no FTP or WWW specific access permissions.

Question 8

There are four types of IIS authentication:

➤ Anonymous

➤ Basic

➤ Digest

➤ Integrated Windows

Match the following qualities with the proper type:

➤ May be used only if clients are using Internet Explorer browsers

➤ Passes login credentials using a hashed value

➤ Users are prompted for logon credentials

➤ Uses the currently logged in user account

➤ Uses the IUSR_*<computername>* account

➤ Will not work through HTTP proxy connections

The correct answers are:

➤ Anonymous

   ➤Uses the IUSR_*<computername>* account

➤ Basic

   ➤Users are prompted for logon credentials

➤ Digest

   ➤May only be used if clients are using Internet Explorer browsers

   ➤Passes login credentials using a hashed value

   ➤Users are prompted for logon credentials

➤ Integrated Windows

   ➤May be used only if clients are using Internet Explorer browsers

   ➤Uses the currently logged-in user account

   ➤Will not work through HTTP proxy connections

Question 9

> Permissions specified in the site masters cannot be overridden by site-level specifications. True or false?
>
> ○ a. True
>
> ○ b. False

Answer b is correct. Lower-level permissions assignments will override higher-level specifications.

Question 10

> Which of the following types of connection is used for connecting to Web folders? [Check all correct answers]
>
> ❑ a. FTP
>
> ❑ b. HTTP
>
> ❑ c. NNTP
>
> ❑ d. SMTP
>
> ❑ e. WebDAV

Answers b and e are correct. Web folder connections use HTTP port 80 protocols to servers that support the WebDAV standards. Answer a is incorrect because the FTP protocol is used for high-speed file transfers. Answer c is incorrect because the NNTP service provides network news group support. Answer d is incorrect because the SMTP service provides basic email support.

Need to Know More?

 Stanek, William R.: *Microsoft Windows 2000 Administrator's Pocket Consultant*. Microsoft Press, Redmond, WA, 2000. ISBN 0-7356-0831-8. This is a helpful reference for network administrators to keep close at hand. The soft-cover trade-sized book is a condensed, easily carried version of many larger tomes of information.

 Microsoft Windows 2000 Server Resource Kit. Microsoft Press, Redmond, WA, 2000. ISBN 1-5723-1805-8. This exhaustive library covers detailed information on all aspects of Windows 2000 Server implementations. It is an invaluable reference for IT departments supporting Microsoft Windows 2000 networks.

 www.microsoft.com/windows2000/techinfo/proddoc/default. asp. *Windows 2000 Product Documentation Online*. This is a complete online copy of the documentation for all versions of the Windows 2000 operating system.

Troubleshooting

Terms you'll need to understand:

✓ Power-On Self Test (POST)
✓ Last Known Good Configuration
✓ Safe mode
✓ Recovery Console
✓ Task Manager
✓ System Monitor
✓ Network Monitor
✓ **ping**
✓ **tracert**
✓ **ipconfig**
✓ **hfnetchk**
✓ **qchain**
✓ Hotfix
✓ Service Pack

Techniques you'll need to master:

✓ Understanding the startup process and files used for Windows 95/98 systems and those running NT-family operating systems such as Windows 2000 and Windows XP
✓ Understanding the use of the advanced startup options, including Safe mode and the Last Known Good Configuration
✓ Identifying the utilities used in network configuration diagnostics such as ping and ipconfig.
✓ Understanding the use of the hfnetchk tool and the qchain utility in maintaining the most recent hotfixes on a system

Previous chapters have discussed the administrative actions to take when all is going well. This chapter will focus on the tools available for times when problems arise. This chapter is not meant as an exhaustive discussion of all possible troubleshooting scenarios, as the possible variety of errors and issues that may arise is too broad a topic for this book. Instead, we will present several useful tools that may be employed by a network administrator to identify and resolve problems

System Startup

When problems arise, often the first signs will appear during system startup. Until the startup process is completed and all settings are applied, a computer is unable to perform its normal functions. Errors arising during this phase may prevent user logon or access to the network, or they may cause a simple outright failure to boot completely.

Initialization

When power is first applied to a system, the basic input/output system (BIOS) chips on the motherboard run a set of self-diagnostic procedures referred to as the *Power-On Self-Test (POST)*. If errors such as a missing CPU or RAM are identified, a series of audio will issue from the system speaker. Each manufacturer's BIOS beep-codes will be different and will be listed in the documentation for the motherboard and BIOS version in use.

Windows 95/98 Startup

Until all legacy systems are upgraded, network administrators may need to know the basics for troubleshooting Windows 95/98 workstation boot errors. In order to properly diagnose errors occurring during the boot process, a network administrator should have a clear understanding of the Windows 95/98 files used in the startup process.

Windows 95/98 utilizes several files during the boot process:

➤ *Autoexec.bat*—An optional startup file that specifies commands and terminate-and-stay-resident (TSR) programs to be executed during the startup process

➤ *Config.sys*—An optional startup file used to specify drivers and system environment variables

➤ *Io.sys*—A hidden, read-only system file required for the boot process to load drivers and TSR programs specified in the config.sys and autoexec.bat files

➤ *Msdos.sys*—A hidden, read-only system file required for the boot process to provide support for older Windows applications

➤ *System.ini*—A required file that provides configuration information for older Windows applications

➤ *Win.ini*—A required file that provides configuration information for older Windows applications

➤ *Win.com*—A required startup file that initiates the Windows 95/98 boot process

Windows 95/98 systems perform their bootup procedure in the following manner:

1. The BIOS performs the POST and initializes connected hardware.

2. Real-Mode startup begins: Io.sys and Msdos.sys begin to load real-mode DOS and drivers such as Himem.sys.

3. Config.sys is processed to initialize environmental variables and load drivers.

4. Autoexec.bat is processed to perform any initialization commands defined.

5. Protected mode begins: Win.com initiates the load of Windows 95/98 components.

6. Win.ini and System.ini are processed to set non-registry-based configuration options.

7. The graphical user interface (GUI) is displayed for system use.

Windows NT/2000/XP Startup

More modern versions of Windows borrow from the NT base and share similar startup procedures. Windows NT and its descendants such as Windows 2000 and Windows XP utilize a boot loader located on the system partition to begin the startup process. This may be configured to provide multi-boot capabilities on systems that have multiple versions of Windows loaded onto the same computer, usually on different partitions, although other options exist.

In order to properly diagnose errors occurring during the boot process of a Windows NT-family system, a network administrator should have a clear understanding of the files used in the startup process.

Windows NT-family systems utilize several files during the boot process:

➤ *Boot.ini*—A hidden, read-only file located on the System partition that is used to specify boot options, including multiboot selection in the Operating System Selection menu displayed during startup.

➤ *Device Drivers*—Drivers required for installed system hardware. These are located on the Boot partition, typically in *%SystemRoot%*\WINNT\ System32\drivers\.

➤ *Hal.dll*—The *Hardware Abstraction Layer (HAL)* file, which is located on the Boot partition. This is a stripped-down version of the kernel responsible for performing translation between platform-specific hardware devices and the Windows kernel.

➤ *Ntbootd.sys*—A hidden, read-only system file located on the System partition on machines that boot using a small-computer system interface (SCSI) type drive.

➤ *Ntdetect.com*—A hidden, read-only system file located on the System partition that is used by Ntldr to provide information on the current system hardware.

➤ *Ntldr*—A required hidden, read-only system file located on the System partition that initiates the boot process for NT-family systems.

➤ *Ntoskrnl.exe*—The Windows system kernel file, located on the Boot partition, typically in *%SystemRoot%*\WINNT\System32\.

➤ *System.dat*—A part of the Windows registry located on the Boot partition and responsible for specifying which device drivers and services will be loaded during the startup process. This is typically located in *%SystemRoot%*\WINNT\System32\Config\.

Windows NT-family systems perform their boot-up procedure in the following manner:

1. The BIOS performs the POST and initializes connected hardware.

2. The Ntldr initializes the CPU.

3. The Boot.ini file is accessed to present the Operating System Selection menu to the user.

4. If a selection is made, or the default-selection timer expires, the appropriate operation system begins to load.

5. Ntdetect.com is run to scan the system hardware.

6. Ntldr loads the Ntoskrnl.exe and Hal.dll files.

7. The System.dat file and Device Driver files are loaded.

8. Ntoskrnl.exe is initialized, starting the Kernel Load phase.

9. During the Kernel Load phase, the Hal.dll is initialized and Device Driver files specified for startup load in the System.dat file are loaded.

10. Kernel Initialization begins, during which the drivers loaded during the Kernel Load phase are initialized, along with any specified in the System.dat file for this phase of the boot process.

11. The Services Load phase begins, loading the session manager (smss.exe), which initializes the memory management key and carries out any required registry entries to start up necessary services and components for Windows operation.

12. The Win32 Subsystem Start process begins after all services are loaded and group policies applied. The Winlogon.exe process is initialized, starting the local security authority (lsass.exe) and displaying the logon dialog box.

Advanced Startup Options

When system startup fails, your first step should be to restart the system using one of the advanced startup options by pressing the F8 key during the system startup process. Table 11.1 details the advanced startup options.

Table 11.1 Windows advanced startup options.	
Option	Description
Command Prompt Only	Windows 95/98-only option that performs only the DOS-based portion of the startup before opening a command prompt.
Debugging Mode	Used in conjunction with a second computer directly connected by a serial cable. Performs detailed low-level debugging of system and kernel-level processes for NT-family machines.

(continued)

Table 11.1 Windows advanced startup options *(continued)*	
Option	**Description**
Enable VGA Mode	Performs a normal startup but prevents the load of video drivers other than the default VGA mode driver.
Last Known Good Configuration	Used to recover to the configuration used during the last successful logon on NT-family systems. Each time a logon occurs, the operating system stores the current configuration so that newly loaded drivers which prevent system startup may be "rolled back" to the Last Known Good Configuration.
Logged	Logs all of the drivers and services loaded at startup into the %*SystemRoot*%\WINNT\Ntbtlog.txt file.
Safe Mode	Loads only the minimum drivers necessary to start the computer, logging all options to the Ntbtlog.txt file. Network, video, and other peripheral device drivers are not loaded, allowing an administrator to log on in Safe mode and remove newly loaded drivers that are preventing successful startup.
Safe Mode With Command Prompt	Starts the system in Safe mode at a command-prompt interface. NT-family systems require a logon before command-prompt access is provided.
Safe Mode With Networking	Performs a Safe mode startup, also loading network drivers in order to allow domain logon or remote-file access during the repair process. This option is not available to Windows 95/98 systems.
Step-By-Step Confirmation	Windows 95/98-only option that allows users to confirm each driver as it is loaded.

* If a driver failure occurs, the Last Known Good Configuration option cannot be used to roll back to a previous configuration if the user logs onto the machine, because this will overwrite the stored configuration with the current one.

Be familiar with the options in Table 11.1, as several questions on the exam may deal with selecting the appropriate Advanced Startup option for specified requirements. In particular, remember that the Last Known Good Configuration only allows driver roll-back to the last successful logon.

Recovery Console

If all advanced startup options fail, the Recovery Console may be used to start the computer and reconfigure services that are preventing the startup process from completing, as well as to format drives, repair the system by copying files from a floppy or CD, repair the boot sector using the **fixboot** command, or repair the master boot record using the **fixmbr** command.

 The Recovery Console allows complete control over the local system. Improper use could render the system unrecoverable. Only experienced administrators should use this tool.

Installing the Recovery Console on a Working System

The Recovery Console may be installed on a functioning Windows 2000 system as an option in the Operating System Selection menu by loading the command console from the Windows 2000 installation CD. Select Run from the Start menu, and then enter the following code:

```
<drivepath>\i386\winnt32.exe /cmdcons
```

Select Yes and follow the prompts to install the Recovery Console. This will only work on a currently functioning Windows 2000 system.

Running the Recovery Console from the Windows 2000 Installation CD

If a system is not currently functional, and the Recovery Console was not previously loaded as a startup option, the Recovery Console may also be run directly from the Windows 2000 installation CD.

The boot order of the system must be configured in its BIOS in order to attempt to boot from the CD before the hard drive, and the Windows 2000 startup CD must be placed in the CD-ROM drive. During initialization, the user will be prompted to Press Any Key To Boot From CD. Pressing a key here will allow the system to boot from the Windows 2000 installation CD.

After the files have loaded, press Enter at the Notification page and select **r** for recovery on the Welcome To Setup page. Then select the current installation to repair and type the password for the Administrator account when prompted.

System Monitoring

Many times, it is necessary to identify system configuration settings and operational details of ongoing processes to identify potential areas of conflict. Windows 2000 and later operating systems provide a variety of utilities that may be used to determine configuration settings, current resource utilization, and network activity.

System Configuration

Microsoft Windows provides several useful GUIs that can be used to determine system configuration settings, including the System Configuration utility and the System Information utility. These utilities may be used to identify the current services and configuration settings on a Windows 2000 or later system.

System Configuration Utility

Windows 98 and Windows XP include the System Configuration utility, which allows an administrator to directly configure many startup options and services. The System Configuration utility (msconfig.exe) and its help file (msconfig.chm) can be copied from a Windows XP system for use on a Windows 2000 system as well.

You can use the System Configuration utility to specify an interactive startup in which device drivers and software are loaded after user response to the prompts for each, or as a selective startup in which certain portions of the configuration are bypassed during setup (see Figure 11.1).

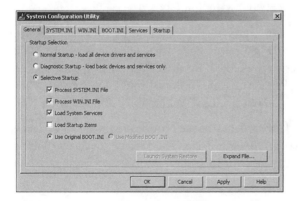

Figure 11.1 System Configuration utility running on a Windows 2000 system.

System Information Utility

You can use the System Information utility to identify currently installed hardware, software, and configuration details. Access this utility by selecting Start I Run and then typing "msinfo32.exe". Figure 11.2 shows an example of this utility in use.

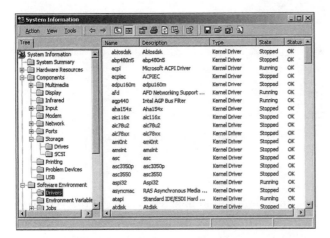

Figure 11.2   System Information utility showing the current software drivers.

Performance and Resource Utilization

When bottlenecks occur at the hardware level, you should first identify resource utilization to determine what aspects of the hardware may require upgrade or replacement. Performance monitoring may be accomplished using the Task Manager, System Monitor, and Network Monitor utilities.

Task Manager

The Windows 2000 Task Manager allows you to access information about currently running applications and processes, as well as performance-related information such as current memory and CPU utilization levels (see Figure 11.3). Selecting Ctrl+Alt+Delete and selecting Task Manager from the options listed will open the Task Manager utility.

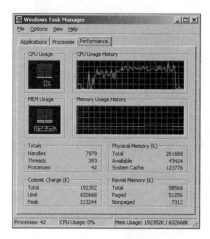

Figure 11.3 Windows Task Manager showing current performance information.

System Monitor

The Windows 2000 System Monitor is an updated version of the Windows NT Performance Monitor utility. You access this MMC snap-in using the Performance option within the Administrative Tools folder located in the Control Panel.

The System Monitor can graphically present information on resource utilization as specified by the administrator (see Figure 11.4) and can also generate alerts and write events to the Event Log to monitor utilization over a period of time.

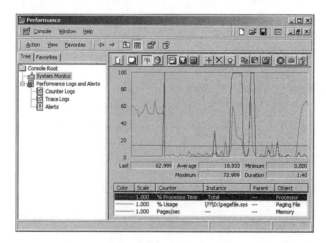

Figure 11.4 System Monitor showing tracking of CPU and Pagefile utilization.

Before making system changes, it is best to establish a *baseline*, or normal level of operations. After changes have been made, a new baseline should be made to compare the effects of the change.

Network Monitor

Windows 2000 Server/Advanced Server systems can be configured to monitor network traffic to and from themselves using the Network Monitor diagnostic utility, which you can select as a Detail option of the Management And Monitoring Tools selection within the Add/Remove Windows Components Wizard accessed through the Add/Remove Programs Wizard found in the Control Panel.

You can use the Network Monitor to inspect packet-level data relating to the system or a particular network protocol (see Figure 11.5). Keep in mind that extended packet logging is very resource intensive and may quickly overrun all available storage space.

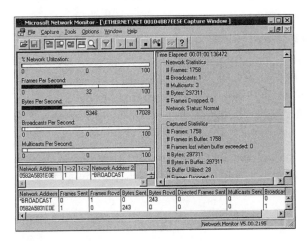

Figure 11.5   Network Monitor logging session.

 A complete version of Network Monitor is available in the Microsoft Systems Management Server (SMS). The complete version allows logging of all traffic within a particular subnet.

Event Viewer

The Event Viewer MMC snap-in, located within the Administrative Tools folder in the Control Panel, allows an administrator to review information logged when events occur within Windows 2000 components and applications, as well as security-related events if auditing has been enabled (detailed in Chapter 13). This is a good place to look to determine which services might have failed during startup. The Event Viewer is described in detail in Chapter 13.

Network Diagnostics

After any startup issues have been resolved, you may discover additional network-related problems preventing access to the Internet, file shares, name resolution services, or other forms of network resources. After checking for hardware and driver issues, you may need to troubleshoot network connectivity using one of the available tools provided by Microsoft.

Network Connectivity

Connections within modern TCP/IP based networks require proper configuration of the TCP/IP settings, as well as the specification of available name resolution servers. DNS, DHCP, and TCP/IP configuration have been discussed in previous chapters (see Chapters 2,4, and 5). If any of these terms are still unclear to you, please review the appropriate chapters as required.

The Windows operating system includes several utilities that are used to verify proper network connectivity, including the **ping**, **pathping**, **tracert**, **ipconfig**, **nbtstat**, **netdiag**, and **netstat** utilities.

ping.exe

To determine if a remote resource is available via TCP/IP networking, use the ping.exe command-line utility. This utility establishes the round-trip time for a connection to a specified remote server, whether specified by FQDN or IP address. See Listing 11.1 for a sample use of the **ping** command.

Listing 11.1 An example of the ping command.

```
C:\>ping myserver.mycorp.com
Pinging myserver.mycorp.com [192.168.1.200] with 32 bytes of data:
Reply from 192.168.1.200: bytes=32 time<10ms TTL=253
Reply from 192.168.1.200: bytes=32 time<10ms TTL=253
Reply from 192.168.1.200: bytes=32 time<10ms TTL=253
```

Listing 11.1   An example of the ping command *(continued)*

```
Reply from 192.168.1.200: bytes=32 time<10ms TTL=253
Ping statistics for 192.168.1.200:
    Packets: Sent = 4, Received = 4, Lost = 0 (0% loss),
Approximate round trip times in milli-seconds:
    Minimum = 0ms, Maximum = 0ms, Average = 0ms
```

You can also use **ping** to verify that the TCP/IP protocol has been bound to the local adapter by specifying the *localhost* address:

```
C:\>ping localhost
Pinging station3.mycorp.com [127.0.0.1] with 32 bytes of data:
Reply from 127.0.0.1: bytes=32 time<10ms TTL=128
Reply from 127.0.0.1: bytes=32 time<10ms TTL=128
Reply from 127.0.0.1: bytes=32 time<10ms TTL=128
Reply from 127.0.0.1: bytes=32 time<10ms TTL=128
Ping statistics for 127.0.0.1:
    Packets: Sent = 4, Received = 4, Lost = 0 (0% loss),
Approximate round trip times in milli-seconds:
    Minimum = 0ms, Maximum = 0ms, Average = 0ms
```

pathping.exe

To test a route over a period of time, use the **pathping.exe** command-line utility. This utility allows multiple testing of each hop along the route over a period of time (the default is 75 seconds). See Listing 11.2 for a sample use of the **pathping** command.

Listing 11.2   An example of the pathping command.

```
C:\>pathping mysrv.mycorp.com
Tracing route to mysrv.mycorp.com [192.168.1.200] over a maximum of 30 hops:
  0  wkstn1.mycorp.com [192.168.0.231]
  1  dallas-1.mycorp.com [192.168.0.1]
  2  newyrk-1.mycorp.com [192.168.1.1]
  3  mysrv.mycorp.com [192.168.1.200]
Computing statistics for 75 seconds...
                Source to Here    This Node/Link
Hop  RTT     Lost/Sent = Pct   Lost/Sent = Pct   Address
  0                                               wkstn1.mycorp.com
[192.168.0.231]
                                0/ 100 =  0%    |
  1    0ms    0/ 100 =  0%      0/ 100 =  0%    dallas-1.mycorp.com
[192.168.0.1]
                                0/ 100 =  0%    |
  2    0ms    0/ 100 =  0%      0/ 100 =  0%    newyrk-1.mycorp.com
[192.168.1.1]
                                0/ 100 =  0%    |
  3    0ms    0/ 100 =  0%      0/ 100 =  0%    mysrv.mycorp.com
[192.168.1.200]
Trace complete.
```

tracert.exe

To determine if a network failure between the local system and a remote resource via TCP/IP networking is affecting performance, use the tracert.exe command-line utility. This utility establishes the time required for each hop in the connection to a specified remote server, whether specified by FQDN or IP address. See Listing 11.3 for a sample use of the **tracert** command.

Listing 11.3 An example of the tracert command.

```
C:\>tracert myserver.mycorp.com
Tracing route to myserver.mycorp.com [192.168.1.200] over a maximum of 30
hops:
  1   <10 ms   <10 ms   <10 ms   dallas-1.mycorp.com [192.168.0.1]
  2   <10 ms   <10 ms   <10 ms   newyork-1.mycorp.com [192.168.1.1]
  3   <10 ms   <10 ms   <10 ms   myserver.mycorp.com [192.168.1.200]
Trace complete.
```

A failure to connect to a router along the path will result in a listing like this:

```
  2      *        *        *       Request timed out.
```

ipconfig.exe

On Windows NT-family systems, you use the ipconfig.exe command-line utility to display current TCP/IP settings and to release and refresh DHCP leases. Table 11.2 details the most common uses of this command.

Table 11.2 Common uses of the ipconfig command.

Use	Purpose
ipconfig	Displays basic information on the current TCP/IP configuration for all network connections.
Ipconfig /?	Displays the help file for this command.
ipconfig /all	Displays detailed current TCP/IP configuration information for all network connections.
ipconfig /release	Releases all currently-held DHCP leases.
ipconfig /renew	Renews DHCP leases for all adapters configured for automatic addressing via DHCP.
Ipconfig /flushdns	Flushes the local DNS name cache.

Windows 98/98 machines use the **winipcfg** command instead of the ipconfig.exe utility.

nbtstat.exe

The nbtstat.exe command-line utility allows viewing and flushing of the NetBIOS name cache, which is populated by broadcast and WINS lookups. Table 11.3 details the most common uses of this command.

Table 11.3 Common uses of the nbtstat command.	
Use	**Purpose**
nbtstat	Displays the help file for this command.
nbtstat -a <*name*>	Lists the contents of a remote system's NBT cache using its FQDN name.
nbtstat -A <*IP address*>	Lists the contents of a remote system's NBT cache using its IP address.
nbtstat -c	Lists the contents of the NBT cache.
nbtstat -r	Lists names resolved by broadcast and WINS lookup.
nbtstat -R	Flushes and reloads the NBT cache.
nbtstat -RR	Sends a Name Release to the WINS server and then performs a refresh.

Netdiag.exe

The netdiag.exe command-line utility functions like an expanded version of the **ipconfig /all** command, adding tests for domain membership and connectivity to a Domain Controller, as well as a basic listing of installed hotfixes, default gateway availability, DNS and WINS server availability, IPSec policy settings, trust verification, and a host of other domain-level diagnostic items.

Netstat.exe

The **netstat** command-line utility displays information on current communications protocols and details of current TCP/IP connections.

Table 11.4 details the most common uses of this command.

Table 11.4 Common uses of the netstat command.	
Use	**Purpose**
netstat /?	Displays the help file for this command.
netstat -a	Lists all current connections and listing ports.
netstat -r	Displays the current local routing table cache.
netstat -s	Provides statistics for each available protocol.

Replication

The Windows 2000 Server/Advanced Server Support Tools and the Windows 2000 Server Resource Kit provide a large number of specific-purpose utilities for identifying and resolving replication issues within an Active Directory environment. It is worth remembering a few utilities and their uses for this exam:

➤ *Gpresult*—This command-line utility from the Windows 2000 Server Resource Kit allows verification of group policy settings for the current user.

➤ *Repadmin*—This command-line utility from the Support Toolsprovides editing capability for Active Directory objects, as well as the ability to manually force server replication.

➤ *Replmon*—This GUI utility from the Support Tools allows you to monitor the replication status of one or more servers within an Active Directory network, as well as the ability to manually force replication.

Security Updates

As soon as a security problem has been identified, Microsoft will work to provide a patch to correct the problem. These single-problem patches are known as *hotfixes*. From time to time, Microsoft will combine all current hotfixes and other non-security-related corrections into a single package known as a *service pack*. Hotfixes are designated by name as belonging to a particular service-pack collection. Hotfixes should never be applied if they predate the most recent service pack. Only the most recent service pack and hotfixes released after it should be applied.

Hotfixes and service packs are provided separately for each operating system, application suite, and application. This means you don't need to download every possible patch when a system only requires an operating system update, for example. Hotfixes and service packs may be obtained through the Downloads button on the Microsoft Security home page, located at **www.microsoft.com/security/**.

Many additional tools to simplify hotfix maintenance are available at the **www.microsoft.com/security/ site** under the Tools And Checklists selection.

Qchain.exe

Currently, each hotfix must be executed and then the system restarted in most cases. Microsoft is working to produce non-reboot patch versions, but for network administrators working with existing software, the requirement to reboot after each hotfix makes deployment of multi-hotfix updates a daunting task.

Microsoft has provided a useful tool to resolve this problem: the qchain.exe utility. This command-line utility allows you to install multiple hotfixes at one time, with the qchain.exe program run last to "squeeze" all the hotfixes together into a single applied patch. This patch can be compiled into a batch-file for easy deployment within a large enterprise network. See Listing 11.4 for a sample batchfile using the qchain utility to apply multiple hotfixes at one time.

Listing 11.4   A sample batchfile using the qchain utility to apply multiple hotfixes at one time.

```
@echo off
q300972_w2k_sp3_x86_en.exe -m -z
q301625_w2k_sp3_x86_en.exe -m -z
q302755_w2k_sp3_x86_en.exe -m -z
q303984_w2k_sp3_x86_en.exe -m -z
q307454_w2k_sp3_x86_en.exe -m -z
qchain.exe
@echo Hotfix Application Completed - Reboot to complete Installation
@echo on
```

Hfnetchk.exe

A useful command-line utility called hfnetchk.exe is available for scanning systems for needed hotfixes. This utility can scan a single computer, a sub-net, or all computers within a domain in order to identify needed hotfixes for each. See Listing 11.5 for a sample scan of the local system using the hfnetchk utility.

Listing 11.5   A sample scan of the local system using the hfnetchk utility.

```
C:\ hfnetchk
Scanning MYSERVER
.............................................................
...
Done scanning MYSERVER
----------------------------
MYSERVER
----------------------------
        WINDOWS 2000 SERVER SP2
                Patch NOT Found MS01-013      Q285156
                WARNING         MS01-022      Q296441
        Internet Explorer 5.5 SP2
                Patch NOT Found MS01-058      Q313675
```

The hfnetchk utility can be used with the default Extensible Markup Language (XML) data file that is automatically downloaded by the utility from Microsoft, or with a customized version created by an administrator to scan for particular items.

Personal Security Advisor

As part of its "Get Secure and Stay Secure" initiative, Microsoft has made available a simple Web-accessible scanning tool that will scan the local system for security issues. The Personal Security Advisor is also available through the Microsoft security Web site, under the Tools And Checklists option. Figure 11.6 shows a sample scan produced using the Personal Security Advisor.

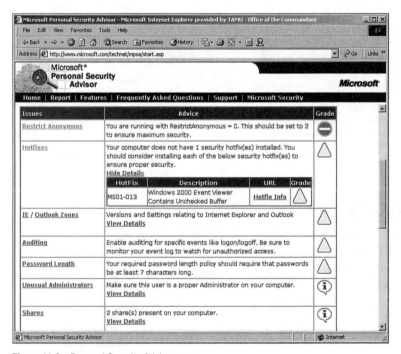

Figure 11.6   Personal Security Advisor scan.

IISLockDown

Another useful tool provided on the Microsoft Security site is the IISLockDown utility, which allows restriction of access to Microsoft's IIS sites using a GUI wizard. This utility provides a simple means to secure an IIS installation using standard pre-tested configuration options.

Practice Questions

Question 1

Arrange in proper order the following steps in a Windows 95/98 startup process:

Autoexec.bat is processed

Config.sys is processed

GUI is displayed

POST occurs

Protected mode begins

Real-mode startup begins

Win.ini is processed

The correct answer is (in order):

POST occurs

Real-mode startup begins

Config.sys is processed

Autoexec.bat is processed

Protected mode beings

Win.ini is processed

GUI is displayed

Question 2

The startup files used by NT-family systems are specified as belonging on the System partition (usually C:\) or the Boot partition and share (usually C:\WINNT\...):

Boot

System

Match the following files with the proper location required for proper system startup:

Boot.ini

Device Drivers

Hal.dll

Ntdetect.com

Ntldr

Ntoskrnl.exe

System.dat

The correct answers are:

Boot

> Device Drivers
>
> Hal.dll
>
> Ntoskrnl.exe
>
> System.dat

System

> Boot.ini
>
> Ntdetect.com
>
> Ntldr

Question 3

The local security authority (lsass.exe) is responsible for the initialization of the memory management key. True or false?

○ a. True

○ b. False

Answer b is correct. The local security authority (lsass.exe) handles the display and use of the logon dialog box. The session manager (smss.exe) is responsible for initializing the memory management key.

Question 4

Which of the following advanced mode startup options will log configuration details to the Ntbtlog.txt file? [Check all correct answers]

❑ a. Command Prompt Only

❑ b. Enable VGA Mode

❑ c. Last Known Good Configuration

❑ d. Logged

❑ e. Safe Mode

❑ f. Safe Mode With Networking

Answers d, e, and f are correct. The Logged and Safe Mode advanced mode startup options will log service and driver configuration information to the *%SystemRoot%*\WINNT\Ntbtlog.txt file. Answer a, b, and c are incorrect because these modes do not log startup configuration information.

Question 5

A local administrator in the Austin office calls to ask you if she should use the Last Known Good Configuration advanced startup mode to roll back a bad video driver that is preventing proper system function. She tells you that after installing the driver, everything was working well, but after the reboot, the user cannot see anything but wavy lines, even after logging into the system. She has tried logging in using a Domain Administrator account and gets the same thing. Will rebooting to the Last Known Good Configuration fix the problem?

○ a. Yes

○ b. No

Answer b is correct. Because the user has logged in successfully since the change was made, the Last Known Good Configuration would have been updated to include the new drivers in the stored configuration. Rebooting and performing the Enable VGA Mode startup option would allow her to access the system and change the video driver settings.

Question 6

> A local administrator in the San Antonio office calls to tell you that he has tried all the advanced startup options and still cannot get a critical system to start up long enough to format a drive and copy files from the user data share. He tells you that he forgot to install the Recovery Console after setting up the machine initially. Can he still get to the Recovery Console now?
>
> ○ a. Yes
>
> ○ b. No

Answer a is correct. He can boot using the Windows 2000 Server installation CD and run the Recovery Console directly from the CD-ROM.

Question 7

> Three resource utilization utilities are available in Windows 2000:
>
> Network Monitor
>
> System Monitor
>
> Task Manager
>
> Match the following characteristics with the appropriate utility:
>
> Can be selected from the options listed when Ctrl+Alt+Delete is selected
>
> Can log data over a period of time
>
> Can collect packet data
>
> Can display current information about current process resource utilization
>
> Can generate alerts when system utilization reaches a specified threshold

The correct answers are:

Network Monitor

Can log data over a period of time

Can collect packet data

System Monitor

Can log data over a period of time

Can display current information about current process resource utilization

Can generate alerts when system utilization reaches a specified threshold

Task Manager

Can be selected from the options listed when Ctrl+Alt+Delete is selected

Can display current information about current process resource utilization

Question 8

Given this output:
```
Reply from 192.168.1.200: bytes=32 time<10ms TTL=253
Reply from 192.168.1.200: bytes=32 time<10ms TTL=253
Reply from 192.168.1.200: bytes=32 time<10ms TTL=253
Reply from 192.168.1.200: bytes=32 time<10ms TTL=253
```

Which utility was used?

O a. ipconfig

O b. netdiag

O c. ping

O d. tracert

Answer c is correct. The ping utility attempts repeated connections to a target address in order to determine connectivity. Answers a and b are incorrect because the ipconfig and netdiag utilities are used to determine local TCP/IP configuration and domain-level connectivity, respectively. Answer d is incorrect because the tracertutility details the connection time for each successive hop in the routing to a target server.

Question 9

Which command should be used to view the TCP/IP settings on a Windows 95/98 machine?

O a. ipconfig

O b. ipconfig /all

O c. ipconfig /win16

O d. ipconfig /9x

O e. winipcfg

Answer e is correct. The **winipcfg** command is used on Windows 95/98 systems to display TCP/IP configuration details. Answers a and b are incorrect because the **ipconfig** command is used on Windows NT-family operating systems. Answers c and d are incorrect because **/win16** and **/9x** are not valid switches for the **ipconfig** command.

Question 10

The hfnetchk utility can identify and install multiple required hotfixes at one time. True or false?

○ a. True

○ b. False

Answer b is correct. The hfnetchk utility can identify any required hotfixes on a system, but to install multiple hotfixes at one time, the hotfixes must be downloaded and applied to the local system. To apply multiple hotfixes at once, you should use the qchain utility.

Need to Know More?

 Stanek, William R.: *Microsoft Windows 2000 Administrator's Pocket Consultant*. Microsoft Press, Redmond, WA, 2000. ISBN 0-7356-0831-8. This is a helpful reference for network administrators to keep close at hand. The soft-cover trade-sized book is a condensed, easily carried version of many larger tomes of information.

 Microsoft Windows 2000 Server Resource Kit. Microsoft Press, Redmond, WA, 2000. ISBN 1-5723-1805-8. This exhaustive library covers detailed information on all aspects of Windows 2000 Server implementations. It is an invaluable reference for IT departments supporting Microsoft Windows 2000 networks.

 www.microsoft.com/security. *Microsoft Security.* This is a dynamic source for all the newest hotfixes, service packs, utilities, and security-related white papers for network administrators working with the Windows environment.

 www.microsoft.com/windows2000/techinfo/proddoc/default. asp. *Windows 2000 Product Documentation Online.* This is a complete online copy of the documentation for all versions of the Windows 2000 operating system.

Remote Access

Terms you'll need to understand:

✓ Virtual Private Network (VPN) Connections
✓ Internet Connection Sharing (ICS)
✓ Point-to-Point Protocol (PPP)
✓ Layer-2 Tunneling Protocol (L2TP)
✓ Point-to-Point Tunneling Protocol (PPTP)
✓ Challenge Handshake Authentication Protocol (CHAP)
✓ Extensible Authentication Protocol (EAP)
✓ Internet Protocol Security (IPSec)
✓ Remote access policies

Techniques you'll need to master:

✓ Understanding the use of virtual private network connections to create secure connections over the Internet
✓ Understanding the process by which LAN protocols tunnel through WAN protocols, which then tunnel through VPN protocols
✓ Recognizing the authentication methods available to Windows 2000 Routing And Remote Access servers
✓ Identifying the three components of remote access properties and how they differ from Active Directory group policies

Previous chapters have covered network connectivity within a contiguous local area network (LAN). Mobile users and telecommuters working from home may also need the same level of access to resources, which will require the use of wide area network (WAN) protocols for connectivity. Windows 2000 uses the Routing And Remote Access Service (RRAS) to allow remote users to establish connections using dial-up or secured virtual private network (VPN) connections through the Internet, to provide support for private network access to Internet resources using network address translation (NAT), and to allow users within a private network to collectively share a single network or dial-up connection using Internet connection sharing (ICS).

This chapter covers the use of the Routing And Remote Access service to provide remote users access to LAN resources through dial-up or VPN connections. It provides instructions for creating and configuring remote access policies and allowing or restricting remote connections. Administrators should be familiar with the basic LAN topics discussed in Chapter 2.

Overview of Remote Acess

Modern network support often requires remote and mobile users to connect to home-office resources as if located within the LAN. Remote users dialup using modem connections over public switched telephone networks, IDSN lines, cable modems, or direct connections to metropolitan area networks (MANs), which provide direct connectivity without the security of a fully internal LAN. To ensure the security of the network and data transmissions between the remote user and the local network, WAN connections use a variety of authentication, communication, and encryption schemes.

Private Networks

To improve security and decrease the number of external IP addresses leased from an Internet service provider (ISP), it is often necessary to separate internal private networks from external public resources or to allow many internal systems to use NAT to share a small number of external IP addresses. In remote offices, a Windows 2000 or XP system with Internet connection sharing (ICS) enabled allows internal computers to share a single external network connection.

Network Address Translation

Windows 2000 servers running the Routing And Remote Access service can allow an internal network using a private addressing scheme to connect to external Internet resources. RRAS also allows external access to distributed internal resources using a small number of external public addresses. Reducing the number of required public addresses reduces the cost of leasing external IP address blocks from ISPs, and gives the administrator control over IP and port connections so that connections made to the same public address can be redirected to different internal servers based on the port used for connection.

For example, suppose that the DNS entry for mainoffice.mycorp.com were assigned to the public leased IP address of 129.4.26.19. Using NAT, all computers within the main office might connect to external Internet resources through this single connection, whereas external users might connect to mainoffice.mycorp.com using FTP and Web connections, that redirect traffic to the FTP and WWW servers within the internal private network (see Figure 12.1).

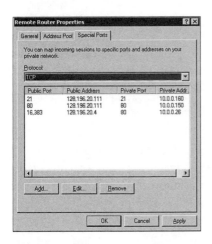

Figure 12.1 NAT configuration showing public to private address and port redirection.

Each public IP address and port can be individually redirected to a different internal IP address and port as desired, so that the administrator can provide common services on nonstandard ports, reducing the ability of hackers to scan public ports and profile a system for attack.

ICS

Using ICS, an external dial-up connection may be shared to multiple machines on an internal LAN. This process uses a limited form of the network address translation capability, configuring the internal network connection of the system to use the private address of 192.168.0.1, which becomes the default gateway for all other machines within the private network (which must use the private network address block starting with 192.168.0.0). You configure this option within the Routing And Remote Access Configuration Wizard. Alternately, from the Control Panel you can use the Network and Dial-up Connections utility in order to configure Routing and Remote Access using the Properties for a dial-up connection (see Figure 12.2).

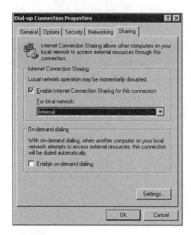

Figure 12.2 Dial-up properties showing Internet connection sharing enabled for the Internal network interface.

A dial-up connection configured for Internet connection sharing can also have on-demand dialing enabled. If enabled, when any client machine within the network tries to connect to external network resources, the private network will trigger the gateway computer to attempt to create a dial-up connection. No user intervention is required on the server for this action to occur.

Remote Access

Previous chapters have discussed establishing connections to shared resources from within a LAN, and creating terminal service sessions to a server configured to support Terminal Service connections. A Terminal Services-enabled server allows the use of client computers unable to run the applications themselves, and simplifies application upgrade because changes to the applications loaded on the server will be available to all users establishing Terminal Services connections.

You will often find it necessary to allow mobile users, telecommuters or users located in remote offices secured connections to main office resources as if they were physically connected to the LAN. You do this using WAN communications protocols to establish dial-up or secured VPN connections over the Internet.

For traveling personnel, it is often significantly less expensive to use a VPN connection through a broadly available ISP that provides local connections to the Internet, because you will avoid the long-distance charges for direct dial-up connections.

WAN Protocols

Remote connections use a combination of both WAN protocols and LAN protocols for communication. A connection is established between the client and server using a WAN protocol, and data traffic occurs by tunneling through this connection using LAN protocols such as TCP/IP, NWLink, NetBEUI, or AppleTalk. These are discussed in detail in Chapter 2.

WAN protocols used by Windows 2000 remote services include:

➤ *AppleTalk Remote Access Protocol (ARAP)*—A proprietary protocol that allows Apple Macintosh systems to connect to a Windows 2000 remote access server using the AppleTalk protocol.

➤ *Microsoft Remote Access Service (RAS) protocol*—A proprietary Microsoft-created protocol that supports NetBEUI connections, allowing legacy systems such as Windows for Workgroups to access local resources. TCP/IP connections are unavailable to these clients, so only local resources will be available.

➤ *Point-to-Point Protocol (PPP)*—The most commonly used protocol, which allows connectivity to any system using PPP.

By default, all LAN protocols configured on the server are enabled for remote access connections when the Routing And Remote Access service is configured.

VPN Protocols

Connections across unsecured connections such as the Internet or shared MANs require additional security to prevent unauthorized access to sensitive data. To provide this security, you enable an additional layer of tunneling with a VPN protocol. The protocol establishes a secured VPN connection between client and server over the Internet, through which a PPP WAN connection is created, which in turn allows the tunneling of data using LAN protocols such as TCP/IP.

VPN protocols used by Windows 2000 include:

➤ *Layer-2 Tunneling Protocol (L2TP)*—Provides a secured connection using tunnel authentication and Internet Protocol Security (IPSec) computer-level authentication for computers running Windows 2000 or later operating systems. This protocol may function across many types of inter-network media including IP, frame-relay, and X.25 dedicated connections.

➤ *Point-to-Point Tunneling Protocol (PPTP)*—Provides a moderately secure tunnel for PPP connections over an IP internetwork. This protocol does not support IPSec encryption natively.

By default, both protocols are enabled when VPN ports are created.

Authentication Protocols

Users must be authenticated before they can connect to remote access servers. The Windows 2000 Routing And Remote Access service provides several standard authentication protocols as well as the EAP used for smart card or biometric authentication devices.

Standard Authentication Methods

The standard authentication protocols available for Windows 2000 remote access include:

➤ *Challenge Handshake Authentication Protocol (CHAP)*—A highly secure challenge-response authentication method used for clients running non-Windows operating systems. CHAP is also known as Message Digest 5 Challenge Handshake Authentication Protocol (MD5 CHAP).

➤ *Microsoft Challenge Handshake Authentication Protocol (MS-CHAP)*—A proprietary, highly secure one-way password authentication method used for clients running Windows 95 or later operating systems.

➤ *Microsoft Challenge Handshake Authentication Protocol version 2 (MS-CHAP v2)*—A proprietary highly secure two-way authentication method used for clients running Windows 98 or later operating systems. This is considered the most secure form of authentication and is offered first when VPN connections are attempted.

➤ *Password Authentication Protocol (PAP)*—A low-security authentication method that uses clear-text passwords for authentication. PAP is used only when no other form of authentication can be used and is not considered secure.

> *Shiva Password Authentication Protocol (SPAP)*—A medium-security form of PAP that requires the use of Shiva-manufactured hardware to provide encryption of password data between client and server.

Extensible Authentication

The EAP supports CHAP authentication using transport layer security for security devices such as smart cards or token cards that provide passwords for authentication of remote connections to secure resources.

The term *extensible* implies that vendors may add their own authentication methods to this authentication protocol, allowing the use of newly developed technologies such as biometric systems using fingerprint or iris scanning to provide unique identification of the user.

 Some new laptops are now available with biometric fingerprint scanners built in, and the use of biometric identification methods is expected to increase in the near future.

Encryption Protocols

To increase the security of remote connections, systems using the MS-CHAP, MS-CHAP v2, and some EAP authentication methods can encrypt data using one of two encryption protocols:

> *Internet Protocol Security (IPSec)*—A cryptographic suite of security protocols that can be used over L2TP connections to provide the most secure communications possible. IPSec settings are configured using the IP Security Policy Management MMC snap-in and are managed using group policy. IPSec uses a 56-bit Data Encryption Standard (DES) encryption scheme for Basic and Strong encryption and the 3DES encryption scheme for Strongest-level encryption.

> *Microsoft Point-to-Point Encryption (MPPE)*—A proprietary encryption scheme that may be used over PPTP connections to provide Basic (40-bit), Strong (56-bit), and Strongest (128-bit) levels of data encryption.

 128-bit MPPE encryption requires the installation of the Windows 2000 High Encryption Pack from the Windows Update site: windowsupdate.microsoft.com.

Configuring Remote Access

Before you can configure RRAS, all hardware and communications protocols must be installed and working, including modem and network interface connections. Also, you should test any form of telecommunications equipment that will provide connectivity to modem banks or networking infrastructure.

 Always check that the phone lines are functional before connecting them to modems so that you will avoid frustration that has nothing to do with the system configuration.

The computer account for the new remote access server must be a member of the RAS and Internet Authentication Service (IAS) Servers security group.

Enabling Inbound Connections

By default, the remote access service is installed on Windows 2000 servers in a disabled state. It is enabled by configuring the server to accept inbound network connections, after which additional settings may be configured.

A member of the Administrators group can enable a server by performing the following steps:

1. Open the Routing And Remote Access MMC snap-in located in the Administrative Tools folder, accessed by Start|Programs|Administrative Tools.

2. Right-click on the server and select Configure And Enable Routing And Remote Access. Click Next when prompted.

3. Several common configurations are presented, allowing simple configuration of the remote access server (see Figure 12.3).

4. Select Remote Access Server to create a new dial-in server. Click Next.

5. You will be presented with a list of LAN protocols that are configured on the server. If all required LAN protocols are present, select Yes; otherwise select No, and you will be able to exit the wizard and install additional protocols. Click Next when you have made a selection.

6. Select the network interface card that inbound dial-up connections should use for network connectivity and click Next.

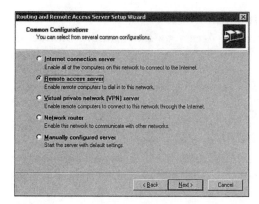

Figure 12.3 Routing and Remote Access setup wizard showing common configuration options.

7. You will be prompted to select whether IP addresses will be automatically assigned by a DHCP server or assigned from a specified pool of addresses. If the remote access server is not configured to use DHCP for addressing on the specified network interface, the local server will automatically be configured to provide addresses. Click Next when you have made your selection.

If you selected automatic IP addressing and no DHCP server is available, DHCP client systems will use addresses from the private address range of 169.254.0.1 through 169.254.255.254. These addresses might prevent access to resources located in the external Internet unless NAT has been configured to allow connections from the private network to the external Internet.

8. If you selected a static address pool, you must configure the pool of available addresses; otherwise, you will be prompted to specify if you wish to configure the server for use with an external Remote Dial-In User Service (RADIUS) server, such as the Internet Authentication Service (IAS). This option is not enabled by default. Click Next and then Finish.

If you configure a remote access server to use an external DHCP server for DHCP addressing, the remote access server will automatically acquire 10 IP addresses, using one for itself and using the additional nine as a temporary address pool for dial-in assignment. If all addresses in the temporary pool are used, the remote access server will acquire ten more from the DHCP server to add to the temporary pool.

Configuring DHCP IP Addressing

To configure Routing And Remote Access to automatically provide IP addresses, perform the following steps in the Routing And Remote Access MMC snap-in:

1. Right-click on the server and select Properties.

2. On the IP tab, configure the server as desired (see Figure 12.4). Select Dynamic Host Protocol (DHCP) to use an external DHCP server for automatic addressing of the selected network interface. A range of static addresses to be used by the selected interface can be configured here as well.

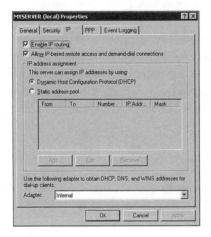

Figure 12.4 IP addressing options within the server Properties interface.

3. Click OK to apply the changes and return to the MMC.

 DHCP leases should be set to a short duration for IP address ranges used by dial-up connections, so that addresses will return to the available pool rapidly enough to provide leases as new connections are made.

Configuring Authentication Modes

To configure authentication modes, perform the following steps in the Routing And Remote Access MMC snap-in:

1. Right-click on the server and select Properties.

2. On the Security tab, click the Authentication Methods button to open the selection interface (see Figure 12.5).

Figure 12.5   Authentication methods available within Routing And Remote Access.

3. Select the desired authentication methods. If you select EAP, you can access vendor-provided options by clicking the EAP Methods button.

4. When you finish choosing all authentication methods, select OK to apply the changes and return to the MMC.

Configuring Ports for VPN Connections

When you enable the Remote Access Server option for inbound, Routing And Remote Access automatically configures five ports each for PPTP and L2TP connections. If you chose the option for Virtual Private Network (VPN) Server, Routing And Remote Access configures 128 ports each for both PPTP and L2TP connections.

To configure ports for VPN connections, perform the following steps in the Routing And Remote Access MMC snap-in:

1. Expand the server and select the Ports node, which will display a listing of available ports configured on the remote access server (see Figure 12.6).

2. Right-click on Ports and select Properties to open a listing of the ports available for VPN connections.

3. Select the desired type of port (such as L2TP, PPTP, or Modem) and click the Configure button.

4. Configure the connection as desired (see Figure 12.7). Interfaces that allow multiple connections may be limited to a specific number of simultaneous connections. You can also specify a phone number for a modem connection.

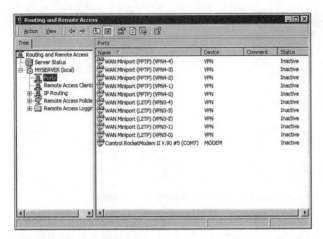

Figure 12.6 Available ports within the Routing And Remote Access MMC snap-in.

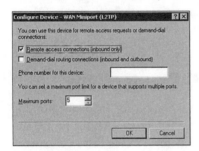

Figure 12.7 Port configuration interface for VPN connections.

5. When all settings have been configured as desired, click OK to close the configuration interface, and then click OK again to return to the MMC.

Remote Access Policies

Administrators restrict or allow user access either by configuring settings on the user account or by setting up remote access policies. Remote access policies can be used only on stand-alone Windows 2000 remote access servers or on those participating in a Windows 2000 native-mode domain. A combination of user account dial-in settings and remote access policy settings will ultimately determine whether a remote connection can be created.

User Account Dial-In Settings

You specify dial-in access permissions within the user account's properties within the Active Directory Users And Computers MMC snap-in. The Dial-In tab provides access to the access permissions, as well as the callback and IP routing settings for the logon account on the Dial-In tab (see Figure 12.8). If the telephone service and all related hardware and drivers support Caller ID, you can enable the Verify Caller-ID to verify the caller's phone number.

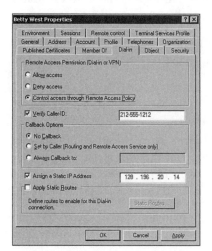

Figure 12.8 User account Properties Dial-In tab.

 The Deny access option cannot be overridden by any other settings.

Manually configuring dial-up access account settings can be used for a small number of accounts, but is unwieldy in the enterprise. In Windows 2000 native-mode domains, you can use group policies to automate the assignment and verification necessary for remote access.

Remote Access Policy Properties

Unlike group policies, remote access policies are not replicated in the Active Directory. Remote access policies are local to the remote access server, allowing different policies to be applied to each remote access server based on its capabilities and utilization. Remote access policies have three components:

➤ *Conditions*—Remote access conditions are attributes of the connection that must all be matched before a connection is allowed. These may include conditional requirements such as the time of day, the groups to which the user's logon account belongs, or the address from which the connection is being attempted.

➤ *Permissions*—Permissions allowing connection to a remote access server are determined by a combination of the dial-in permissions set for the user account and those specified in remote access policies. When the option for access is set to Control Access Through Remote Access Policy in the user account dial-in settings, the policy alone determines access.

➤ *Profile*—The profile includes the settings to be applied to a connection, such as authentication type, maximum length of connection time, and encryption modes to be used.

Remote Access Policy Evaluation

When a connection to a Windows 2000 remote access server is initiated, the connection will be evaluated for matches to all three properties in the following order:

1. The attempted connection is matched against all sets of conditions to determine if any of them match. If no match is found, the connection will be refused. Only if there is a complete match will the connection attempt continue.

2. The user account's permissions will be evaluated. If Deny Access is present, the connection will terminate. If Allow Access is set and other conditions such as Verify Caller-ID are completed, the profile will be applied. If Control Access Through Remote Access Policy is set, the policy whose conditions were matched will be evaluated for access permissions. If allowed, the profile will be applied; otherwise the connection will be refused.

3. The settings for the policy's profile will be applied to the connection. If authentication or encryption modes are required and the client is unable to establish a connection using the proper protocol, the connection will be refused. If these are successful, the connection will be made.

Applying Access Policies

The default policy is applied if the conditions are evaluated for all other policies and all fail. If the user account is configured to Allow Access, access will be granted. Otherwise, the default policy will refuse all other connection attempts. If user accounts are configured to Control Access Through

Remote Access Policy and only the default policy is present, all connections
will be refused.

 If all policies are deleted, including the default, then all connections will be refused,
regardless of whether the Allow Access option was configured for the user account.

Multiple remote access policies can be configured on the remote access server. Connection attempts are evaluated against all of them in order until a
match is found. Evaluation occurs from the top of the list down, so the
default policy should be the bottom one if it is not removed.

You can alter the order of remote access policies within the Routing And
Remote Access MMC snap-in by selecting the appropriate remote access
policy in the Remote Access Policies node and using the small arrows in the
header to move the policy up or down in the list(see Figure 12.9).

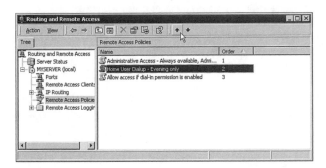

Figure 12.9   Remote access policies listing.

You can create new policies here by performing the following steps:

1. Right-click the Remote Access Policies node and select New Remote
   Access Policy to open the wizard.

2. Provide a meaningful name for the policy and click Next.

3. Add conditions for the new policy by clicking the Add button to open
   the conditions interface (see Figure 12.10).

4. Select a restriction to be applied to this policy and click Add.

5. Specify the appropriate settings for the condition and click OK.

6. Repeat steps 3 through 5 until all desired conditions have been specified
   for the policy and then click Next.

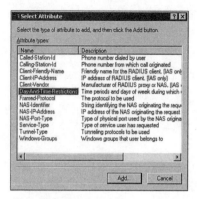

Figure 12.10 Remote access policy conditions attribute selection window.

7. Select whether this policy will Grant or Deny access permissions if matched. To create a new access policy allowing users to connect, select Grant Remote Access Permission and click Next.

Keep in mind that the first policy whose conditions match fully will be the one evaluated for the connection attempt. A policy may be created to deny access to members of specific groups during particular times of the day, for example, and if that is the first matched policy, those users will be denied access.

8. Click the Edit Profile button to configure settings for authentication modes, encryption protocols, or dial-in constraints such as idle logoff settings and maximum session timing (see Figure 10.11).

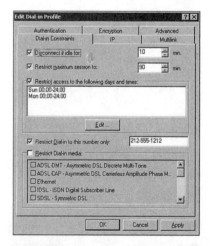

Figure 12.11 Remote access policy profile Dial-in Contraints.

9. When all settings have been properly configured, select Apply to enable the changes and OK to close the profile settings page.

10. Click Finish to complete the policy creation, and then arrange the policy within the list as desired.

Configuring Client Connections

You can configure access to a remote access server by going to the Control Panel, double-clicking on Network And Dial-Up Connections, and then double-clicking on the Make New Connection option. Double-clicking this icon will begin the New Connection Wizard, which provides several options for the new connection:

➤ Accept Incoming Connections—Allows other computers to dial into the local system and attempt a connection.

➤ Connect Directly To Another Computer—Creates a direct connection to another computer using the serial, parallel, USB, or infrared ports.

➤ Connect To A Private Network Through The Internet—Creates a VPN connection.

➤ Dial Up To A Private Network—Creates a modem connection to a remote access server.

➤ Dial Up To The Internet—Creates a modem connection to an Internet service provider.

Dialing Up to a Private Network

If you specify Dial Up To A Private Network, you will be prompted for a phone number to dial and optional area or country codes for dialing, if needed. You can then select if the connection will be available to all users on this computer or only for the current user account. Give the account a meaningful name and click Finish.

To configure connection specifications such as the number of times to attempt to connect if busy, encryption and security settings, or ICS, right-click the new connection in the Network And Dial-up Connections folder and select Properties.

To open the connection, double-click the appropriate shortcut in the Network And Dial-up Connections folder.

Connecting to a Private Network Through the Internet

When creating a VPN connection, you will be prompted to select whether the connection will be created using a dial-up specification or through the Internet. You can select a previously configured dial-up connection to dial into a private network using a remote access server.

You must specify the host name or IP address of the remote access server you wish to connect to, and then you can select if the connection will be available for all users on this computer or only for the current user account. Assign the account a meaningful name and click Finish to complete the New Connection Wizard.

You can configure specifications for the new VPN connection by right-clicking New Connection in the Network And Dial-Up Connections folder and selecting Properties.

To open the VPN connection, double-click the appropriate shortcut in the Network And Dial-Up Connections folder.

Practice Questions

Question 1

Which of the following allows a remote access server to share one external connection for multiple internal private addresses? [Check all correct answers]

- ❏ a. ICS
- ❏ b. NAT
- ❏ c. Remote access policy
- ❏ d. Tunneling
- ❏ e. VPN

Answers a and b are correct. ICS allows a single system to serve as a gateway for private address hosts to access external resources through a single connection. NAT allows the use of a small number of public addresses for access by a larger number of private internal addresses, and may be used to share a single public address with multiple private address hosts. Answer c is incorrect because a remote access policy defines conditions for connection attempts to a remote access server. Answer d is incorrect because tunneling is the process by which LAN protocols are passed through WAN protocols, or WAN protocols through secured VPN protocols. Answer e is incorrect because a VPN connection allows a remote user to establish a remote secured connection to a LAN as if directly connected.

Question 2

Which of the following is the private address assigned to a server providing shared Internet connection support to a local subnet?

- ○ a. 10.0.0.1
- ○ b. 169.254.0.1
- ○ c. 192.168.0.1
- ○ d. 255.255.128.0
- ○ e. 255.255.255.0

Answer c is correct. Although answer a is also another private network address, it is incorrect because the proper gateway IP address assigned to the ICS server is 192.168.0.1. Answer b is incorrect, because it is the first address in the range of private addresses issued by a remote access server when automatic IP addressing has been selected but no DHCP server is available. Answers d and e are incorrect because they are examples of subnet masks.

Question 3

> For traveling users, VPN connections using the Internet may be preferable to using direct dial-up to a corporate server. True or false?
>
> ○ a. True
>
> ○ b. False

Answer a is correct. Local dialup to an ISP may provide a less expensive option because it will avoid the long-distance charges incurred in dialing into a remote access server.

Question 4

> Three types of connection protocol are involved in establishing remote access connections:
>
> LAN protocols
>
> WAN protocols
>
> VPN protocols
>
>
> Match the following protocols with the appropriate type:
>
> AppleTalk   L2TP
>
> PPP
>
> PPTP
>
> TCP/IP

The correct answers are:

LAN protocols

      AppleTalk

      TCP/IP

WAN protocols

      PPP

VPN protocols

      L2TP

      PPTP

Question 5

For which purpose would you specifically use the EAP?

○ a. Authenticating biometric identification

○ b. Authenticating non-Windows connections

○ c. Connecting to Windows 95 and later operating systems

○ d. Connecting to Windows 98 or later operating systems

Answer a is correct. The EAP is used with technologies such as biometric identification systems. Answer b is incorrect because CHAP is also able to authenticate non-Windows connections. Answer c is incorrect because MS-CHAP version 1 and higher can be used for Windows connections on Windows 95 and later operating systems. Answer d is incorrect because MS-CHAP version 2 and higher can be used for Windows connections on Windows 98 and later operating systems.

Question 6

Which of the following authentication methods is considered the most secure method for Windows connections?

○ a. CHAP

○ b. MD5 CHAP

○ c. MS-CHAP

○ d. MS-CHAP v2

○ e. PAP

Answers d is correct. MS-CHAP v2 is considered the most secure authentication method. Answers a and b are incorrect because MD5 CHAP and CHAP are the same protocol, which is used to support non-Windows client access. Answer c is incorrect because version 1 of the MS-CHAP protocol does not provide two-way password encryption. Answer e is incorrect because PAP sends authentication passwords in clear text.

Question 7

How many IP address leases will a remote access server claim if configured for DHCP IP addressing and automatic IP assignment?

○ a. None

○ b. 1

○ c. 5

○ d. 10

○ e. 20

Answer d is correct. A remote access server will claim IP address leases in blocks of 10.

Question 8

The Deny Access Dial-Up setting can be overridden by remote access policy settings. True or false?

○ a. True

○ b. False

Answer b is correct. The Deny Access setting cannot be overridden.

Question 9

Arrange the three components of remote access policies in the order in which they are evaluated:

Profile

Conditions

Permissions

The correct answer is, in order:

      Conditions

      Permissions

      Profile

Question 10

If all access policies have been deleted, but the user account has been configured with the Allow Access Dial-Up setting, will the user be able to connect to the remote access server?

○ a. Yes

○ b. No

Answer b is correct. The user will not be able to establish a connection to the server if no policies exist. It is important to create at least one policy or leave the default policy in place or no connections can be made to the server.

Need to Know More?

 Stanek, William R.: *Microsoft Windows 2000 Administrator's Pocket Consultant.* Microsoft Press, Redmond, WA, 2000. ISBN 0-7356-0831-8. This is a helpful reference for network administrators to keep close at hand. The soft-cover trade-sized book is a condensed, easily carried version that contains the information of many larger tomes.

 Microsoft Windows 2000 Server Resource Kit. Microsoft Press, Redmond, WA, 2000. ISBN 1-5723-1805-8. This exhaustive library covers detailed information on all aspects of Windows 2000 Server implementations. It is an invaluable reference for IT departments supporting Microsoft Windows 2000 networks.

 www.microsoft.com/windows2000/techinfo/proddoc/default. asp. *Windows 2000 Product Documentation Online.* This is a complete online copy of the documentation for all versions of the Windows 2000 operating system.

 www.microsoft.com/technet/treeview/default.asp?url=/ technet/itsolutions/network/Default.asp. *Networking and RAS Documentation Online.* A detailed RAS-focused site within the Technet online documentation, including a number of useful "How to" articles.

13

Network Security

. . . .

Terms you'll need to understand:

✓ Authentication strength

✓ Brute force attack

✓ Password

✓ Security templates

✓ Account policies

✓ Password policy

✓ Account lockout policy

✓ Auditing

✓ Security Log

✓ Filtering

Techniques you'll need to master:

✓ Understanding the purpose and use of the common security templates provided by Microsoft

✓ Recognizing the MMC snap-ins used to import and apply security templates and the scope of application for each

✓ Identifying and understanding the use of Password and Account Lockout policy settings

✓ Enabling auditing and using the Event Viewer and Security Log in order to identify common security concerns

Previous chapters have discussed the methods for creating increasingly more interconnected networks of computing systems. As network complexity and availability of resources increase, security of these resources requires more attention. This chapter covers the basics involved in securing a Windows 2000 network—it is in no way a rigorous coverage of all possible security options. Additional references are listed at the end of the chapter.

Introduction to Network Security

It has often been said that the only way to truly secure a computer is to unplug it from the wall, put it back in its box, and lock that box in a safe place. Although there is some truth to the idea that any computer connected to a network is inherently less secure than one that is not, there are some actions a network administrator can take in order to minimize the potential for unauthorized access to resources within Windows 2000 domains.

Terminology

Before delving into the built-in options available for network security with the Active Directory environment, it is helpful to know a few common terms:

➤ *Authentication strength*—The strength of a password or other form of authentication is measured by how easily it can be guessed or obtained by someone seeking unauthorized access to network resources. Exceptionally weak passwords include any common words ("password," "love," "sex," "money," and "god"); the names of family, pets, or friends; or words commonly associated with the user such as a nickname, alma mater, or fraternal organization. Authentication methods should be as strong as possible, in order to prevent unauthorized access to the network.

➤ *Brute force attack*—This is an automated attack in which all possible combinations of username and passwords are attempted using some type of cracking tool. This is typically combined with a dictionary attack to reduce the time needed to find easily guessable passwords. Automated brute force attacks against the Administrator account are the most common. It is best to rename the Administrator account in a production environment, and use that account only when performing Admin-level actions. Network administrators should always use a nonprivileged user account for normal day-to-day operations, such as reading email or Web browsing. This allows easier auditing of all Admin-level accounts' access to better protect against unauthorized access.

▶ *Dictionary attack*—An attack that involves the use of an automated cracking tool that attempts many possible password combinations utilizing a
dictionary of known terms as the basis for each attempt. Dictionaries are
available to crackers (persons attempting to obtain unauthorized access to
network resources) that include all of the words in the English language,
and passwords based on these are considered to be very weak.

▶ *Password*—A "secret" code word, composed of letters, numbers, and sym-
bols, which only the user and the computer know. In combination with a
user logon account ID, a password allows the computer to verify that the
user attempting to log on is the correct user. Passwords must be kept
secret or they are of little use.

▶ *Smart card*—A strong logon authentication device used in combination
with a personal identification number (PIN) to verify the identity of the
user attempting to log on. Smart cards are considered strong security
because access to a physical card may be limited more easily than to a simple password.

Smart card use is enabled using the Active Directory Users And Computers MMC
snap-in. Open the Properties of the user account and select Smart Card Required For
Interactive Logon on the Account tab.

▶ *Trojan horse*—A program that appears to perform a desired task, but which
also provides a "back door" through which a cracker can gain access to a
system or even take over the user interface using built-in remote access
tools.

▶ *Virus*—The general term for any self-propagating code. Viruses can be
written to access user files, damage critical components of operating
systems, or even to take over computers and use them to assault other
computers in turn. Control of remote-controlled machines, also called
"*zombies*," is often traded between crackers for use in attacking other
portions of the Internet.

Securing the Network

Windows 2000 provides several built-in tools that will enable the network
administrator to improve security against unauthorized access. These
include the use of Group Policy to implement enterprise-wide security conventions and the Event Log, which allows access to the Security Event Log,
showing events specified in the domain auditing policy settings.

Educating Users

The first and best line of defense against unauthorized access to your network lies in the education of your users. Users must be made aware of new security threats, such as email-borne viruses like the Melissa or Anna Kournikova packages. These packages propagate themselves via email to all of a user's contacts, so that the recipients think the package is from a known source. If users have not been warned against such incoming messages, they are more likely to open an unexpected attachment, introducing an undesirable program into the network.

New users should be provided with company security policies during their orientation. This should include, but not be limited to, the following:

➤ Always log out or lock a workstation when it's not in use. If a user walks away from her terminal without closing or locking the session, anyone else may sit down and use that machine with the full access rights and capabilities of the absent user. With more remote-access tools becoming available to crackers, an open terminal session may provide a ready conduit for an assault against a network—one in which most of the safeguards have already been bypassed because the user is already logged in.

NOTE

You can lock a Windows NT or later computer by pressing Ctrl+Alt+Delete at the same time, and then selecting Lock Computer from the presented list of tasks. The user's programs are maintained in their current state, but a password for the current logon must be provided before the console is again accessible.

➤ Do not run programs from the Web. Viruses are often propagated using programs packaged as "shareware" or "freeware" that users may find interesting. Users should be cautioned against running any unknown packages from any source.

➤ Never open unexpected email attachments. Many viruses propagate themselves using email, and may come from a known source whose system was inadvertently infected.

➤ Never share passwords. Passwords and logon accounts used by multiple people make it difficult or impossible to identify the responsible party if a security breach occurs. If resources must be accessed by other users, they should contact a network administrator who can grant their logon account access rights over the appropriate file or folder.

➤ Never transmit passwords, logon accounts, credit card numbers, or other forms of sensitive data using email or instant messaging services. Crackers may intercept data transmitted using unsecured methods and use the data in order to compromise network security.

Maintaining Security Updates

Due to the large number of crackers in the world who are constantly working to produce ever-more-capable viruses and exploits allowing unauthorized access into networks, you need to always install the most recent security updates available. Manufacturers of operating systems and application suites will provide security patches, known as *hotfixes* for Microsoft patches, which must be applied to all appropriate systems in order to protect against newly discovered threats. On a regular basis, many hotfixes and other non-security-related updates will be combined into a single update package known as a service pack. The installation of hotfixes and service packs was detailed in Chapter 11.

Hotfixes should never be installed on a system running a later service pack than the hotfix version.

Updating Virus Definitions

Viruses can compromise almost a quarter of a million machines within the first few hours of their release. New forms of a new virus can be re-released within hours or days, often combined with functionality borrowed from other viruses. These hybrid packages are often capable of spreading themselves through networks in several ways, and they move with frightening speed.

As new viruses are released, antivirus manufacturers create new virus definition files to identify and protect against newly released viruses. Regular updates to virus definitions must be included in any network security plan, simply due to the rapidity of virus release and the potential harm that may be wrought by these self-replicating viruses.

Security Using Group Policy

The most powerful tool for defining and enforcing network security settings is the Windows 2000 Group Policy. You can create group policy settings by hand using the Group Policy MMC snap-in, or import them from several standard tested template files (.inf) provided by Microsoft. Group policies can also be used to enable and define event auditing in order to further monitor access or actions taken within the Active Directory structure.

NOTE Pre-Service Pack 2 versions of Windows 2000 may have trouble utilizing group policy security settings if the domain name includes the letters "inf" together (example: info.mycorp.com).

Security Templates

Microsoft provides a number of security template files (.inf) that have been extensively tested in order to provide a simple method of establishing a basic configuration for security according to the level required. Security templates are provided for workstation, member server, and domain controllers based on the level of security required. Table 13.1 details the most commonly used templates included with Windows 2000.

Table 13.1	Commonly used security template files.		
Template	**Platform**	**File**	**Description**
Basic	Workstation	basicwk.inf	The Basic template, which specifies default security settings. This is not considered a secure environment.
Basic	Member Server	basicsv.inf	Identical to basicwk.inf, only used for a Member Server.
Basic	Domain Controller	basicdc.inf	Identical to basicws.inf, only used for Domain Controllers.
Compatibility	Workstation	compatws.inf	A variation of the Basic template, which is configured to allow greater local permissions in order to improve the ability of legacy applications to function. This is not considered a secure environment.
High Security	Workstation	hisecws.inf	A highly secure template for Windows 2000 native-mode domains without down-level operating system Windows clients.
High Security	Member Server	hisecsv.inf	Identical to highsecws.inf, but used for a Member Server.
High Security	Domain Controller	hisecdc.inf	Identical to highsecws.inf, but used for domain controllers.

(continued)

Table 13.1	Commonly used security template files *(continued)*		
Template	**Platform**	**File**	**Description**
Secure	Workstation	securews.inf	A medium-security form of the Basic template that includes simple auditing as well as automatic removal of all users from the Power Users group.
Secure	Member Server	securesv.inf	Identical to securews.inf, but used for a Member Server.
Secure	Domain Controller	securedc.inf	Identical to securews.inf, but used for domain controllers.

The commonly used template files are stored in this directory:

`%SystemRoot%/WINNT/System32/Security/Templates`

Additional templates are available for the restriction of rights for Terminal Services users (notssid.inf), the return of default Terminal Services user rights (defltsv.inf), and other configurations. Administrators csn also create their own custom security setting templates and export them as INF files for use elsewhere.

Security templates should only be applied to Windows 2000 systems that are cleanly installed on an NTFS partition. Upgraded systems only have the Basic template available.

Importing Security Templates

You can mport security template files using the following tools, based on the applicable scope of the settings:

➤ *Domain Controllers Security Policy MMC snap-in*—Allows application of security template settings to all domain controllers within a domain.

➤ *Domain Security Policy MMC snap-in*—Applies security template settings to an entire domain.

➤ *Group Policy MMC snap-in*—Applies security template settings to specific group policy objects.

➤ *Local Security Policy MMC snap-in*—Imports security template settings for use on stand-alone systems. Local settings apply only when logons use machine Local accounts.

Be able to recognize all four snap-ins and their scope for security settings.

You can import security templates by opening the appropriate MMC snap-in, right-clicking on the Security Settings node, and selecting Import Policy from the available options. You can choose to clear the current security settings if desired, before selecting Open to begin the settings importation. Once completed, simply close the MMC.

Analyzing Changes to Security Settings

Before importing new security settings from a template file, you can evaluate the effects of the new settings by using the Security Configuration And Analysis MMC snap-in to compare the settings in a template to those currently configured. Simply follow these steps:

1. Once loaded, select Open Database and provide a new path and name for the snap-in's database file.

2. Select the desired template for analysis by right-clicking on the Security Configuration And Analysis node and selecting Import Template.

3. Select the proper template, and right-click the node again and select Analyze Computer Now. You can see the effects of this change in Figure 13.1.

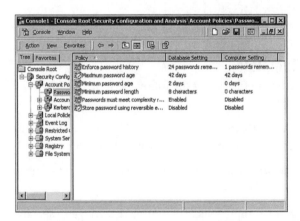

Figure 13.1 Security Configuration and Analysis MMC snap-in comparing security template settings.

After the changes have been reviewed and deemed acceptable, you can apply the changes using the proper MMC, or from within the Security Configuration And Analysis MMC snap-in by right-clicking the node and selecting Configure Computer Now from the available options.

The Security Configuration And Analysis MMC may also be used to verify current settings. This is useful for troubleshooting and as a part of the regular security audit process.

Account Policies

If further customization of security settings is required, or an Administrator wants to create a new security policy, the appropriate MMC snap-in should be used based on the desired scope of application for the new settings.

Security settings involving Account Policies are the most likely to need reconfiguration to suit specific organizational requirements. You can find these within the MMC by expanding the Security Settings, and then the Account Policies branch below. Three types of settings can be modified:

➤ *Password Policy*—Configure settings involving the length, lifespan, and complexity of logon passwords here.

➤ *Account Lockout Policy*—Configure settings involving the effects of repeated failed attempts to log on here.

➤ *Kerberos Policy*—Configure Kerberos ticket authentication policy settings here.

Defining Password and Account Lockout policies to increase password complexity and limit the number of times a user can attempt to log on and fail before being locked out will improve security against brute force cracking attempts.

Account policies for password and lockout duration are applied at the domain level. In a multidomain tree or forest, the same group policy object can be assigned to each domain container, or separate ones can be assigned to each as dictated by business rules.

Password Policy Settings

Password settings allow for stronger security against unauthorized access by requiring complex passwords of limited lifespan. Changes to password settings do not apply to current passwords. They will take effect the next time a password is reset by an administrator or changed by the user. Table 13.2 details the password policy settings and the purpose of each.

Table 13.2 Account policy password settings.	
Setting	**Purpose**
Enforce Password History	Maintains a historical listing of up to 24 past passwords that may not be reused. This prevents users from simply reusing the same password each time the old one expires, effectively bypassing password expiration and allowing crackers unlimited time in which to attempt to break the user's password.
Maximum Password Age	Sets the maximum lifespan of a password. Shortening this time gives crackers less of an opportunity to attempt brute force attacks against a particular password before the password is changed. Microsoft recommends 30 days for secure configurations, and 42-45 for medium-security network requirements.
Minimum Password Age	Sets a minimum time before users may change their passwords after the last change. Used in combination with the option to Enforce Password History, this option prevents a user from rapidly entering temporary passwords until the history cache has been flushed, and reentering a favorite password again.
Minimum Password Length	Configures the minimum length for an acceptable password, from 0 to 14 characters in length. Setting this to 0 allows for a blank password to be entered, which is considered highly unsecure.
Passwords Must Meet Complexity Requirements	Requires complex passwords with characters from at least three of the available four categories: English uppercase letters (A-Z), English lowercase letters (a-z), western Arabic numerals (0-9), and symbols (%, !, ?, etc.). Configuring this will set an automatic minimum of three characters for a new password, even if the Minimum Password Length was set below three characters.
Store Passwords Using Reversible Encryption	Stores passwords using a reversible password hashing method. This setting is disabled by default.

* Passwords should be longer than seven characters in order to improve security within mixed-mode domains or domains utilizing LAN Manager–style password hashing, such as those with Windows 95/98 clients. LAN Manager passwords are hashed as two seven-digit codes using well-known algorithms. Passwords of less than eight characters reduce the cracking effort required by half or more. Windows 2000 native-mode domains with only Windows NT or Windows 2000 and later operating systems may be configured to use a more secure form of password hashing.

Account Lockout Policy Settings

Account lockout settings define the behavior for authentication of user logons that have been repeatedly attempted and failed due to incorrect passwords. Increasing security here will defend against automated brute force cracking attempts by limiting the number of times a logon and password may be attempted within a short time span before being locked out and requiring administrative intervention to reset. Table 13.3 details the account lockout policy settings and the purpose of each.

Table 13.3 Account lockout policy settings.	
Setting	**Purpose**
Account Lockout Duration	Configures the duration for which the account logon will be locked out after reaching the number of failed attempts specified in the threshold, from 0 to 99,999 minutes. A setting of zero minutes will require an Administrator to reset the account before it can be used.
Account Lockout Threshold	Configures the maximum number of failed logon attempts that may occur before account lockout occurs, from 0 to 999 attempts. A setting of zero effectively disables this setting.
Reset Account Lockout Counter After	Allows the Administrator to configure the amount of time before the failed attempt counter is returned to zero. Microsoft recommends a setting of one day (1,440 minutes) for high-security configurations, and a value of 30 minutes for medium-security configurations. Failed logon attempts that reach the threshold value within the duration specified by this setting will be locked out.

All three settings must be configured or account lockout protection will not occur.

Auditing for Security

Auditing allows details to be written to the Event Log when specific actions occur, such as logon attempts, alterations of rights, system shutdown, or file and folder access. These events can then be viewed within the Security Log, allowing an Administrator or any user account granted the Manage auditing and security log permission to troubleshoot potential security breaches.

TIP

Enable auditing of as few event types as possible. Auditing too many events will rapidly overfill the Security log file, and may impact system performance.

Configuring Auditing

Windows 2000 provides the ability to perform auditing on many types of events, generating entries in the event logs when logon attempts fail or succeed, when a policy change occurs, when a system event occurs, when object access succeeds or fails, or following account management events. Auditing can be configured at the domain, system, folder, or file level in order to provide granular control over which events will be monitored. Remember that auditing can rapidly overfill the Security Log file, so remember to limit auditing to only necessary events.

Domain and System Auditing

Auditing can be enabled at the domain or local system level using group policy settings from within the appropriate MMC snap-in by expanding the Security Settings node, and then the Local Policies And Audit Policy branches below. Figure 13.2 shows the available Audit Policy options for the newcorp.com domain.

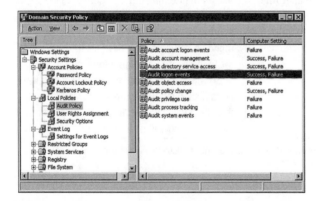

Figure 13.2 Domain Security Policy MMC snap-in showing the available Audit Policy options.

File and Folder Auditing

Auditing can be enabled within the Properties of a file or folder by selecting Advanced on the Security tab and then selecting the Auditing tab. Figure 13.3 shows the available Audit Policy options for the MyDir folder.

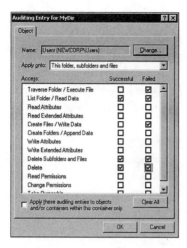

Figure 13.3   Folder Properties for the MyDir folder, showing the available Audit Policy options.

In order to enable object-level auditing, either Audit Directory Service Access (for auditing on a domain controller) or Audit Object Access (for auditing on a member server) must be enabled using group policy.

Event Logs

Auditing events are written into the security log of the appropriate system. They may be viewed using the Event Viewer MMC snap-in. Within this snap-in, several log types are viewable:

➤ *Application Log*—Provides information on events recorded by applications running on the computer.

➤ *Security Log*—Provides information on events generated by auditing.

➤ *System*—Provides information on events recorded by the Windows 2000 operating system and its components.

➤ *Directory Service*—Available only on domain controllers. This log provides details on domain events such as directory replication.

➤ *DNS Server*—Available only on servers running the DNS service. This log provides information on DNS server events such as DNS file replication.

➤ *File Replication Service*—Available only on domain controllers. This log provides information on distributed file system and group policy replication events.

Events within the Security Log

Events written to the Security Log are recorded as a success—identified by a gold key icon—or a failure—identified by a gold padlock icon. Figure 13.4 shows a sample Security Log listing. Each event is listed with an Event ID code, which identifies the type of action that has been logged. Table 13.4 lists a few of the more common events to look for in the Security Log.

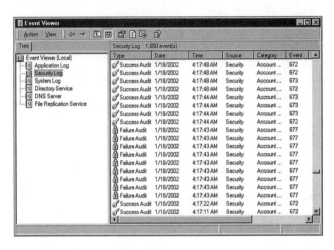

Figure 13.4   The Event Viewer MMC snap-in showing the Security Log file.

Table 13.4	Common important Security Log events.
Event ID	**Meaning**
513	System shutdown generates a 513 event. Permissions to shut down systems may be restricted in an organization, in order to avoid down-time or accidental restart of critical ongoing processes. Monitoring for event 513 may reveal errors in assigned access permissions.
517	When the security log is cleared, an event 517 is generated. Security event logs should be archived before being cleared, and any administrator who is clearing the security logs should properly document and justify their actions. Clearing a security log is one way that a successful cracker may attempt to cover his tracks.
528	Successful user logon event.
529	Failed logon attempt due to incorrect logon or password.
539	Failed logon attempt caused by account lockout. A listing of several 529s followed by many 539s is a good indicator of a brute force attack.

(continued)

Table 13.4	Common important Security Log events *(continued)*
Event ID	**Meaning**
578	A change in file ownership will generate a 578 event. Ownership conveys control over an object, so users with incorrect permissions who can take ownership of files may reveal errors in assigned access permissions.
672	A Kerberos authentication ticket has been granted upon initial successful logon.
673	A service ticket grant event, which occurs after an authentication ticket has been granted. This indicates the service to which access has been granted.
677	An attempt was made to connect from a system that does not support Kerberos authentication.

Filtering the Security Log

It is often helpful to view only a portion of the Security Log dealing with a specific event type, or involving a specific computer or user account. The Event Viewer provides the ability to filter out a subset of the event log by right-clicking on the desired log type and selecting Properties, and then selecting the Filter tab to open the log filtering dialog box (see Figure 13.5).

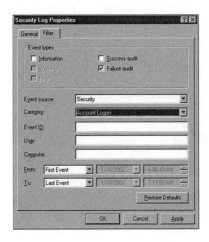

Figure 13.5   Security Log Filter settings to show only Account Logon failures.

Select Apply to apply the filter and OK to return to the Event Viewer MMC. To remove the filter, repeat the process and select (All) for the Event Source and then Apply and OK again to return to the unfiltered Event Viewer.

Practice Questions

Question 1

A brute force attack is an attempt to gain unauthorized access by attempting all possible combinations of password characters along with a known user account. True or false?

○ a. True

○ b. False

Answer a is correct. Brute force attacks are typically enacted using an automated tool that can attempt millions of possible password combinations for a user's logon name until the account lockout threshold is reached, or access is gained. Answer b is thus incorrect.

Question 2

Arrange the following forms of identification in order of their strength from highest to lowest:

➤ Anonymous access

➤ Password: <blank>

➤ Password: %sh1nyd0g!

➤ Password: password

➤ Smart card

The correct answer is, in order:

➤ Smart card (strongest authentication)

➤ Password: %sh1nyd0g!

➤ Password: password

➤ Password: <blank>

➤ Anonymous access (no authentication)

Anonymous access provides no authentication. Passwords are considered to be "stronger" as they increase in length and complexity, because brute force cracking attempts will take longer to guess the proper combination. The most secure of the options listed would be the use of a security token such as a smart card along with a personal identification number (PIN). Access to a physical token such as a smart card is much easier to restrict than a virtual security key such as a password.

Question 3

Which of the following should be applied on a regular basis? [Check all correct answers]

❑ a. Hotfixes

❑ b. Service packs

❑ c. Virus definitions

Answers a, b, and c are all correct. Security updates such as hotfixes, as well as larger updates bundled into service packs, should be applied on a regular basis to provide the highest level of operating system and application security. Virus definitions are constantly updated to include protection against newly released viral programs. Antivirus software must have an up-to-date virus definitions file in order to provide the best protection.

Question 4

Microsoft provides security templates for use on three types of systems:

➤ Domain controllers

➤ Member Servers

➤ Workstations

Match the following template files with the appropriate type of system:

➤ basicdc.inf

➤ basicsv.inf

➤ basicwk.inf

➤ compatws.inf

➤ hisecdc.inf

➤ hisecsv.inf

➤ hisecws.inf

➤ securedc.inf

➤ securesv.inf

➤ securews.inf

The correct answers are:

➤ Domain controllers

    ➤ basicdc.inf

    ➤ hisecdc.inf

    ➤ securedc.inf

➤ Member Servers

    ➤ basicsv.inf

    ➤ hisecsv.inf

    ➤ securesv.inf

➤ Workstations

    ➤ basicwk.inf

    ➤ compatws.inf

    ➤ hisecws.inf

    ➤ securews.inf

Question 5

> A local domain administrator contacts you saying that he has finished upgrad-
> ing the PDC to Windows 2000, and then all of the BDCs, and has switched the
> domain to native mode. He now wants to apply the Secure template on his
> domain controllers, and has opened the Domain Controllers Security Policy
> MMC snap-in. He says he can only load the Basic template, rather than the
> Secure one, and asks that you send him the Secure template files. Will this fix
> his problem?
>
> ○ a. Yes
> ○ b. No

Answer b is correct. Only the Basic template can be used on systems that are
not cleanly installed on a Windows 2000 NTFS partition. His upgraded
servers will not have been cleanly installed on a new Windows 2000 NTFS
partition.

Question 6

> There are four MMC snap-ins used for applying imported security template files:
> - Domain Controllers Security Policy
> - Domain Security Policy
> - Group Policy
> - Local Security Policy
>
> Match the following scope of application with the appropriate MMC:
> - Applies settings to all computers within a domain
> - Applies settings on a stand-alone system
> - Applies settings to all domain controllers within a domain
> - Applies settings to a specific group policy object
> - Settings affect domain accounts
> - Settings affect local user accounts only

The correct answers are:

- Domain Controllers Security Policy
    - Applies settings to all domain controllers within a domain
    - Settings affect domain accounts
- Domain Security Policy
    - Applies settings to all computers within a domain
    - Settings affect domain accounts
- Group Policy
    - Applies settings to a specific group policy object
    - Settings affect domain accounts
- Local Security Policy
    - Applies settings on a stand-alone system
    - Settings affect local user accounts only

Question 7

Account policies specify three categories of settings:

➤ Password Policy

➤ Account Lockout Policy

➤ Kerberos Policy

Match the following settings with the appropriate account policy category:

➤ Account Lockout Duration

➤ Account Lockout Threshold

➤ Enforce Password History

➤ Maximum Password Age

➤ Minimum Password Age

➤ Minimum Password Length

➤ Passwords Must Meet Complexity Requirements

➤ Reset Account Lockout Counter After

The correct answers are:

➤ Password Policy

  ➤ Enforce Password History

  ➤ Maximum Password Age

  ➤ Minimum Password Age

  ➤ Minimum Password Length

  ➤ Passwords Must Meet Complexity Requirements

➤ Account Lockout Policy

  ➤ Account Lockout Duration

  ➤ Account Lockout Threshold

  ➤ Reset Account Lockout Counter After

➤ Kerberos Policy

Question 8

> You should enable auditing wherever possible, so as to have a better log of all possible security-related events. True or false?
>
> ○ a. True
> ○ b. False

Answer b is correct. Enabling Auditing can rapidly overrun the Security Log file. Enable only the minimum items required.

Question 9

> Which of the following log types may be found on domain controllers? [Check all correct answers]
>
> ❏ a. Application Log
> ❏ b. Directory Service Log
> ❏ c. DNS Service Log
> ❏ d. Exchange Server Log
> ❏ e. File Replication Service Log
> ❏ f. Security Log
> ❏ g. System Log
> ❏ h. SQL Server Log

Answers a, b, c, e, f, and g are correct. Answers d and h are incorrect because events from applications such as Exchange and SQL Server are written to the Application Log.

Question 10

> A client reports that they cannot log on to the network. You have looked through the Security Log for events relating to the user's logon account. You have found a large number of 529 events the night before and then several hundred 539 events, ending after an hour. You assume that this was a brute force attack, and plan to reset the user's account. Will this correct the user's logon problem?
>
> ○ a. Yes
> ○ b. No

Answers a is correct. A series of 529 events followed by 539s is a good indicator of some type of password guessing, and several hundred events of that type within an hour's time indicates the use of an automated tool. Resetting the user account should allow a return of logon capability—at least until another brute force attack is attempted using that account.

Need to Know More?

 Stanek, William R.: *Microsoft Windows 2000 Administrator's Pocket Consultant*. Microsoft Press, Redmond, WA, 2000. ISBN 0-7356-0831-8. A helpful reference for network administrators to keep close at hand. The soft-cover trade-size book is a condensed, easily carried version of many larger tomes of information.

 Microsoft Windows 2000 Server Resource Kit. Microsoft Press, Redmond, WA, 2000. ISBN 1-5723-1805-8. An exhaustive library covering detailed information on all aspects of Windows 2000 Server implementations. An invaluable reference for IT departments supporting Microsoft Windows 2000 networks.

 www.microsoft.com/windows2000/techinfo/proddoc/default. asp. *Windows 2000 Product Documentation Online*. A complete online copy of the documentation for all versions of the Windows 2000 operating system.

Sample Test

You will have 150 minutes to complete the exam, which is comprised of 60 questions. The score given will be either Pass or Fail, without numerical scoring provided. Care should be taken in reading each question, looking for details that would rule out any of the answers. Pay particular attention to exam exhibits, and consider side effects that may occur if each solution is attempted. Many times there will be two or more apparently correct answers, while only one correct answer is acceptable due to the changes that will occur as a result of the alternatives presented.

Test Questions

Question 1

You have a Unix print server that supports three printers. You need to publish these printers in the Active Directory. You have installed the Unix File And Print connectivity component. What must you do additionally in order to accomplish this task?

○ a. Nothing. It is not possible to use a Unix system as a print server for a Windows 2000 Active Directory network.

○ b. Nothing. The Unix print server will publish its printers automatically using the File And Print services.

○ c. Manually publish the printer using the Active Directory Sites And Services MMC snap-in.

○ d. Manually publish the printer using the Active Directory Users And Computers MMC snap-in.

Question 2

In which of the following should you add static FQDN listings?

○ a. LMHOSTS

○ b. HOSTS

○ c. RIP

○ d. IGMP

○ e. AppleTalk

Question 3

Your company has decided to use the internal addressing range of 192.168.0.0/13. You have been told to plan the internal subnetting to allow for up to 500 subnets of 1,000 hosts each. What is the broadcast address and subnet mask for a host located in the first subnet of this configuration? [Check all correct answers]

- ❑ a. 255.248.0.0
- ❑ b. 255.255.252.0
- ❑ c. 255.255.255.0
- ❑ d. 192.168.3.255
- ❑ e. 192.168.175.255
- ❑ f. 192.168.255.255

Question 4

Which entry below is the correct LMHOSTS entry that will cache at boot the name resolution value for the server myserver.mycorp.com, with an IP address of 128.176.244.10?

- ○ a. 128.176.244.10 myserver
- ○ b. 128.176.244.10 myserver #PRE
- ○ c. 128.176.244.10 myserver.mycorp.com
- ○ d. 128.176.244.10 myserver.mycorp.com #PRE
- ○ e. myserver 128.176.244.10
- ○ f. myserver.mycorp.com 128.176.244.10

Question 5

What is the correct subnet mask for the 194.161.240.0 subnet after being divided into four smaller subnets?

- ○ a. 255.255.128.0
- ○ b. 255.255.192.0
- ○ c. 255.255.255.0
- ○ d. 255.255.255.128
- ○ e. 255.255.255.192

Question 6

> Within the following domain types:
>
> NT 4
>
> Windows 2000 mixed mode
>
> Windows 2000 native mode
>
>
> Match the following server roles with the domain type each may be found within (some may be used more than once):
>
> Backup Domain Controller
>
> Global Catalog server
>
> Member server
>
> PDC Emulator
>
> Primary Domain Controller

Question 7

> The delay between when a change is made to one copy of the Global Catalog and when it is updated on all other copies is called what?
>
> O a. Convergence
>
> O b. Latency
>
> O c. Replication
>
> O d. Annoying

Question 8

In a new test domain, you set up a single server in the root domain, and a single server as the only controller in a child domain. You are about to deploy a third server in order to correct several event log errors on the root domain's controller that detail failures to update name and SID information. How should you install the new server to eliminate this problem?

- ○ a. Install the new server as a member server of the root domain and move the DNS and WINS services to the new server. Direct both of the other servers to this new server for name resolution.

- ○ b. Install the new server as a domain controller in the child domain and move the Schema Master role to the new server.

- ○ c. Install the new server as a domain controller of the root domain and move the Infrastructure Master role to the new server.

- ○ d. Install the new server as a second Global Catalog server in the root domain.

- ○ e. Install the new server as a domain controller in a parent domain to the current Root. Enable DNS service in this server, and direct both of the other servers to this new server for name resolution.

Question 9

If users in Domain A can access resources in Domain B, then it is said that Domain A _____ Domain B.

- ○ a. Is shared by
- ○ b. Is trusted by
- ○ c. Shares
- ○ d. Trusts

Question 10

Several container levels are available within an Active Directory deployment:

Domains

Forests

Nested organizational units

Organizational units

Trees

Arrange these in order from largest to smallest.

Question 11

What is the relative distinguished name of this LDAP name:

CN=station1,OU=dallas,DC=mycorp,DC=com

○ a. CN=station1

○ b. OU=dallas

○ c. DC=mycorp

○ d. DC=com

○ e. DC=mycorp,DC=com

Question 12

You have been tasked with setting up a DNS Active Directory Integrated lookup zone that will allow IP addresses to be resolved to their FQDNs. Which type of zone do you need to create?

○ a. Forward Lookup

○ b. Reverse Lookup

○ c. Standard Primary

○ d. Standard Secondary

Question 13

You are combining the old public Web server (public.mycorp.com) and the new production Web server (prod.mycorp.com), while allowing developers to continue using the name public.mycorp.com. You have removed the DNS entry for the old Web server, and now need to create a record that will direct users looking for publc.mycorp.com to the new server's current IP address. What type of record should you create?

○ a. Host (A) record

○ b. CNAME record

○ c. MX record

○ d. PTR record

○ e. WWW record

Question 14

Which utility should be used in order to test DNS lookup functionality?

○ a. ipconfig

○ b. nbtstat

○ c. nslookup

○ d. ping

○ e. pathping

○ f. tracert

Question 15

A client configured to use DHCP addressing will first attempt to renew its lease when what percentage of the lease's term has expired?

○ a. 25 percent

○ b. 50 percent

○ c. 75 percent

○ d. 90 percent

○ e. 95 percent

○ f. When it expires

Question 16

During which phase of the DHCP lease process will a client assign itself an address in the 169.254.0.1-169.254.255.254 range if no DHCP servers provide the client with a potential lease?

○ a. Discovery

○ b. Offer

○ c. Request

○ d. Acknowledgement

Question 17

A new DHCP server has been installed in a subnet in order to reduce bottlenecks at the existing DHCP server. All IP addresses within the subnet have been split into the two separate scopes. Everything was working well for a little over a week, and then some clients report that they cannot connect to the network. There is no pattern to this that you can discern, and you can ping the DHCP servers from the machines having a problem using their NetBIOS names. What do you need to do in order to resolve this problem?

○ a. Separate the two portions of the subnet into separate sites and place one DHCP server in each site using the Active Directory Sites And Services MMC snap-in.

○ b. Place a Global Catalog server with DNS and WINS services in the local subnet and configure all machines to use the new server for all name service support.

○ c. Remove the old server in order to eliminate potential scope conflicts.

○ d. Authorize the new DHCP server for the domain.

○ e. Configure the affected client systems for static IP addressing.

Question 18

It is not possible to know which IP address a DHCP server will provide to a particular client before the lease has been granted. True or false?

○ a. True

○ b. False

Question 19

A client reports he is unable to access the Manager's file share. You check his account and note that the account is a member of the Managers, Sales, and Domain Users groups. The Sales group is a child of the Front Office group. You examine the permissions on each of these groups with regards to the Manager's file share and find that the Managers group is allowed Read and Write permissions, Sales is allowed Write permissions, the Front Office group is denied Full Access, and the Domain Users group has no specified permissions set for the Manager's file share. Which group's access permissions must be changed to allow the user to access the Manager's file share?

○ a. Domain Users

○ b. Front Office

○ c. Managers

○ d. Sales

○ e. None of the above

Question 20

You have created a custom Taskpad for your assistants located in each city's main office. What methods can you use to distribute the Taskpad file? [Check all correct answers]

❏ a. Email

❏ b. Instant Messenger

❏ c. File Share

❏ d. CD-ROM

Question 21

Which permission type will override the others if a conflict occurs?

○ a. Explicit allow

○ b. Explicit denial

○ c. Implicit denial

Question 22

Which portion of a group policy object is a folder hierarchy located in the %*SystemRoot*%\WINNT\SYSVOL\sysvol\<*domain*>\Policies\ directory?

○ a. Group policy container

○ b. Group policy template

○ c. Group policy scope

Question 23

What is the default group policy refresh interval for domain controllers?

○ a. 5 minutes

○ b. 30 minutes

○ c. 60 minutes

○ d. 90 minutes

○ e. 120 minutes

Question 24

You have specified new computer policy settings and allowed sufficient time for all domain controllers to receive a replicated copy of the changes. A user calls to complain that the changes are still not working on her system, even though she has logged out and back in. What is the simplest of the available steps you should try in order to check the proper group policy application?

○ a. From the user's computer, use the gpresult utility to verify that the proper group policy is being assigned to the user.

○ b. From the nearest domain controller, attempt to ping the client computer to verify network connectivity.

○ c. From the user's computer, use the netdiag utility to verify domain membership and the availability of a domain controller.

○ d. Reboot the nearest domain controller to force replication of the group policy objects to occur.

○ e. Have the user reboot her computer and log on again.

○ f. Have the user log off, wait five minutes, and log on again.

Question 25

Which permissions must be assigned to an account to allow a group policy to be applied to the account? [Check all correct answers]

- ❏ a. Full Control
- ❏ b. Read
- ❏ c. Write
- ❏ d. Apply Group Policy

Question 26

You are responsible for applying an update to 1,000 systems throughout an enterprise network deployment. How should you handle this deployment most efficiently?

- ○ a. Create a custom MSI file and publish it to all users using group policy.
- ○ b. Create a custom MSI file and assign it to all users using group policy.
- ○ c. Create a custom MSI file and publish it to the computers using group policy.
- ○ d. Create a custom MSI file and assign it to the computers using group policy.

Question 27

What is the proper CIDR notation for the base subnet including the address 128.176.224.13 with a subnet mask of 255.255.255.128?

- ○ a. 128.176.224.0/7
- ○ b. 128.176.224.0/25
- ○ c. 128.176.224.13/25
- ○ d. 128.176.224.127/25
- ○ e. 128.176.224.255/25

Question 28

The _____ favorable combination is used for NTFS and Share access permission resolution, and the _____ favorable combination for both is used for determining the final access rights.

○ a. most; most

○ b. least; most

○ c. least; least

○ d. most; least

Question 29

For the following printer reference options:

Connect

Move

Open

Properties

Match the following descriptions with the appropriate reference option:

Allows job and print queue management

Allows the addition of available drivers.

Allows the location of a published printer reference to be changed to a different organizational unit.

Performs installation of a printer on a computer.

Question 30

A user connecting through Terminal Services complains that his local printer is not available during the session, but is available when not using the Terminal Services client. What do you need to do to give him access to his local printer while using Terminal Services?

○ a. Add a network printer reference to the printer on the local machine.

○ b. Share the local printer, making sure the user's account has the proper access permissions to the share.

○ c. Install the proper printer driver on the server.

○ d. Update the printer driver on the local system.

Question 31

> Which port must be opened through a firewall to allow remote access using Terminal Services?
>
> ○ a. 21
> ○ b. 25
> ○ c. 80
> ○ d. 3389
> ○ e. 8080

Question 32

> For the following RAID types:
>
> RAID-0
>
> RAID-1
>
> RAID-5
>
> Match the following qualities with the appropriate type (some may be used more than once):
>
> Also called mirroring
>
> Also called striping
>
> Also called striping with parity
>
> Fastest RAID access type
>
> Fault tolerant
>
> Least efficient RAID storage type
>
> Slowest RAID access type

Question 33

> You have been charged with migrating an existing NT 4 domain to Windows 2000. After upgrading the PDC and the BDC, your assistant accidentally changed the domain mode from mixed mode to native mode while several Windows NT 4 member servers remained. Will this change cause problems?
>
> ○ a. Yes
> ○ b. No

Question 34

Placing organizational units within organizational units is called:

- ○ a. Compiling
- ○ b. Budding
- ○ c. Nesting
- ○ d. Spawning

Question 35

Which ports must be opened through a firewall to allow FTP and WWW access, respectively?

- ○ a. 21, 25
- ○ b. 21, 80
- ○ c. 21, 8080
- ○ d. 25, 3389
- ○ e. 80, 3389

Question 36

For the following site identification methods:

Custom port

Host headers

Multiple IP

Match the following characteristics with the appropriate method (some may be used more than once):

Allows a registered alias to be used to identify a site

Allows sharing of a single IP address for multiple sites

Allows the association of one or more IP addresses to a site

Provides enhanced security against port scanning

Question 37

Which account is used in anonymous FTP connections?

O a. Administrator

O b. Guest

O c. IUSR_<*domain name*>

O d. IUSR_<*computer name*>

O e. IWAM_<*domain name*>

O f. IWAM_<computer name>

Question 38

A local administrator has called you to ask your advice on recovering data from a system. She has determined that the master boot record has been corrupted, and plans to use the Recovery Console to correct the problem long enough to copy all user files off the system. Which of the following is the proper command to use to rebuild the master boot record?

O a. fixboot

O b. Logged

O c. Safe Mode

O d. fixmbr

O e. Debugging Mode

Question 39

For the following monitoring utilities:

System Monitor

Task Manager

Network Monitor

Match the following characteristics with the appropriate utility (some may be used more than once):

Can be used to stop processes that are consuming too many system resources

Captures data packets

Can be used to log data over a period of time

Provides current process resource utilization statistics

Question 40

The following code segment is example output from which command?

```
1 <10 ms <10 ms <10 ms d-1.crp.com [10.0.0.1]
2 <10 ms <10 ms <10 ms ny-1.crp.com [10.0.1.1]
3 <10 ms <10 ms <10 ms srv.crp.com [10.0.1.2]
```

- ○ a. ping
- ○ b. tracert
- ○ c. pathping
- ○ d. ipconfig
- ○ e. netdiag

Question 41

You have been hired as a consultant to set up a small office network so that the existing dialup connection can be shared by three other systems located in the same office. The ISP providing service to the office has a maximum connection time of two hours, and some employees work outside of normal hours and may not have direct access to the computer that is connected to the dial-up service. You decide to put Ethernet NICs in each of the systems and connect all of the systems using a hub and a static addressing scheme, using TCP/IP. You plan to configure the gateway computer to provide ICS with no other options selected. Is there anything else you will need to do to allow all of the systems to share the single external dial-up connection?

- ○ a. Yes
- ○ b. No

Question 42

Which of the following authentication methods is considered the least secure, and used only as a last resort?

- ○ a. CHAP
- ○ b. MS-CHAP
- ○ c. MS-CHAP v2
- ○ d. PAP
- ○ e. SPAP

Question 43

Which use of the **route** command will create a persistent route to a destination address of 10.1.50.4/16, through the next gateway address of 10.50.1.1?

○ a. route add 10.1.50.4 mask 255.255.0.0 10.50.1.1

○ b. route add 10.50.1.1 mask 255.255.0.0 10.1.50.4

○ c. route -p add 10.1.50.4 mask 255.255.0.0 10.50.1.1

○ d. route -p add 10.1.50.4 mask 255.255.255.0 10.50.1.1

○ e. route -p add 10.50.1.1 mask 255.255.0.0 10.1.50.4

Question 44

Which of the following password and logon settings must be configured to enable password lockout? [Check all correct answers]

❑ a. Complexity Requirements

❑ b. Enforce History

❑ c. Account Lockout Duration

❑ d. Reset Lockout Counter After

❑ e. Account Lockout Threshold

Question 45

> For the following event log types:
>
> Application Log
>
> Security Log
>
> System
>
> Directory service
>
> DNS Server
>
> File replication service
>
> Match the following characteristics with the appropriate type (some may be used more than once):
>
> Includes details on events such as directory replication
>
> Only found on DNS servers
>
> Only found on domain controllers
>
> Provides events logged by programs such as Exchange or SQL Server
>
> Provides information on events generated by auditing
>
> Provides information on group policy replication

Question 46

> You have been tasked with changing all workstations in your company to use dynamic addressing. After configuring a DHCP server with active scopes for both subnets in your company, you configure all workstations within for dynamic IP configuration. The DHCP server is located in Subnet-B.
>
> Users of systems located in Subnet-A report that they are unable to access the Internet, while users of systems in Subnet-B are having no difficulties. You perform an **ipconfig /all** on several systems within Subnet-A and find that all have failed to obtain a DHCP lease. Which of the following options will correct this problem?
>
> ○ a. Reconfigure the workstations in Subnet-A to use static IP addressing.
>
> ○ b. Place a Caching DNS server in Subnet-A and redirect clients in Subnet-A to use this for name resolution.
>
> ○ c. Place a DHCP Proxy in Subnet-A.
>
> ○ d. Configure all workstations in Subnet-A with the IP address of the DHCP server.

Question 47

Which of the following commands will create a route to the destination 10.5.0.0/16 with the next hop address of 10.2.0.1 that will remain after the TCP/IP protocol is restarted?

○ a. route add 10.5.0.0 mask 16 10.2.0.1

○ b. route add 10.5.0.0 mask 255.255.0.0 10.2.0.1

○ c. route –p add 10.5.0.0 mask 16 10.2.0.1

○ d. route –p add 10.5.0.0 mask 255.255.0.0 10.2.0.1

○ e. route –p add 10.2.0.1 10.5.0.0 mask 255.255.0.0

Question 48

You have been told to configure the main office printer so that when the CEO prints, his documents will be printed ahead of other pending jobs. You create a second share for the printer, which only the CEO's account will be able to access. In order to move his documents ahead of all other outstanding jobs, which of the following values should be set of the print priority of the new share?

○ a. Immediate

○ b. 1

○ c. 50

○ d. 99

○ e. 100

Question 49

You have configured a dual-boot system, placing the Windows XP operating system on the first partition of the first drive on the first IDE controller, and Windows 2000 on the first partition of the second drive on the same controller. Which of the following boot.ini entries would be used to access Windows 2000?

○ a. multi(0)disk(0)rdisk(0)partition(1)

○ b. multi(0)disk(0)rdisk(0)partition(2)

○ c. multi(1)disk(0)rdisk(0)partition(1)

○ d. multi(0)disk(1)rdisk(0)partition(1)

○ e. multi(0)disk(0)rdisk(1)partition(1)

Question 50

Which of the following commands would reset the computer GPO settings immediately? [Check all correct answers.]

- ❏ a. gpupdate
- ❏ b. gpupdate /target:computer
- ❏ c. secedit /refreshpolicy computer_policy /enforce
- ❏ d. secedit /refreshpolicy machine_policy /enforce

Question 51

For the three group types:

Domain local groups

Global groups

Universal groups

Match the following characteristics with the appropriate type (some may be used more than once):

May be used to grant permissions only in the local domain.

May be used to grant permissions within any domain within a forest.

May have only local-domain users and groups as members.

May have users and computers from any domain within the forest as members.

Not available in Mixed-mode Windows 2000 domains.

Question 52

Admin-A creates a new user AUser within the SalesTemps organizational unit. Before this creation has been propagated, Admin-B deletes the SalesTemps OU. When all replication has been completed, the OU has been removed. Where is the orphaned AUser account?

- ○ a. In the default Users container.
- ○ b. In the lostandfound container.
- ○ c. In the recycle bin container.
- ○ d. It is lost.

Question 53

Which of the following profile options would be the most efficient for use by IT personnel who operate throughout the company, testing desktop and system settings on many machines and running many diagnostic programs each maintains?

○ a. Local profile

○ b. Local profile with GPO folder redirection

○ c. Mandatory profile

○ d. Roaming profile

Question 54

Which of the following commands will remove all routes to internal subnets within the 10.0.0.0/8 address space?

○ a. route delete 10.0.0.0 mask 255.0.0.0

○ b. route delete 10.*

○ c. route delete 10.0.0.0/8

○ d. route –p delete 10.0.0.0 mask 255.0.0.0

Question 55

Which boot.ini syntax would specify the second partition on the first drive on the third SCSI controller?

○ a. scsi(0)disk(3)rdisk(0)partition(2)

○ b. scsi(2)disk(0)rdisk(0)partition(1)

○ c. scsi(2)disk(0)rdisk(0)partition(2)

○ d. scsi(2)disk(1)rdisk(0)partition(2)

○ e. scsi(3)disk(1)rdisk(0)partition(2)

Question 56

Your department shares network address space with two other departments. All three departments maintain their own DHCP servers. A user reports a message from his system that states a duplicate IP address has been detected. You suspect DHCP scope address overlap and want to contact the systems admin for the proper department, so need to determine which computers are sharing the same address. From the client computer experiencing the error, which of the following commands would allow you to find the other system claiming the same IP address?

- ○ a. arp -a
- ○ b. nbtstat -c
- ○ c. netstat -s
- ○ d. ipconfig /release
- ○ e. nslookup mycorp.com

Question 57

A remote salesperson reports that when their laptops are connected via the office wireless network, everything works well, but when they are dialing in from some hotels their logon scripts are not running properly. The user says that their desktop settings are being configured properly all the time, and that everything works normally from other dial-in locations. They have already checked with their ISP and the firewall and network configurations at all hotels involved are the same. What is the most likely problem?

- ○ a. An inherited group policy setting from a higher-level assignment is overriding the script settings.
- ○ b. The dial-up connection is too slow in some locations.
- ○ c. The DNS server is overloaded.
- ○ d. The firewall is preventing access by the user when dialing in from certain locations.
- ○ e. The group policy object is not properly configured.

Question 58

What is the largest number of hosts listed that may operate within the 10.0.0.0/23 subnet?

○ a. 50

○ b. 100

○ c. 250

○ d. 500

○ e. 1000

Question 59

You suspect that a system that has been left powered off for two months may need security and anti-virus updates. You plan to use the hfnetchk tool to check for any needed updates and then obtain the appropriate patches from the Microsoft Security site.

Will this complete the stated requirement?

○ a. Yes

○ b. No

Question 60

You have been told to configure a new server to use RAID in the most efficient fault-tolerant configuration possible using a pair of identical 100GB IDE drives. Which RAID type would be the best choice?

○ a. Mirroring (RAID 1)

○ b. Striping (RAID 0)

○ c. Striping with parity (RAID 5)

Answer Key

1. d	21. b	41. a
2. b	22. b	42. d
3. b, d	23. a	43. c
4. b	24. e	44. c, d, e
5. e	25. b, d	45. See answer
6. See answer	26. d	46. c
7. b	27. b	47. d
8. c	28. d	48. d
9. b	29. See answer	49. e
10. See answer	30. c	50. b,d
11. a	31. d	51. See answer
12. b	32. See answer	52. b
13. b	33. b	53. b
14. c	34. c	54. b
15. b	35. b	55. c
16. a	36. See answer	56. b
17. d	37. d	57. b
18. b	38. d	58. d
19. b	39. See answer	59. b
20. a, b, c, d	40. b	60. a

Question 1

The correct answer is d. You must manually publish the printer using the Active Directory Users And Computers MMC snap-in. Answers a and b are incorrect because it is possible to manually publish a printer shared from a Unix platform, though Unix will not automatically publish to the Active Directory. Answer c is incorrect because the Active Directory Sites And Services MMC snap-in is not used for printer publication.

Question 2

Answer b is the correct answer. Static fully qualified domain naming (FQDN) entries are entered into the HOSTS file, which is checked before external name resolution is attempted. Answer a is incorrect because the LMHOSTS file is used for static NetBIOS name assignment. Answers c and d are incorrect because RIP and IGMP are routing protocols used by routers for communications. Answer e is incorrect because AppleTalk is a LAN protocol used by Macintosh computers.

Question 3

Answers b and d are correct. You can determine the correct internal subnet mask by first calculating the original subnet mask provided. 192.168.0.0/13 specifies a 13-bit subnet mask:

11111111.11111000.00000000.00000000 (255.248.0.0)

Answer a is incorrect for the final subnet mask, because this matches the initial mask value. This leaves 19 bits remaining for internal subnetting. In order to have at least 500 internal subnets, the next-highest factor of 2 must be calculated, which is in this case 512, or 2^9. This requires 9 additional bits for the internal subnet mask:

11111111.11111000.00000000.00000000 (original subnet mask of 13 bits)

00000000.00000111.11111100.00000000 (internal network ID mask of 9 bits)

11111111.11111111.11111100.00000000   (final   subnet   mask   -> 255.255.252.0)

This leaves 10 bits for host addressing within each subnet. $2^{10} = 1,024$ host addresses per subnet. This is sufficient to the requirement of at least 1,000 hosts per subnet. Answer c is incorrect because a subnet mask of 255.255.255.0 would leave only 8 bits available for host addressing per subnet, which would leave only 256 possible host addresses, less the default gateway and broadcast addresses, and would result in only 254 possible host addresses per subnet, which is less than the requirement.

Given the original starting address of 192.168.0.0 and the subnet mask of 255.255.252.0, the broadcast address for the first subnet range can be easily calculated by setting all host address bits to 1's for the first subnet:

11000000.10101000.00000000.00000000 (base address of 192.168.0.0)

11111111.11111111.11111100.00000000 (subnet mask of 255.255.252.0)

11000000.10101000.000000 (network address of the first subnet)

00000000.00000000.00000011.11111111 (all 1's for the host address within the subnet)

11000000.10101000.00000011.11111111 (broadcast address for the first subnet: 192.168.3.255)

Answers e and f are incorrect because they specify more than 10 bits for their host addresses.

Question 4

Answer b is correct. The proper LMHOSTS entry should specify the association of the IP address and the NetBIOS name (myserver) with the flag #PRE set in order to cache the information at boot. Answer a is incorrect because it lacks the #PRE designation. Answers c and d are incorrect because they specify a fully qualified name (myserver.mycorp.com) rather than the proper NetBIOS flat namespace name (myserver). Answer e is incorrect because it reverses the order of the NetBIOS name and the IP address. Answer f is incorrect because it is formatted as a HOSTS entry, associating the fully qualified name (myserver.mycorp.com) with the IP address.

Question 5

Answer e is correct. The specified subnet 194.161.240.0 is a Class C address, which means it has a default subnet mask of 255.255.255.0. This could also be written as 194.161.240.0/24. Dividing this into four smaller subnets would require 2 bits for subnet network addressing, yielding a final subnet mask of 255.255.255.192 (11111111.11111111.111111111.11000000), which leaves 6 bits for host addressing. The maximum number of host addresses per subnet is therefore $2^6 = 64$ addresses. With the first and last assigned to the default gateway and broadcast for each subnet, a maximum of 62 host addresses are available in each of the four subnets.

Question 6

The correct answers are:

NT 4.0

   Backup Domain Controller

   Member server

   Primary Domain Controller

Windows 2000 mixed mode

   Member server

   Global Catalog server

   PDC Emulator

Windows 2000 native mode

   Member server

   Global Catalog server

   PDC Emulator

Question 7

The correct answer is b. The delay between when a change is first made and when it is propagated to all other copies of the Global Catalog is called latency. Answers a and c are incorrect because the goal of having all changes distributed everywhere is called convergence, and the process of distributing a change is called replication. Answer d is incorrect because, though it is often annoying, the process of replication until convergence is reached allows for a multimaster structure such as the Active Directory to operate.

Question 8

The correct answer is c. The errors shown occur when the Infrastructure Master and Global Catalog exist on the same server. Moving the Infrastructure Master role to another domain controller in the root domain will relieve this conflict. Answer a is incorrect because this is not a DNS-related problem. Answer b is incorrect because the Schema Master role is not involved, and must remain in the root domain of the forest. Answer d is incorrect because it does not specify removing the Global Catalog service from the original root domain server, so the conflict with the Infrastructure Master will continue to occur. Answer e is incorrect because you cannot create a parent to the Root domain, and this is not a DNS-related problem.

Question 9

The correct answer is b. If users in Domain A can access resources located in Domain B, then it is said that Domain A is trusted by Domain B. Answers a and c are incorrect because the term sharing applies to making resources available to remote users. Answer d is incorrect because Domain B trusts Domain A, not the other way around.

Question 10

The correct answer is, in order:

Forests

Trees

Domains

Organizational units

Nested organizational units

Question 11

The correct answer is a. The relative distinguished name is the portion of the LDAP name that is unique to the target object. Answers b, c, d, and e are all portions of the distinguished name, but are not unique to the target object.

Question 12

The correct answer is b. A Reverse Lookup zone allows IP addresses to be translated into their equivalent FQDNs. Answer a is incorrect because a Forward Lookup zone translates a specified FQDN into its associated IP address. Answers c and d are incorrect because this was specified as an Active Directory Integrated zone, whereas a Standard Primary zone is stored in a local text file, and a Standard Secondary zone is simply a read-only copy of a Standard Primary zone's lookup file. A Reverse Lookup zone could be created as either an Active Directory Integrated zone, a Standard Primary zone, or a Standard Secondary zone. In this case, however, Active Directory Integrated was specified.

Question 13

The correct answer is b. Creating a CNAME (Alias) record for the name public.mycorp.com, as an alias for the current production server's IP Host (A) record, will allow both names to resolve to the same address. Answer a is incorrect because it is unnecessary to create a new Host (A) record for an already-in-use IP address, and this may cause unexpected behavior when attempting a reverse lookup from IP address to FQDN naming. Answer c is incorrect because an MX record is used for mail redirection. Answer d is incorrect because a PTR record is created in a Reverse Lookup zone and associates an IP address with its equivalent FQDN. Answer e is incorrect because WWW is not a valid DNS record type.

Question 14

The correct answer is c. The nslookup utility can be used to verify DNS functionality. Answers a and b are incorrect because the ipconfig and nbtstat utilities are used to display information about the current TCP/IP configuration of a system. Answers d, e, and f are incorrect because the ping, pathping, and tracert utilities are used to verify proper network connectivity.

Question 15

The correct answer is b. A client will first attempt to renew its DHCP lease when 50 percent of the lease's lifespan has passed. Answers a, c, d, e, and f are incorrect.

Question 16

The correct answer is a. A client will broadcast a DHCPDISCOVER message during the Discovery phase, and await the first DHCPOFFER from available servers in its local area network. If it does not receive an offer, it will utilize a private address and continue to check for available DHCP servers every five minutes until one becomes available. Answer b is incorrect because the Offer phase occurs when the servers send the DHCPOFFER back to the requesting client. Answer c is incorrect because the Request phase occurs when the client sends a DHCPREQUEST back to the offering server. Answer d is incorrect because the Acknowledgement phase occurs when the offering server responds to the client's request by providing the addressing and configuration information in a new lease.

Question 17

The correct answer is d. Because client systems will respond to the first offer they receive from a DHCP server, some may be provided will lease offers from DHCP servers not authorized for the Active Directory domain. DHCP servers must be authorized before they can provide leases to domain clients. Answer a is incorrect because a site includes one or more subnets, and DHCP servers will respond to DHCPDISCOVER broadcast messages automatically. Answer b is incorrect because the issue is not a name service problem. Answer c is incorrect because the scopes have already been separated to avoid conflicts between the two servers. Answer e is an incorrect solution because static addressing would require a free address in the subnet, and all addresses have already been included in the DHCP scopes, so later conflicts between two systems with the same IP address may result.

Question 18

The correct answer is b. It is possible to preassign a particular IP address to a specific system by creating a DHCP reservation within the server's scope.

Question 19

The correct answer is b. Denying Full Access includes denial of all other types of access. An inherited access denial will override any inherited allow permissions. Answers a and c are incorrect because neither the lack of permissions assigned to the Domain Users group nor the allow permissions granted to the Managers group would prevent access. Answer d is incorrect because, although the denial is inherited from the Front Office through the Sales group, the denial assigned to the parent group is the cause of the error. Answer e is incorrect because the removal of the denial from the Front Office group will resolve this conflict.

Question 20

Answer a, b, c, and d are all correct. It is possible to distribute a custom MMC just as you would distribute any other type of file. You may also need to distribute the adminpak.msi file in order to install all of the appropriate snap-ins onto the local administrator's systems.

Question 21

The correct answer is b. An explicit denial will override any other permission assignments. Answer a is incorrect because an explicit denial will override an explicitly granted allow. Answer c is incorrect because an implicit denial is the default in which no access is granted without an explicit allow. Any explicit assignment will override an implicit denial.

Question 22

The correct answer is b. The group policy template is a folder hierarchy containing settings and scripts for the group policy. Answer a is incorrect because the group policy container is an Active Directory object. Answer c is incorrect because the scope of a group policy is the level at which it may be assigned.

Question 23

The correct answer is a. In order to ensure that domain controllers maintain the most updated version of group policies, the refresh interval is five minutes. Answers b, c, d, and e are incorrect, although the default refresh interval for non-domain controllers is 60 minutes, plus or minus a random interval up to 30 minutes. This equates to a random interval between 30 and 90 minutes.

Question 24

The correct answer is e. Because the changes were computer policy settings, they will not be reloaded until the next reboot of the system. Answers a, b, c, and d are incorrect because they all involve going to the user's system or to the domain controller, which should not be the first thing attempted in this case. Answer f is incorrect because the user has already attempted a logoff/logon cycle, and computer settings will not be refreshed until the next reboot cycle.

Question 25

The correct answers are b and d. In order for a group policy to be applied to an account, it must have the Read and Allow Group Policy permissions. Answers a and c are incorrect because they are not specifically required for this purpose.

Question 26

The correct answer is d. The custom MSI file should be assigned to the computer as an automatic installation to ensure that all systems will obtain the new settings upon their next reboot. Answers a and b are incorrect because we cannot control which systems users will log on to, and a necessary update should be applied to all computers. Answer c is incorrect because software packages cannot be published to computers, only assigned.

Question 27

The correct answer is b. The given subnet mask (255.255.255.128) translates into a 25-bit mask: 11111111.11111111.11111111.10000000, which leaves 7 bits remaining for host addressing. This translates to 128 possible addresses for each subnet. The address 128.176.224.13 is in the first 128 addresses of the range 0-127. The first address is assigned to the default gateway, while the last is assigned to the broadcast address for the subnet. Therefore, the address of the default gateway is 128.176.224.0, with a 25-bit subnet mask. This is written in CIDR notation as 128.176.224.0/25.

Answer a is incorrect because it specifies only a 7-bit subnet mask. Answer c is incorrect because it specifies the original network host address. Answer d is incorrect because it specifies the broadcast address for the target subnet. Answer e is incorrect because it specifies the broadcast address for the upper 128-address subnet: 128.176.224.128-255.

Question 28

The correct answer is d. The most favorable combination of access permissions is used for NTFS and Share level access resolution, and the least favorable combination for both is used when determining final access rights. Therefore, answers a, b, and c are incorrect.

Question 29

The correct answer is:

Connect

Performs installation of a printer on a computer

Move

Allows the location of a published printer reference to be changed to a different organizational unit

Open

Allows job and print queue management

Properties

Allows the addition of available drivers

Question 30

The correct answer is c. When a Terminal Services connection is made, the server will check for a printer driver of the appropriate type. If the driver is not installed, the printer will be unavailable during the Terminal Services session. Answer a is incorrect because the printer is a local printer, not a network printer. Answers b and d are incorrect because the user can already use the printer when not using Terminal Services.

Question 31

The correct answer is d. Terminal Services connections require access to port 3389. Answers a, b, c, and e are incorrect. If using the TSAC Web-based client, port 80 must be open to the Web server providing access to the TSAC client, which does not need to be the same machine accessed using Terminal Services through the TSAC client.

Question 32

The correct answers are:

RAID-0

  Also called striping

  Fastest RAID access type

RAID-1

  Also called mirroring

  Fault tolerant

  Least efficient RAID storage type

RAID-5

  Also called striping with parity

  Fault tolerant

  Slowest RAID access type

Question 33

The correct answer is b. Native mode requires that all domain controllers be upgraded to Windows 2000. Member servers can be Windows NT 4 or later operating systems.

Question 34

The correct answer is c. Placing organizational units within other organizational units is called nesting. Answers a, b, and d are incorrect.

Question 35

The correct answer is b. FTP access requires port 21, while default access using a Web browser requires port 80. Answers a, c, d, and e are incorrect.

Question 36

The correct answer is:

Custom port

    Allows sharing of a single IP address for multiple sites

    Provides enhanced security against port scanning

Host headers

    Allows a registered alias to be used to identify a site

    Allows sharing of a single IP address for multiple sites

Multiple IP

    Allows the association of one or more IP addresses to a site

Question 37

The correct answer is d. The IUSR_*<computer name>* account provides anonymous access via FTP and Web site connections. Answers a and b are incorrect because a machine-specific account is used for anonymous access. Answers c and e are incorrect because account naming for anonymous access accounts is machine specific, not domain-specific . Answer f is incorrect because the IWAM_*<computer name>* account is used to run certain types of Web-deployed applications, rather than for anonymous access authentication.

Question 38

The correct answer is d. The **fixmbr** command is used within the recovery console to rebuild a corrupted master boot record. Answer a is incorrect because the **fixboot** command is used to repair the boot sector rather than the master boot record. Answers b, c, and e are incorrect because Logged, Safe Mode, and Debugging Mode are all advanced startup options and not commands within the Recovery Console.

Question 39

The correct answer is:

System Monitor

  Can be used to log data over a period of time

  Provides current process resource utilization statistics

Task Manager

  Can be used to stop processes that are consuming too many system resources

  Provides current process resource utilization statistics

Network Monitor

  Captures data packets

  Can be used to log data over a period of time

Question 40

The correct answer is b. The **tracert** command provides a rapid test of each hop between the source and a target host. Answers a and c are incorrect because the **ping** and **pathping** commands repeatedly test connectivity to the same target address. Answers d and e are incorrect because the **ipconfig** and **netdiag** commands provide information on current TCP/IP settings, rather than connectivity details to a target host.

Question 41

The correct answer is a. To allow all employees to reconnect after the ISP's automatic timeout, the gateway computer should be configured to Enable Demand Dialing, so that any attempts to connect to the Net will cause the gateway system to perform a connection to the dial-up service.

Question 42

The correct answer is d. The Password Authentication Protocol (PAP) transmits password data in clear text and is not considered a secure method of authentication. Answers a, b, and c are incorrect because the Challenge Handshake Authentication Protocol variations (CHAP, MS-CHAP, and MS-CHAP v2) are considered highly secure. Answer e is incorrect because the Shiva Password Authentication Protocol (SPAP) provides moderate security through Shiva hardware password encryption.

Question 43

The correct answer is c. The address 10.1.50.4/16 has a 16-bit subnet mask, which translates to 255.255.0.0. In order to specify a persistent route, the **-p** designator is required. The proper command to add this route is:

```
route -p add 10.1.50.4 mask 255.255.0.0
  10.50.1.1 (route -p <address> mask <mask> <next hop>)
```

Answers a and b are incorrect because they do not specify a persistent route (they lack the **-p** flag). Answer d is incorrect because it specifies the wrong subnet mask. Answer e is incorrect because the target address and next hop are reversed.

Question 44

Answers c, d, and e are correct. All three of the account lockout settings must be configured: Account Lockout Duration, Account Lockout Threshold, and Reset Account Lockout Counter After. If any of these are not configured, account lockout will not function. Answers a and b are incorrect because they are password settings rather than account lockout settings. Passwords must meet complexity requirements and enforce password history.

Question 45

The correct answers are:

Application Log

  Provides events logged by programs such as Exchange or SQL Server

Security Log

  Provides information on events generated by auditing

System

Directory service

  Includes details on events such as directory replication

  Only found on domain controllers

DNS Server

  Only found on DNS servers

File replication service

  Only found on domain controllers

  Provides information on group policy replication

Question 46

Answer c is correct. Since broadcasts typically do not pass routers, only systems within the subnet local to the DHCP server are able to obtain DHCP leases properly. A DHCP Proxy within Subnet-A will redirect DHCP lease requests from broadcasts in Subnet-A to the DHCP server located within Subnet-B. Answer a is incorrect because the specification details the need to use dynamic addressing. Answer b is incorrect because the failure to obtain a DHCP lease is not a name resolution issue. Answer d is incorrect because each host must have its own unique IP address.

Question 47

Answer d is correct. To create a persistent (lasting) route to the detination network 10.5.0.0/16 through the gateway 10.2.0.1, the correct command would be: route –p add 10.5.0.0 mask 255.255.0.0 10.2.0.1. Answers a and b are incorrect because they do not include the –p flag necessary to establish a persistent route. Answers a and c are incorrect because they do not specify a subnet mask in the proper format, here 255.255.0.0. Answer e is incorrect because the next hop is out of order. The correct order is: route [-p] add *<network address>* mask *<subnet mask> <next hop>*.

Question 48

Answer d is correct. The highest-priority setting for a print share is 99. Answers a and e are incorrect because the print priority must be a numerical value between 1 and 99. Answer b is incorrect because 1 is the default (lowest priority) setting. Answer c is incorrect because it is possible that other shares for the printer may have a value above 50. It would be necessary to ensure that all other shares for this printer had a print priority value of 98 or less, in order to be certain that the CEO's documents would print first in the queue.

Question 49

Answer e is correct. In order to open the first partition on the second drive on the first IDE controller, the proper boot.ini entry would be multi(0)disk(0)rdisk(1)partition(1). Answer a is incorrect because rdisk(0) specifies the first drive. Answer b is incorrect because partition(2) specifies the second partition, in this case, on the first drive. Answer c is incorrect because multi(1) specifies the second IDE controller. Answer d is incorrect because disk(1) would only be used to specify a SCSI drive. IDE specifications will always have a disk() value of 0.

Question 50

Answers b and d are correct. The **secedit /refreshpolicy machine_policy** command may be used to enforce GPO settings immediately. This is being replaced by the **gpupdate /target:computer** command in the most recent versions of Windows. Answer a is incorrect because the default for the **gpupdate** command is to update both user and computer GPO settings. Answer c is incorrect because the **secedit /refreshpolicy** command may be used to refresh the **machine_policy** or **user_policy** settings. There is not a **computer_policy** option for this command.

Question 51

The correct answers are:

Domain local groups

May be used to grant permissions only in the local domain.

May have users and computers from any domain within the forest as members.

Global groups

May be used to grant permissions only in the local domain.

May have only local-domain users and groups as members.

Universal groups

May be used to grant permissions within any domain within a forest.

May have users and computers from any domain within the forest as members.

Not available in Mixed-mode Windows 2000 domains.

Question 52

Answer b is correct. Orphaned objects within the Active Directory are placed in the lost and found container. Answer a is incorrect. Newly created user accounts will be created within this container by default, but orphaned user account objects will not be relocated here. Answer c is incorrect because the recycle bin is used to hold deleted file references until emptied, and is not used by Active Directory for object storage. Answer d is incorrect because the orphaned object continues to exist within the Active Directory database.

Question 53

Answer b is correct. A local profile with GPO-redirected folders would allow the IT staff to access their diagnostic programs from any system within the company while minimizing network bandwidth requirements. Answer a is incorrect because each local profile copy would be different, preventing easy access to all of the standard diagnostic programs for each. Answer c is incorrect because a mandatory profile is used to restrict changes to the profile, and the IT staff is responsible for testing multiple settings and configurations. Answer d is incorrect because a roaming profile copies all files within the profile from the server to the client system during logon, and then synchronizes these files again at logout. This is highly bandwidth intensive.

Question 54

Answer b is correct. To delete all routes to subnets located within the 10.0.0.0/8 address space, the proper format is: route delete 10.*. Answers a and d are incorrect because they specifies the deletion of only the route to the 10.0.0.0 subnet. Routes to additional subnets within the address space such as 10.5.0.0 would be unaffected. Answer d is also incorrect because the –p flag is only used to create routes. All route deletions are persistent, since deletions remove the relevant routing entries. Answer c is incorrect because the mask is not specified in the proper form, and if properly formatted as in answer a, the result would remove routing to only the one subnet.

Question 55

Answer c is correct. In order to open the second partition on the first drive on the third SCSI controller, the proper boot.ini entry would be scsi(2)disk(0)rdisk(0)partition(2). Answer a is incorrect because scsi(0) specifies the first SCSI controller, and disk(3) specifies the fourth physical disk. Answer b is incorrect because partition(1) specifies the first partition. Answers d and e are incorrect because disk(1) specifies the second disk on the controller. Answer e is also incorrect because scsi(3) specifies the fourth SCSI controller.

Question 56

Answer b is correct. The nbtstat –c command will list the current contents of the NetBIOS lookup cache, including the IP addresses of all cached local system announcement broadcasts. Answer a is incorrect because the arp –a command will simply display the current IP to MAC configuration details for the local network interfaces. Answer c is incorrect because the netstat –s command will list the by-protocol communications statistics for all network adapters. Answer d is incorrect because ipconfig /release will only release any current DHCP leases and will not provide information on conflicting leases. Answer e is incorrect because the nslookup *<domain>* command will provide the IP addresses of authoritative DNS servers for the specified domain.

Question 57

Answer b is correct. The most likely cause of this problem is that a slow network connection (under 500kbps) has been detected, so that only the Administrative Templates, Security, and EFS settings are being evaluated from the GPO. Dial-up connections are limited in transmission rate based on many factors, which may vary from location to location. Answer a is incorrect because an inherited higher-level setting would function always, regardless of the method of connection or source location. Because the GPO settings work properly at times, the settings are not in conflict. Answer c is incorrect because name resolution errors would not cause a partial GPO assignment. Connectivity to a server would either be able to provide the GPO settings or not, and would only be affected by DNS failure if no other method of name resolution to identify a domain controller was available. Answer d is most likely incorrect. It is possible to filter by source IP address at a firewall, but the ISP of the hotels has verified that the network configuration is the same. This is not the best possible answer from those listed. Answer e is incorrect because an incorrect GPO configuration would be applied in the same manner regardless of the connection method.

Question 58

Answer d is correct. A subnet mask of 23 bits leaves 9 bits for host addressing (000000000-111111111), which provides 512 possible addresses. Answer a is incorrect because more than 6 bits are available for host addressing, allowing more than 64 possible addresses. Answer b is incorrect because more than 7 bits are available, allowing more than 128 host addresses. Answer c is incorrect because more than 8 bits are available, allowing more than 256 host addresses. Answer e is incorrect because 10 bits would be required for host addressing of 1024 addresses.

Question 59

Answer b is correct. This will update all of the Microsoft operating system security patches and hotfixes, but you will also need to update the anti-virus definitions as well, along with any Office Suite updates that have come out. Hfnetchk does not check for application updates, only for operating system and certain service updates such as those for SQL Server.

Question 60

Answer a is correct. RAID-1 (mirroring) would be the most efficient fault-tolerant solution possible using two drives. Answer b is incorrect because RAID-0 (striping) is not a fault-tolerant storage solution. Answer c is incorrect because RAID-5 (striping with parity) requires three or more drives.

What's on the CD-ROM

This appendix is a brief rundown of what you'll find on the CD-ROM that comes with this book. For a more detailed description of the *PrepLogic Practice Tests, Preview Edition* exam simulation software, see Appendix B, "Using *PrepLogic Practice Tests, Preview Edition* Software." In addition to the *PrepLogic Practice Tests, Preview Edition*, the CD-ROM includes the electronic version of the book in Portable Document Format (PDF), several utility and application programs, and a complete listing of test objectives and where they are covered in the book. Finally, a pointer list to online pointers and references are added to this CD. You will need a computer with Internet access and a relatively recent browser installed to use this feature.

PrepLogic Practice Tests, Preview Edition

PrepLogic is a leading provider of certification training tools. Trusted by certification students worldwide, we believe PrepLogic is the best practice exam software available. In addition to providing a means of evaluating your knowledge of the Exam Cram material, *PrepLogic Practice Tests, Preview Edition* features several innovations that help you to improve your mastery of the subject matter.

For example, the practice tests allow you to check your score by exam area or domain to determine which topics you need to study more. Another feature allows you to obtain immediate feedback on your responses in the form of explanations for the correct and incorrect answers.

PrepLogic Practice Tests, Preview Edition exhibits most of the full functionality of the *Premium Edition* but offers only a fraction of the total questions. To get the complete set of practice questions and exam functionality, visit PrepLogic.com and order the *Premium Edition* for this and other challenging exam titles.

Again, for a more detailed description of the *PrepLogic Practice Tests, Preview Edition* features, see Appendix B.

Exclusive Electronic Version of Text

The CD-ROM also contains the electronic version of this book in Portable Document Format (PDF). The electronic version comes complete with all figures as they appear in the book. You will find that the search capabilities of the reader comes in handy for study and review purposes.

Easy Access to Online Pointers and References

The Suggested Reading section at the end of each chapter in this Exam Cram contains numerous pointers to Web sites, newsgroups, mailing lists, and other online resources. To make this material as easy to use as possible, we include all this information in an HTML document titled "Online Pointers" on the CD. Open this document in your favorite Web browser to find links you can follow through any Internet connection to access these resources directly.

Using the *PrepLogic Practice Tests, Preview Edition* Software

This Exam Cram includes a special version of PrepLogic Practice Tests—a revolutionary test engine designed to give you the best in certification exam preparation. PrepLogic offers sample and practice exams for many of today's most in-demand and challenging technical certifications. This special *Preview Edition* is included with this book as a tool to use in assessing your knowledge of the Exam Cram material, while also providing you with the experience of taking an electronic exam.

This appendix describes in detail what *PrepLogic Practice Tests, Preview Edition* is, how it works, and what it can do to help you prepare for the exam. Note that although the *Preview Edition* includes all the test simulation functions of the complete, retail version, it contains only a single practice test. The *Premium Edition*, available at PrepLogic.com, contains the complete set of challenging practice exams designed to optimize your learning experience.

Exam Simulation

One of the main functions of *PrepLogic Practice Tests, Preview Edition* is exam simulation. To prepare you to take the actual vendor certification exam, PrepLogic is designed to offer the most effective exam simulation available.

Question Quality

The questions provided in the *PrepLogic Practice Tests, Preview Edition* are written to the highest standards of technical accuracy. The questions tap the content of the Exam Cram chapters and help you to review and assess your knowledge before you take the actual exam.

Interface Design

The *PrepLogic Practice Tests, Preview Edition* exam simulation interface provides you with the experience of taking an electronic exam. This enables you to effectively prepare yourself for taking the actual exam by making the test experience a familiar one. Using this test simulation can help to eliminate the sense of surprise or anxiety you might experience in the testing center because you will already be acquainted with computerized testing.

Effective Learning Environment

The *PrepLogic Practice Tests, Preview Edition* interface provides a learning environment that not only tests you through the computer, but also teaches the material you need to know to pass the certification exam. Each question comes with a detailed explanation of the correct answer and often provides reasons the other options are incorrect. This information helps to reinforce the knowledge you already have and also provides practical information you can use on the job.

Software Requirements

PrepLogic Practice Tests requires a computer with the following:

➤ Microsoft Windows 98, Windows Me, Windows NT 4.0, Windows 2000, or Windows XP

➤ A 166MHz or faster processor is recommended

➤ A minimum of 32MB of RAM

➤ As with any Windows application, the more memory, the better your performance

➤ 10MB of hard drive space

Installing *PrepLogic Practice Tests, Preview Edition*

Install *PrepLogic Practice Tests, Preview Edition* by running the setup program on the *PrepLogic Practice Tests, Preview Edition* CD. Follow these instructions to install the software on your computer:

1. Insert the CD into your CD-ROM drive. The Autorun feature of Windows should launch the software. If you have Autorun disabled, click the Start button and select Run. Go to the root directory of the CD and select setup.exe. Click Open, and then click OK.

2. The Installation Wizard copies the *PrepLogic Practice Tests, Preview Edition* files to your hard drive; adds *PrepLogic Practice Tests, Preview Edition* to your Desktop and Program menu; and installs test engine components to the appropriate system folders.

Removing *PrepLogic Practice Tests, Preview Edition* from Your Computer

If you elect to remove the *PrepLogic Practice Tests,, Preview Edition* product from your computer, an uninstall process has been included to ensure that it is removed from your system safely and completely. Follow these instructions to remove PrepLogic Practice Tests, Preview Edition from your computer:

1. Select Start, Settings, Control Panel.

2. Double-click the Add/Remove Programs icon.

3. You are presented with a list of software currently installed on your computer. Select the appropriate *PrepLogic Practice Tests, Preview Edition* title you wish to remove. Click the Add/Remove button. The software is then removed from you computer.

Using *PrepLogic Practice Tests, Preview Edition*

PrepLogic is designed to be user friendly and intuitive. Because the software has a smooth learning curve, your time is maximized, as you will start practicing almost immediately. *PrepLogic Practice Tests, Preview Edition* has two major modes of study: Practice Test and Flash Review.

Using Practice Test mode, you can develop your test-taking abilities, as well as your knowledge through the use of the Show Answer option. While you are taking the test, you can reveal the answers along with a detailed explanation of why the given answers are right or wrong. This gives you the ability to better understand the material presented.

Flash Review is designed to reinforce exam topics rather than quiz you. In this mode, you will be shown a series of questions, but no answer choices. Instead, you will be given a button that reveals the correct answer to the question and a full explanation for that answer.

Starting a Practice Test Mode Session

Practice Test mode enables you to control the exam experience in ways that actual certification exams do not allow:

➤ **Enable Show Answer Button**—Activates the Show Answer button, allowing you to view the correct answer(s) and a full explanation for each question during the exam. When not enabled, you must wait until after your exam has been graded to view the correct answer(s) and explanation(s).

➤ **Enable Item Review Button**—Activates the Item Review button, allowing you to view your answer choices, marked questions, and facilitating navigation between questions.

➤ **Randomize Choices**—Randomize answer choices from one exam session to the next; makes memorizing question choices more difficult, therefore keeping questions fresh and challenging longer.

To begin studying in Practice Test mode, click the Practice Test radio button from the main exam customization screen. This will enable the options detailed previously.

To your left, you are presented with the options of selecting the preconfigured Practice Test or creating your own Custom Test. The preconfigured test has a fixed time limit and number of questions. Custom Tests allow you to configure the time limit and the number of questions in your exam.

The *Preview Edition* included with this book includes a single preconfigured Practice Test. Get the compete set of challenging PrepLogic Practice Tests at PrepLogic.com and make certain you're ready for the big exam.

Click the Begin Exam button to begin your exam.

Starting a Flash Review Mode Session

Flash Review mode provides you with an easy way to reinforce topics covered in the practice questions. To begin studying in Flash Review mode, click the Flash Review radio button from the main exam customization screen. Select either the preconfigured Practice Test or create your own Custom Test.

Click the Best Exam button to begin your Flash Review of the exam questions.

Standard *PrepLogic Practice Tests, Preview Edition* Options

The following list describes the function of each of the buttons you see. Depending on the options, some of the buttons will be grayed out and inaccessible or missing completely. Buttons that are accessible are active. The buttons are as follows:

➤ **Exhibit**—This button is visible if an exhibit is provided to support the question. An exhibit is an image that provides supplemental information necessary to answer the question.

➤ **Item Review**—This button leaves the question window and opens the Item Review screen. From this screen you will see all questions, your answers, and your marked items. You will also see correct answers listed here when appropriate.

➤ **Show Answer**—This option displays the correct answer with an explanation of why it is correct. If you select this option, the current question is not scored.

➤ **Mark Item**—Check this box to tag a question you need to review further. You can view and navigate your Marked Items by clicking the Item Review button (if enabled). When grading your exam, you will be notified if you have marked items remaining.

➤ **Previous Item**—This option allows you to view the previous question.

➤ **Next Item**—This option allows you to view the next question.

➤ **Grade Exam**—When you have completed your exam, click this button to end your exam and view your detailed score report. If you have unanswered or marked items remaining you will be asked if you would like to continue taking your exam or view your exam report.

Time Remaining

If the test is timed, the time remaining is displayed on the upper right corner of the application screen. It counts down the minutes and seconds remaining to complete the test. If you run out of time, you will be asked if you want to continue taking the test or if you want to end your exam.

Your Examination Score Report

The Examination Score Report screen appears when the Practice Test mode ends—as the result of time expiration, completion of all questions, or your decision to terminate early.

This screen provides you with a graphical display of your test score with a breakdown of scores by topic domain. The graphical display at the top of the screen compares your overall score with the PrepLogic Exam Competency Score.

The PrepLogic Exam Competency Score reflects the level of subject competency required to pass this vendor's exam. While this score does not directly translate to a passing score, consistently matching or exceeding this score does suggest you possess the knowledge to pass the actual vendor exam.

Review Your Exam

From Your Score Report screen, you can review the exam that you just completed by clicking on the View Items button. Navigate through the items viewing the questions, your answers, the correct answers, and the explanations for those answers. You can return to your score report by clicking the View Items button.

Get More Exams

Each *PrepLogic Practice Tests, Preview Edition* that accompanies your Exam Cram contains a single PrepLogic Practice Test. Certification students worldwide trust PrepLogic Practice Tests to help them pass their IT certification exams the first time. Purchase the *Premium Edition* of PrepLogic Practice Tests and get the entire set of all new challenging Practice Tests for this exam. PrepLogic Practice Tests—Because You Want to Pass the First Time.

Contacting PrepLogic

If you would like to contact PrepLogic for any reason, including information about our extensive line of certification practice tests, we invite you to do so. Please contact us online at **http://www.preplogic.com.**

Customer Service

If you have a damaged product and need a replacement or refund, please call the following phone number:

800-858-7674

Product Suggestions and Comments

We value your input! Please email your suggestions and comments to the following address:

feedback@preplogic.com

License Agreement

YOU MUST AGREE TO THE TERMS AND CONDITIONS OUT-LINED IN THE END USER LICENSE AGREEMENT ("EULA") PRESENTED TO YOU DURING THE INSTALLATION PROCESS. IF YOU DO NOT AGREE TO THESE TERMS DO NOT INSTALL THE SOFTWARE.

Glossary

. . . .

Active Directory

An integrated multimaster hierarchical domain model, available beginning with Windows 2000, which can be queried using the Lightweight Directory Access Protocol (LDAP).

administrative templates

Preconfigured collections of settings for easy administration of common group policy configuration types.

auditing

Allows events to be written to the Security Log when specific audited actions occur.

authentication

The process by which a user's identity is verified for the purposes of allowing a connection to be created to a site or service.

authorization

The registration process for a DHCP server that allows the server to provide automatic addressing support for members of a domain.

backup domain controller

Windows NT 4 server that maintains a read-only copy of user and computer account settings provided by the primary domain controller.

bridgehead server

A domain controller responsible for inter-site replication of the Active Directory catalog.

Classless Inter-Domain Routing (CIDR) notation

A simplified non-class-based system for efficient subnet expression. In CIDR notation, the complex numerical subnet mask is replaced by a suffix of the number of bits in the effective mask (for example, 128.176.242.0/24 instead of 128.176.242.0 mask 255.255.255.0).

domain

A collection of systems that share a membership in a common, server-supported grouping. Domains provide common user logon accounts and centralized management of resource access.

drivers

Custom software-interface packages that provide translation between hardware devices and the Hardware Abstraction Layer (HAL).

dynamic addressing

Host name and IP addressing that can change with each reconnection of a computer. It is facilitated by a Dynamic Host Configuration Protocol (DHCP) server.

Flexible Single-Master Operation (FSMO) roles

Roles that can be assigned to particular domain controllers to provide specific services that must be coordinated by a single master system.

folder redirection

A process enabled using group policies that will allow common folders such as the My Documents or Desktop folders to be redirected from their default locations to remote file shares, which continue to behave as if still local to the computer.

forest

A structure of domains sharing a discontinuous namespace, configured as one or more trees.

fully qualified domain name (FQDN)

A hierarchical namespace host designation that includes the domain and host identification (for example, myserver.mycorp.com).

Global Catalog

A distributed multimaster database used in Active Directory domains to maintain information on user and computer accounts.

groups

Groups are logical groupings in which user and computer accounts can be granted membership. These are used to easily administer permissions assignments to common groupings of accounts. A Group may also be a member of other groups, allowing nested inheritance of permissions.

Group Policy

Collections of settings that can be assigned to groups or containers to simplify centralized administration, configuration, and software deployment within Active Directory networks.

Hardware Abstraction Layer (HAL)

A software layer that protects the kernel from direct interaction with the hardware and its drivers.

Hotfix

A patch provided by Microsoft to correct an identified security error.

initialization
Testing of hardware by the system BIOS and assignment of default values during the software loading process.

kernel
The compiled software modules that make up the operating system.

linking group policies
The process of assigning a group policy to a particular object or container. A single container can have multiple policies linked to it, and a single group policy can be linked to multiple containers.

local area network (LAN)
A network spanning a small geographic area, often as small an area as a single building.

logging
The collection of data for later analysis.

Media Access Control (MAC) identifier
A unique hexadecimal (base 16) alpha-numeric identifier assigned to a network interface card by its manufacturer.

Microsoft Management Console (MMC)
A common interface that can be customized to provide a single point of control over multiple administrative tasks.

mixed-mode domain
An Active Directory domain that can support NT 4 backup domain controllers.

native-mode domain
An Active Directory domain that cannot contain any NT 4 backup domain controllers.

NetBIOS name
An older flat-namespace naming system used by Windows systems, which utilizes only the host name for identification.

organizational units
Subdomain groupings into which user, computer, and other organizational units can be placed in order to easily grant administrative control over a limited grouping of resources without requiring full domain administration capability.

partition
A logical section defined on a disk drive. Each partition can be independently formatted using the FAT32 or NTFS file system.

permissions
Access rights granted or denied to security principles such as user and computer accounts either directly or by way of inheritance through group membership.

publishing resources
Publication of a resource creates a reference to the object in the global catalog. Each published resource can have its own discretionary access control list (DACL).

primary domain controller

Windows NT 4 server responsible for maintaining all changes to domain user and computer account settings.

querying

The process by which a client system requests the resolution of a name to its associated IP address using a name resolution service such as a Domain Name Service (DNS) server.

scope

A defined address pool and configuration settings appropriate to addresses leased from this pool within a DHCP server.

service pack

A collection of current hotfixes and other non-security-related updates and patches gathered into a single package.

site

One or more subnets connected using reliable, high-speed connections.

static addressing

An association of name and IP address that does not change without administrative intervention.

subnet

A group of host addresses that share a network address in common.

subnet mask

A bit pattern that defines the portion of an IP address that specifies the network address.

subnetting

The process of creating smaller subnets from larger address blocks.

Taskpad

A customized MMC console that contains very user-friendly shortcuts to specified tasks, hiding the full complexity of the MMC.

Terminal Services

A remote-control interface that allows remote access to a virtual terminal as if directly connected to a server. Each session is maintained separately from all others, and users can utilize all programs on the server using a thin client interface.

Transmission Control Protocol/Internet Protocol (TCP/IP)

A suite of common protocols that has become the default common language for Internet connectivity.

tree

A hierarchical structure of parent and child domains sharing a common namespace.

trust

A logical connection between domains that allows accounts from one domain to be granted access permissions to resources located within another.

virus

A program capable of self-replication and automatic distribution, which may be benign or highly destructive based on the intent of its creator.

wide area network (WAN)

A network spanning a large geographic area, providing communications between higher-speed local-area networks.

workgroup

A collection of computers within a peer-to-peer network, in which all systems can provide access for any others within the workgroup.

zone

A logical namespace grouping managed by a DNS server.

Index

. . . .

A

A (address) resource record (DNS), 74
access permissions
   filtering, group policies, 137-138
   shared folders, 164
   user authentication, IIS, 207-210
access rights, Active Directory, 112-113
accessing
   FTP sites, IIS, 216-217
   Web sites, IIS, 216-219
account policies, 285-287
accounts, managing, 188-190
Acknowledgement procedure, DHCP lease
   generation, 93-94
Active Directory, 40-41, 347
   administration, 110
      access rights, 112-113
      assignments, 114-115
      delegated permissions, 110-111
      delegation of authority, 115-118
      management tools, 118-123
      permissions, 111-112
   attributes, 46
   custom consoles, 118
   domain controllers, 40-41
      FSMO (Flexible Single-Master
        Operation) roles, 42-43
      GC (global catalog), 41-42
      trusts, 43-46
   group policies, 130-131
      access permission filtering, 137-138
      administraion, 142-147

      application, 134
      block inheritance, 136
      containers, 131
      creating, 138-141
      default inheritance modification, 136
      domain controllers, 141-142
      domain-level settings, 134
      editing, 140-141
      linking, 138-141
      objects, 130
      organizational unit settings, 135
      overriding, 137
      removing, 141
      same-container settings, 135-136
      scope, 132-134
      settings, 132-133
      site-level settings, 134-142
      slow network connections, 142
      software deployment, 147-150
      template, 131
   Integrated zones, 76
   objects, 46
   schema changes, 46
Active Directory Integrated zones (DNS),
   71
Active Directory Users and Computers
   MMC snap-in, smart cards, enabling, 279
AD (Active Directory). *See* Active Directory,
   41
adaptive exams, 13-14
   fixed-length exams, compared, 15
   short-form exams, compared, 15
   strategies, 15, 18

address classes, IP addressing, 29-30
address resolution protocol (ARP). *See* ARP
(address resolution protocol)
addresses, DNS, registering, 69
addressing
    dynamic addressing, DHCP, 91
    IP addressing, 29
        address classes, 29-30
        subnetting, 30-31
    static addressing, DHCP, 90-91
administration
    Active Directory, 110
        access rights, 112-113
        assignments, 114-115
        delegated permissions, 110-111
        delegation of authority, 115-118
        management tools, 118-123
        permissions, 111-112
    group policies, 142
        folder redirection, 145-147
        scripting, 144-145
        settings, 144
        templates, 143-144
administrative templates, 347
Administrative Templates setting (group
    policies), 132
advanced options, system startup, 231-232
AppleTalk, 25
AppleTalk Remote Access Protocol (ARAP).
    See ARAP (AppleTalk Remote Access
    Protocol)
Application log (auditing), 289
applications, group policies, 134
ARAP (AppleTalk Remote Access Protocol),
    257
ARP (address resolution protocol), 27
ARPANET, 24
Assignments, Active Directory, 114-115
attributes, Active Directory, 46
auditing, 287-291, 347
    configuring, 288-289
    enabling, 288
    event logs, 289-291
authentication, 347
    users, IIS, 205-210
authentication protocols, remote access,
    258-259
authentication strength, 278
authority, delegating, 115-118
authorization, 347
    DHCP servers, 96-97
Autoexec.bat file, 228

B

backup domain controllers, 347
Balter, Dan, 197
baselines, establishing, 237
basic disks, 181
block inheritance, group policies, 136
bridgehead servers, 50, 347
brute-force attacks, 278
build-list-and-reorder questions, exams, for-
    mat, 6-8

C

Cache-Only DNS servers, 70
CAL (Client Access License), 179
case studies, 13-14
    layout, 4-5
    strategies, 15-16
certification exams
    adaptive exams, strategies, 18
    build-list-and-reorder questions, 6-8
    case studies
        layout, 4-5
        strategies, 15-16
    create-a-tree questions, 8-10
    drag-and-connect questions, 10-11
    fixed-length, strategies, 16-17
    formats, 13-14
        strategies, 15
    multiple-choice questions, 5-6
    practice exams, taking, 19-20
    question handling, strategies, 18-19
    readiness, assessing, 2
    resources, 20-22
    select-and-place questions, 11-12
    short-form, strategies, 16-17
    testing centers, 3-4
Challenge Handshake Authentication
    Protocol (CHAP). *See* CHAP (Challenge
    Handshake Authentication Protocol)
change permissions, shared foders, 164
CHAP (Challenge Handshake
    Authentication Protocol), 258
CIDR (Classless Inter-Domain Routing),
    162, 347
classes, IP addressing, 29-30
Classless Inter-Domain Routing (CIDR).
    See CIDR (Classless Inter-Domain
    Routing)
Client Access License (CAL). *See* CAL
    (Client Access License)

clients
     connections, configuring, 269-270
     reserving, DHCP servers, 101-102
     Terminal Services, 180
CNAME (Canonical) resource record
     (DNS), 74
Command Prompt Only option (Windows
     startup), 231
command-line utilities
     fixboot command, 233
     fixmbr command, 233
     gpresult command, 242
     ipconfig command, 77, 240
     nbtstat command, 78, 241
     net command, 78
     netdiag command, 241
     netstat command, 241
     nslookup, 79
     pathping command, 239
     ping command, 79, 238
     repadmin command, 242
     replmon command, 242
     tracert command, 80, 240
     winipcfg command, 240
components, Windows components, adding,
     178
computer accounts, managing, 188
Config.sys file, 228
configuring
     auditing, 288-289
     DHCP servers, 95-96
          authorization, 96-97
          scope, 97-101
     DNS servers, 72-73
     DNS zones, 75-76
     domains, 185-190
     drives, 180-182
     dynamic volumes, 182-185
     IIS servers, 204
     Internet Explorer, proxy servers,
          218-219
     ports, VPN connections, 263-264
     remote access, 260-264
          client connections, 269-270
     servers, 185-187
     system configuration, 234-235
     Terminal Services, 179-180
     zones, FQDN, 76
connections
     clients, configuring, 269-270
     networks, troubleshooting, 238-242
     private networks via Internet, 270

Web sites, establishing, 216
WebDAV, IIS (Internet Information
     Service), 217-218
consoles
     Active Directory, custom consoles, 118
     sending, 167-168
containers
     group policies, 131
     inheritance, 113
Create All Child Objects permission (Active
     Directory), 111
create-a-tree questions, exams, formats,
     8-10

D

DACL (discretionary access control list),
     160
DARPA (Defense Advanced Research
     Projects Agency), 24
DC (domain controller). *See* domain con-
     trollers
dcpromo command-line utility, 185
Debugging Mode option (Windows start-
     up), 231
default inheritance, group policies, modify-
     ing, 136
Defense Advanced Research Projects
     Agency (DARPA), 24
delegated permissions, Active Directory,
     110-111, 115-118
Delegation of Control wizard, 115-118
Delete All Child Objects permission (Active
     Directory), 111
deleting group policies, 141
delta loss, files, 167
deploying software, group policies, 147-150
DHCP (Dynamic Host Configuration
     Protocol), 90
     dynamic addressing, 91
     leasing, 91
          duration, 94-95
          generating, 92-94
     static addressing, 90-91
*DHCP Handbook: Understanding, Deploying,
     and Managing Automated Configuration
     Services*, 108
DHCP servers
     clients, reserving, 101-102
     configuring, 95-96
          authorization, 96-97
          scope, 97-101

diagnostic testing, logging, 66
dialing up, private networks, remote access, 269
dialog boxes
  Internet Information Service components dialog box, 203
  New Object - Computer dialog box, 188
  New Share dialog box, 164
  Properties dialog box, 163
  Send Console Message dialog box, 167-168
  Sharing dialog box, 162
dictionary attacks, 279
directory browsing permissions, IIS, 208
Directory Service logs (auditing), 289
Discovery procedure, DHCP lease generation, 92-93
discretionary access control list (DACL). *See* DACL (discretionary access control list)
Disk Management node (Computer Management MMC snap-in), 180
disks
  basic disks, 181
  dynamic disks, 181
  RAID (redundant array of independent disks), 183-185
DNS (domain name system) servers, 31
  addresses, registering, 69
  caches, FQDN host naming, 68
  configuring, 72-73
  logs, auditing, 289
  name resolution, 69-70
  properties, 73-74
  querying, 70-71
  resource records, 74-75
  types, 70
  zones, 71-72
    configuring, 75-76
    creating, 73-74
    support, 71
documentation, IIS, 203
domain controllers
  Active Directory, 40-41
    FSMO (Flexible Single-Master Operation) roles, 42-43
    GC (global catalog), 41-42
    trusts, 43-46
  BDCs (backup domain controllers), 40
  creating, 186
  group policies, specifying, 141-142
  names, changing, 68
  PDCs (primary domain controllers), 40

Domain Controllers Security Policy MMC snap-in, 283
domain name system (DNS) servers. *See* DNS (domain name system) servers
Domain Naming Master role (FSMO), 42
Domain Security Policy MMC snap-in, 283
domain-level settings, group policies, 134
domains, 46-47, 348
  configuring, 185-190
  forests, 50
  groups, 47
  member services, 48
  membership
    changing, 68
  mixed-mode domains, 186, 349
  modes, 186-187
  native-mode domains, 349
  objects, 47
  OUs (organizational units), 48-49
  trees, 49-50
  users, 46
drag-and-connect questions, exams, format, 10-11
drivers, 348
drives
  configuring, 180-182
  logical drives, 181-182
Droms, Ralph E., 108
duration, leases, DHCP, 94-95
dynamic addressing, 348
  DHCP, 91
dynamic disks, 181
Dynamic Host Configuration Protocol (DHCP). *See* DHCP (Dynamic Host Configuration Protocol)
dynamic volumes, configuring, 182-185

E

editing group policies, 140-141
educating users, security issues, 280
Enable VGA Mode option (Windows startup), 232
encryption protocols, remote access, 259
establishing trusts, 187
event logs, auditing, 289-291
Event Viewer, 289-291
Event Viewer MMC snap-in, 238
Events, Security Log, 290
exams
  adaptive exams, strategies, 18
  build-list-and-reorder questions, 6-8

case studies
    layout, 4-5
    strategies, 15-16
create-a-tree questions, 8-10
drag-and-connect questions, 10-11
fixed-length exams, strategies, 16-17
formats, 13-14
    strategies, 15
multiple-choice questions, 5-6
practice exams, taking, 19-20
question handling, strategies, 18-19
readiness, assessing, 2
resources, 20-22
select-and-place questions, 11-12
short-form exams, strategies, 16-17
testing centers, 3-4
Extensible Markup Language (XML). *See*
  XML (Extensible Markup Language)
Extranets, IIS (Internet Information
  Service), 200-202, 209

F

failures, networks, checking, 240
File Replication Service logs (auditing), 289
File Transfer Protocol (FTP). *See* FTP (File
  Transfer Protocol)
files
  Autoexec.bat file, 228
  Config.sys file, 228
  delta loss, 167
  Io.sys file, 229
  Msdos.sys file, 229
  sharing, 163
    shared folders, 163-169
  System.ini file, 229
  Win.com file, 229
  Win.ini file, 229
filtering
  access permissions, group policies,
    137-138
  Security Log, 291
fixboot command, 233
fixed-length exams, 13-14
  adaptive exams, compared, 15
  strategies, 15-17
fixmbr command, 233
flags, nbtstat utility, 78
Flexible Single-Master Operation (FSMO).
  See FSMO (Flexible Single-Master
  Operation)

folder redirection, 348
Folder Redirection setting (group policies),
  132
folders
  IIS, 204
  redirecting, group policies, 145-147
  shared folders
    access permissions, 164
    creating, 163-164
    managing, 166-167
    publishing, 165
    sharing, 163-169
    virtual folders, creating, 214-215
    Web sharing, 215
forests, 348
  domains, 50
formats
  adaptive exams, strategies, 18
  case studies, strategies, 15-16
  exams, 13-15
  fixed-length exams, strategies, 16-17
  short-form exams, strategies, 16-17
forward lookup queries (DNS), 71
FQDNs (fully qualified domain names),
  28-29, 58, 348
  host naming, 67-68
    DNS cache, 68
    HOSTS file, 68-69
    resource records, 75
    zone configuration, 76
  name resolution, 32, 59-60
    LDAP (Lightweight Directory
      Access Protocol), 59
FrontPage 2000 Server extensions, IIS, 203
FSMO (Flexible Single-Master Operation)
  roles, 42-43, 348
FTP (File Transfer Protocol), 26, 200-203
  access, IIS, 216-217
Full Control permission (Active Directory),
  112, 164
fully qualified domain names (FQDNs). *See*
  FQDNs (fully qualified domain names)

G

GC (global catalog), Active Directory,
  41-42, 348
generating leases, DHCP, 92-94
globally unique identification (GUID). *See*
  GUID (globally unique identification)
gpresult command-line utility, 242

group policies, 130-131
  access permissions, filtering, 137-138
  administration, 142
    folder redirection, 145-147
    scripting, 144-145
    settings, 144
    templates, 143-144
  application, 134
  block inheritance, 136
  containers, 131
  creating, 138-141
  default inheritance, modifying, 136
  domain controllers, specifying, 141-142
  domain-level settings, 134
  editing, 140-141
  linking, 138-141, 349
  objects, 130
  organizational unit settings, 135
  overriding, disabling, 137
  removing, 141
  same-container settings, 135-136
  scope, 132-134
  security, 281-287
    account policies, 285-287
    security templates, 282-285
  settings, 132-133
  site-level settings, 134-142
  slow network connections, 142
  software deployment, 147-150
  template, 131
  unlinked group policy objects, creating,
    138
Group Policy MMC snap-in, 283, 348
groups, 348
  domains, 47
  permissions, resolving, 113
GUID (globally unique identification), 130

H

HAL (Hardware Abstraction Layer), 348
hfnetchk command-line utility, 243
Holme, Dan, 197
host IDs, 29
hosts
  identifying, 27-29
  naming, FQDN, 67-69, 76
HOSTS file, FQDN host naming, 68-69
hotfixes, 242-243, 281, 348
HTTP (Hypertext Transfer Protocol), 26,
  200

I

ICS (Internet Connection Sharing), 254
  remote access, 255-256
identifying
  hosts, 27-29
  sites, IIS, 201-202
IIS (Internet Information Service), 200
  components, 203-204
  documentation, 203
  extranets, 200-202, 209
  folders, 204
    Web sharing, 215
  FrontPage 2000 Server extensions, 203
  FTP servers, 203
  installation, 203-204
  Internet, 200-202, 209
  Internet Explorer, configuring to use
    proxy servers, 218-219
  Internet Services Manager, 204
  intranets, 200-202, 209
  maintenance, 219
  Master Properties, 210-211
  NNTP service, 204
  servers, configuring, 204
  site masters, 201
  sites, 201
    accessing, 216-219
    connection establishment, 216
    creating, 210-215
    identification, 201-202
  SMTP service, 204
  snap-ins, 204
  user authentication, 205-207
    access permissions, 207-210
    authentication types, 206-207
    Web methods, 205-206
  virtual folders, 201
    creating, 214-215
  virtual sites, 201
  WebDAV (Web Distributed Authoring
    and Versioning), 201
    connections, 217-218
  World Wide Web server, 204
IISLockDown utility, 244
importing security templates, 283-284
inbound connections, enabling, remote
  access, 260-263
Infrastructure Master role (FSMO), 43
inheritance
  containers, 113
  group policies

block inheritance, 136
  modifying, 136
initialization, 349
  system startup, 228
installing
  IIS, 203-204
  Recovery Console, 233
Integrated zones (DNS), 76
interactive queries (DNS), 71
Internet, 24
  history of, 24
  IIS (Internet Information Service),
    200-202, 207-209
  private networks, connecting to, 270
Internet Connection Sharing (ICS). See ICS
  (Internet Connection Sharing)
Internet Explorer, configuring, proxy
  servers, 218-219
Internet Explorer Maintenance setting
  (group policies), 132
Internet Information Service (IIS). See IIS
  (Internet Information Service)
Internet Information Service components
  dialog box, 203
Internet Protocol (IP). See IP (Internet
  Protocol)
Internet Protocol Security (IPSec). See
  IPSec (Internet Protocol Security)
Internet service providers (ISPs). See ISPs
  (Internet service providers)
Internetwork Packet Exchange (IPX). See
  IPX (Internetwork Packet Exchange)
intranets, IIS (Internet Information
  Service), 200-202, 209
Io.sys file, 229
IP (Internet Protocol), 25-26, 29
  addressing
    address classes, 29-30
    composition, 28
    subnetting, 30-31
ipconfig utility, name resolution, 77
ipconfig.exe command-line utility, 240
IPSec (Internet Protocol Security), 259
IPX (Internetwork Packet Exchange), 25
ISPs (Internet service providers), 25

J–K–L

kernels, 349
Knight, Natasha, 197

L2TP (Layer-2 Tunneling Protocol), 258
LANs (local area networks), 24, 349

Last Known Good Configuration option
  (Windows startup), 232
Layer-2 Tunneling Protocol (L2TP). See
  L2TP (Layer-2 Tunneling Protocol)
LDAP (Lightweight Directory Access
  Protocol)
    FQDN (fully qualified domain name)
      resolution, 59
leasing, DHCP, 91
  duration, 94-95
  generating, 92-94
Lemon, Ted, 108
levels, scope, DHCP servers, 101
lifecycles, software, 147-149
linking, group policies, 138-141, 349
LMHOSTS file, NetBIOS, 61-62
local area networks (LANs). See LANs (local
  area networks)
Local Security Policy MMC snap-in, 283
locations, references, 161
Logan, Todd, 197
Logged option (Windows startup), 232
logging, 349
  diagnostic testing, 66
logical drives, 181-182
longer duration, DHCP leases, 94

M

MAC (media access control), 27-29, 349
mailservers, 28
maintenance, IIS, 219
management tools, Active Directory,
  118-123
managing
  accounts, 188
  shared folders, 166-167
Master Properties (IIS), 210-211
*MCSE Windows 2000 Professional Exam
  Cram*, 197
MCSE Windows 2000 Server Exam Cram,
  197
media access control (MAC). See MAC
  (media access control)
member services, domains, 48
membership, domains, changing, 68
messages, console messages, sending,
  167-168
Microsoft certification exams
  adaptive exams, strategies, 18
  build-list-and-reorder questions, 6-8

case studies
  layout, 4-5
  strategies, 15-16
create-a-tree questions, 8-10
drag-and-connect questions, 10-11
fixed-length exams, strategies, 16-17
formats, 13-15
multiple-choice questions, 5-6
practice exams, taking, 19-20
question handling, strategies, 18-19
readiness, assessing, 2
resources, 20-22
select-and-place questions, 11-12
short-form exams, strategies, 16-17
testing centers, 3-4
Microsoft Certified Professional pages,
  20-22
Microsoft Challenge Handshake
  Authentication Protocol (MS-CHAP). *See*
  MS-CHAP (Microsoft Challenge
  Handshake Authentication Protocol)
Microsoft Challenge Handshake
  Authentication Protocol version 2
  (MS-CHAP v2). *See* MS-CHAP v.2
Microsoft Management Console (MMC).
  See MMC (Microsoft Management
  Console)
Microsoft Point-to-Point Encryption
  (MPPE). *See* MPPE (Microsoft Point-to-
  Point Encryption)
Microsoft Security Web site, 251
*Microsoft Windows 2000 Administrator's
  Pocket Consultant*, 38, 55, 87, 128, 157,
  176, 251, 276, 299
Microsoft Windows 2000 Server Resource Kit,
  38, 55, 87, 108, 128, 157, 176, 197, 251,
  276, 299
mixed-mode domains, 186, 349
MMC (Microsoft Management Console), 349
  custom consoles, 118-121
  snap-ins, 119-121
modes, domains, 186-187
MPPE (Microsoft Point-to-Point
  Encryption), 259
MS-CHAP (Microsoft Challenge
  Handshake Authentication Protocol), 258
MS-CHAP v.2 (Microsoft Challenge
  Handshake Authentication Protocol ver-
  sion 2), 258
Msdos.sys file, 229
multiple-choice questions, exams, format, 5-6
MX (Mail Exchange) resource record
  (DNS), 75

N

name caches, NetBIOS, 61
name resolution, 31, 58
  command-line utilities, 76-77
    ipconfig, 77
    nbtstat, 78
    net, 78
    nslookup, 79
    ping, 79
    tracert, 80
  DNS, 69-70
    queries, 70-71
    resource records, 74-75
    server configuration, 72-73
    server properties, 73-74
    server types, 70
    types, 70
    zones, 71-76
  FQDN (fully qualified domain name),
    32, 58-60
    host naming, 67-69, 75-76
    LDAP (Lightweight Directory
      Access Protocol), 59
  NetBIOS, 31-32, 58-60
    LMHOSTS file, 61-62
    name caches, 61
    WINS resolution, 62-63
    WINS service configuration, 64-67
names, domains, changing, 68
NAT (network address translation), 254-255
native-mode domains, 349
nbtstat.exe command-line utility, 78, 241
net utility, name resolution, 78
NetBIOS, 29
  name resolution, 31-32, 58, 60
    LMHOSTS file, 61-62
    name caches, 61
    WINS resolution, 62-63
    WINS service configuration, 64-67
  names, 349
netdiag.exe command-line utility, 241
netstat command-line utility, 241-242
network address translation (NAT). *See*
  NAT (network address translation)
network addressing protocols, 25
network administrators, job description, 24
network IDs, 29
network interface cards (NICs). *See* NICs
  (network interface cards)
Network Monitor, 237
Network News Transfer Protocol (NNTP).
  See NNTP (Network News Transfer
  Protocol)

Networking and RAS Documentation
Online, 276
networking protocols, 25-27
networks
    connectivity, troubleshooting, 238-242
    failures, checking, 240
    protocols
        network addressing protocols, 25
        TCP/IP suite protocols, 26
    security, 278-287
        auditing, 287-291
        authentication strength, 278
        brute-force attacks, 278
        dictionary attacks, 279
        group policies, 281-287
        passwords, 279
        smart cards, 279
        trojan horses, 279
        updates, 281
        user education, 280
        virus definitions, 281
        viruses, 279
New Object - Computer dialog box, 188
New Scope Wizard, 99
New Share dialog box, 164
NICs (network interface cards), 27
NNTP (Network News Transfer Protocol),
200, 204
nontransitive trusts (domains), 44-45
NS (Name Server) resource record (DNS),
75
nslookup utility, name resolution, 79

O

objects
    Active Directory, 46
    domains, 47
    group policies, 130
    unlinked group policy objects, creating,
    138
Offer procedure, DHCP lease generation,
93
one-way trust relationships (domains),
44-45
options, scope, DHCP servers, 99-101
organizational unit settings, group policies,
135
OUs (organizational units), 48-49, 190, 349
overriding group policies, disabling, 137

P

PAP (Password Authentication Protocol),
258
parameters, scope, DHCP servers, 97-98
partitions, 181-182, 349
Password Authentication Protocol (PAP).
See PAP (Password Authentication
Protocol)
passwords, 279
pathping.exe command-line utility, routes,
testing, 239
PDC Emulators, 42-43
PDCs (primary domain controllers), 40, 350
performance utilization, 235-237
permissions, 349
    access permissions
        filtering, 137-138
        shared folders, 164
    Active Directory, 111-112
        delegated permissions, 110-111
    resolution, 113, 168-169
Permissions wizard, 209
Personal Security Advisor, 244
ping.exe command-line utility
    name resolution, 79
    remote resources, availability checks,
    238-239
Point-to-Point Protocol (PPP). See PPP
(Point-to-Point Protocol)
Point-to-Point Tunneling Protocol (PPTP).
See PPTP (Point-to-Point Tunneling
Protocol)
policies
    account policies, 285-287
    group policies, 130-131
        access permission filtering, 137-138
        administration, 142-147
        application, 134
        block inheritance, 136
        containers, 131
        creating, 138-141
        default inheritance modification, 136
        domain controllers, 141-142
        domain-level settings, 134
        editing, 140-141
        linking, 138-141
        objects, 130
        organizational unit settings, 135
        removing, 141
        same-container settings, 135-136
        scope, 132-134

security, 281-287
settings, 132-133
site-level settings, 134-142
slow network connections, 142
software deployment, 147-150
template, 131
remote access, 264-269
properties, 265-269
user-account dial-in settings, 265
POP3 (Post Office Protocol v3), 26
ports, configuring, VPN connections,
263-264
POST (Power-On Self-Test), 228
Post Office Protocol v3 (POP3). *See* POP3
(Post Office Protocol v3)
Power-On Self-Test (POST). *See* POST
(Power-On Self-Test)
PPP (Point-to-Point Protocol), 26, 257
PPTP (Point-to-Point Tunneling Protocol),
26, 258
practice exams, taking, 19-20
Primary DNS servers, 70
primary domain controllers (PDCs). *See*
PDCs (primary domain controllers)
printers, sharing, 169-170
private networks
connecting to via Internet, 270
remote access, 254-256, 269
properties
DNS servers, 73-74
remote access policies, 265-269
Properties dialog box, 163
protocols
See also specific protocols
authentication protocols, remote access,
258-259
encryption protocols, remote access, 259
networking protocols, 25-27
network addressing protocols, 25
TCP/IP suite protocols, 26
VPNs, remote access, 257-258
WANs, remote access, 257
proxy servers, Internet Explorer, configuring to use, 218-219
PTR (pointer) resource record (DNS), 75
publishing
resources, 160-162
shared folders, 165
publishing resources, 349

Q-R

qchain.exe utility, 243
queries, DNS servers, 70-71, 350
question-handling strategies, 18-19
RAID (redundant array of independent
disks), 183-185
RAS (Remote Access Service) protocol, 257
Read permission (Active Directory), 112
read permissions
IIS, 208
shared folders, 164
readiness, exams, assessing, 2
Recovery Console, 233
installing, 233
Windows 2000 installation CD, running
from, 233
recursive queries (DNS), 71
redirecting folders, group policies, 145-147
redundant array of independent disks
(RAID). *See* RAID (redundant array of
independent disks)
references, locations, 161
registering addresses, DNS, 69
remote access, 254-257
authentication protocols, 258-259
client connections, configuring, 269-270
configuring, 260-264
encryption protocols, 259
ICS, 255-256
inbound connections, enabling, 260-263
NAT (network address translation),
254-255
policies, 264-269
properties, 265-269
user-account dial-in settings, 265
private networks, 254-256
VPN protocols, 257-258
WAN protocols, 257
Remote Access Service (RAS) protocol. *See*
RAS (Remote Access Service) protocol
Remote Installation Services setting (group
policies), 132
repadmin command-line utility, 242
replication partners, WINS server, 66-67
replmon command-line utility, 242
Request procedure, DHCP lease generation, 93
reserving clients, DHCP servers, 101-102
resolution
See also name resolution
permissions, 168-169

groups, 113
    users, 113
resource records, DNS, 74-75
resources
    DHCP Handbook Understanding,
        Deploying, and Managing Automated
        Configuration Services, 108
    exam strategies, 20-22
    MCSE Windows 2000 Professional Exam
        Cram, 197
    MCSE Windows 2000 Server Exam Cram,
        197
    Microsoft Security Web site, 251
    Microsoft Windows 2000 Administrator's
        Pocket Consultant, 38, 55, 87, 128, 157,
        176, 251, 276, 299
    Microsoft Windows 2000 Server Resource
        Kit, 38, 55, 87, 108, 128, 157, 176,
        197, 251, 276, 299
    publishing, 160-162
    utilizing, 235-237
    Windows 2000 Product Documentation
        Online, 38, 55, 87, 108, 128, 157, 197,
        251, 299
    Windows 2000 System Administrator's
        Handbook, 55
    Windows Scripting Host Web page, 157
reverse lookup queries (DNS), 71
Reverse Lookup zones (DNS), 71
RID Master role (FSMO), 43
routes, testing, pathping.exe , 239
Routing and Remote Access Service
    (RRAS). *See* RRAS (Routing and Remote
    Access Service)
Routing and Remote Access setup wizard,
    261
RRAS (Routing And Remote Access
    Service), 254

S

Safe Mode option (Windows startup), 232
Safe Mode with Command Prompt option
    (Windows startup), 232
Safe Mode with Networking option
    (Windows startup), 232
Salmon, Laurie, 197
same-container settings, group policies,
    135-136
Schema Master role (FSMO), 43

scope, 350
    DHCP servers, 97
    activation, 99
    creating, 98-99
    options, 99-101
    parameters, 97-98
    group policies, 132-134
script source access permissions, IIS, 208
scripting group policies, 144-145
scripts and executables permission, IIS, 209
scripts only permissions, IIS, 209
Scripts setting (group policies), 132
Secondary DNS servers, 70
secure socket layer (SSL). *See* SSL (secure
    socket layer)
security
    access rights, Active Directory, 112-113
    assignments, Active Directory, 114-115
    auditing
        configuring, 288-289
        enabling, 288
        event logs, 289-291
    authentication, IIS, 205-210
    authentication strength, 278
    delegation of authority, Active Directory,
        115-118
    group policies, 130-131, 281-287
        access permission filtering, 137-138
        account policies, 285-287
        administration, 142-147
        application, 134
        containers, 131
        creating, 138-141
        domain controllers, 141-142
        editing, 140-141
        linking, 138-141
        removing, 141
        scope, 132-134
        security templates, 282-285
        settings, 132-133
        site-level settings, 134-142
        slow network connections, 142
        software deployment, 147-150
        template, 131
    networks, 278-287
        auditing, 287-291
        authentication strength, 278
        brute-force attacks, 278
        dictionary attacks, 279
        passwords, 279
        smart cards, 279
        trojan horses, 279

updates, 281
user education, 280
virus definitions, 281
viruses, 279
permissions
Active Directory, 111-112
delegated permissions, 110-111
resolution, 168-169
security templates, 282-285
updates, 242-244
Security Configuration and Analysis MMC
snap-in, 284
Security Log
events, 290
filtering, 291
Security log (auditing), 289
security principles, 40
Security Settings setting (group policies),
132
security templates, 282-285
importing, 283-284
select-and-place questions, exams, format,
11-12
Send Console Message dialog box, 167-168
sending console messages, 167-168
Serial Line Internet Protocol (SLIP). *See*
SLIP (Serial Line Internet Protocol)
servers, configuring, 185-187, 204
service packs, 350
settings, group policies, 132-133, 144
domain-level settings, 134
organizational unit settings, 135
same-container settings, 135-136
shared folders, 163-169
access permissions, 164
creating, 163-164
managing, 166-167
publishing, 165
sharing
files, 163
shared folders, 163-169
folders, Web sharing, 215
printers, 169-170
Sharing dialog box, 162
Shiva Password Authentication Protocol
(SPAP). *See* SPAP (Shiva Password
Authentication Protocol)
short duration, DHCP leases, 94
short-form exams, 13-14
adaptive exams, compared, 15
strategies, 15-17
Simple Mail Transfer Protocol (SMTP). *See*
SMTP (Simple Mail Transfer Protocol)

Simple Network Management Protocol
(SNMP). *See* SNMP (Simple Network
Management Protocol)
site masters, IIS, 201
site-level settings, group policies, 134-142
sites
accessing, IIS, 216-219
creating, IIS, 210-215
identifying, IIS, 201-202
SLIP (Serial Line Internet Protocol), 26
slow network connections, group policies,
142
smart cards, 279
SMTP (Simple Mail Transfer Protocol), 27,
200, 204
SNMP (Simple Network Management
Protocol), 27
SOA (start of authority) resource record
(DNS), 75
software
deployment, group policies, 147-150
lifecycles, 147-149
Software Installation setting (group policies), 133
spanned volumes, 182
SPAP (Shiva Password Authentication
Protocol), 259
SRV (service) resource record (DNS), 75
SSL (secure socket layer), 210
Standard Primary zones (DNS), 71, 76
Standard Secondary zones (DNS), 72
Stanek, William R., 38, 55, 87, 128, 157,
176, 251, 276, 299
startup
advanced options, 231-232
initialization, 228
Recovery Console, 233
Windows 95/98, 228-229
Windows NT/2000/XP, 229-231
static addressing, 350
DHCP, 90-91
static mappings, WINS server, 66
Step-By-Step Confirmation option
(Windows startup), 232
storage
drives, configuring, 180-182
dynamic volumes, configuring, 182-185
Strahan, Tillman, 55
striped volumes, 183
subnet, 350
subnet masks, 30, 350
subnetting, 350
IP addressing, 30-31

System Configuration utility, 234
System Information utility, 235
System log (auditing), 289
System Monitor, 236
system monitoring, 234
  configuration, 234-235
  performance utilization, 235-237
  resource utilization, 235-237
system startup
  advanced options, 231-232
  initialization, 228
  problems, troubleshooting, 228-233
  Recovery Console, 233
  Windows 95/98, 228-229
  Windows NT/2000/XP, 229-231
System.ini file, 229

T

Task Manager, 235-236
Taskpad, 350
TCP (Transmission Control Protocol), 27
TCP/IP (Transmission Control
  Protocol/Internet Protocol), 24, 350
TCP/IP suite protocols, 26
Telnet, 27
templates
  administration templates, group policies,
    131, 143-144
  security templates, 282-285
Terminal Services, 350
  clients, 180
  configuring, 179-180
Terminal Services Advanced Client (TSAC).
  See TSAC (Terminal Services Advanced
  Client)
Terminal Services Client Creator, 180
testing centers, environment, 3-4
tests. See exams
tracert utility, name resolution, 80
tracert.exe command-line utility, network
  failures, checking, 240
transitive trusts (domains), 44
Transmission Control Protocol (TCP). See
  TCP (Transmission Control Protocol)
Transmission Control Protocol/Internet
  Protocol (TCP/IP). See TCP/IP
  (Transmission Control Protocol/Internet
  Protocol)
trees, domains, 49-50, 350
trojan horses, 279

troubleshooting
  network connectivity, 238-242
  problems, system startup, 228-233
trusts, 350
  domains, Active Directory, 43-46
  establishing, 187
TSAC (Terminal Services Advanced Client),
  180
two-way trusts (domains), 44

U

UDP (User Datagram Protocol), 27
unlimited duration, DHCP leases, 95
unlinked group policy objects, creating, 138
updates, security, 242-244
  maintaining, 281
User Datagram Protocol (UDP). See UDP
  (User Datagram Protocol)
users
  accounts, managing, 189-190
  authenticating, IIS, 205-210
  domains, 46
  educating, security, 280
  permissions, resolving, 113

V

virtual folders, IIS, 201
  creating, 214-215
virtual sites, IIS, 201
viruses, 279, 351
  virus definitions, updating, 281
volumes
  dynamic volumes, configuring, 182-185
  spanned volumes, 182
  striped volumes, 183
VPNs (virtual private networks)
  ports, configuring, 263-264
  remote access, protocols, 257-258

W

WANs (wide area networks), 24, 351
  remote access, protocols, 257
Watts, David, 55
Web access permissions, IIS, 207-208
Web authentication methods, IIS, 205-206
Web Distributed Authoring and Versioning
  (WebDAV). See WebDAV (Web
  Distributed Authoring and Versioning
Web sharing, folders, 215

Web sites
accessing, IIS, 216-219
connections, establishing, 216
Web-based resources, 21-22
Microsoft Security Web site, 251
Windows 2000 Product Documentation
Online, 38, 55, 87, 108, 128, 157, 197,
251, 299
Windows Scripting Host Web page, 157
WebDAV (Web Distributed Authoring and
Versioning), 201
IIS (Internet Information Service), 201,
217-218
wide area networks (WANs). *See* WANs
(wide area networks)
Willis, Will, 55
Win.com file, 229
Win.ini file, 229
Windows, system startup
advanced options, 231-232
Recovery Console, 233
Windows 2000, system startup, 229-231
Windows 2000 installation CD, Recovery
Console, running from, 233
Windows 2000 Product Documentation
Online, 38, 55, 87, 108, 128, 157, 176,
197, 251, 276, 299
*Windows 2000 Software Installation and
Maintenance Technology*, 147
*Windows 2000 System Administrator's
Handbook*, 55
Windows 95/98, system startup, 228-229
Windows Component wizard, 178
Windows components, adding, 178
Windows Installer, 147
Windows Internet Naming Service
(WINS). *See* WINS (Windows Internet
Naming Service)
Windows NT, system startup, 229-231
Windows Scripting Host Web page, 157
Windows XP, system startup, 229-231
winipcfg command, 240
WINS (Windows Internet Naming
Service), 31, 64-67
replication partners, 66-67
resolution, 62-63
static mappings, 66
wizards
Delegation of Control wizard, 115-118
New Scope wizard, 99
Permissions wizard, 209

Routing and Remote Access setup wiz-
ard, 261
Windows Component wizard, 178
workgroups, 351
World Wide Web, 24
World Wide Web server, IIS, 204
Write permission (Active Directory), 112
write permissions, IIS, 208

X–Y–Z

XML (Extensible Markup Language), 244

zones (DNS), 71, 351
configuring, 75-76
creating, 73-74
DNS, 71-72